John Nelson DARBY

Max S. Weremchuk

John Nelson DARBY

Max S. Weremchuk

LOIZEAUX BROTHERS
Neptune, New Jersey

John Nelson Darby

The English Edition Is
A Publication of Loizeaux Brothers, Inc.,
A Nonprofit Organization Devoted to the Lord's Work
and to the Spread of His Truth.

The 1988 German edition is published by
Christliche Literatur-Verbreitung.

The 1990 Dutch edition is published by
Uitgeverij H. Medema.

Library of Congress Cataloging-in-Publication Data

Weremchuk, Max S.
[John Nelson Darby und die Anfänge einer Bewegung. English]
John Nelson Darby / Max S. Weremchuk.
Translation of: John Nelson Darby und die Anfänge einer Bewegung.
Includes bibliographical references.
ISBN: 0-87213-923-9
1. Darby, J. N. (John Nelson), 1800-1882. 2. Plymouth Brethren-
-England—Clergy—Biography. 3. Plymouth Brethren—History.
I. Title.
BX8809.D3W47 1992
289.9—dc20
[B] 92-2688

Printed in the United States of America
10 9 8 7 6 5 4 3 2 1

To Captain Al Scabbard

If Darby had occupied Abraham's position, he might have left behind him hardly less than Abraham's fame. It is easy to picture him dwelling in the land of promise as in a strange country, the contented heir of the promises of the world to come; or communing with God in the night-watches, by the lonely tent and altar that mark the stages of his faithful pilgrimage; or despising the gifts of the King of Sodom, and extending a covenant of peace to Philistine Abimelech.

W. B. Neatby

"Oh, the joy of having nothing and being nothing, seeing nothing but a living Christ in glory, and being careful for nothing but His interests down here." J. N. Darby

(This photo is from Souvenez-vous de vos conducteurs *and is the earliest known photo of Darby.)*

Contents

Foreword

TO THE GERMAN EDITION

My purpose and goal when I began work on this biography back in 1980 were relatively simple. I was a most ardent Darby follower and the accounts that I had been reading of him by modern authors did not present him in a favorable light. This greatly disturbed me. It was a distorted and unfair picture that the others presented, I thought. Several older books, now difficult to obtain, were accessible to me and so the idea was born to extract accounts from these older works and group them together in an effort to present Darby in a more pleasing and attractive light. I was encouraged in this by others and set to work.

Not long after beginning my work I had the opportunity to travel to England and Ireland with a good friend of mine, and to visit various places connected with Darby's past. I still have very pleasant memories of the beautiful Irish countryside and the trip did much to give me a feeling for the "atmosphere" needed for the background of the planned book.

Through the kind support of another, I was brought into contact with Ulrich Bister of Herborn/Hörbach, who has a vast collection of historical Brethren material. He was kind enough to let me make use of what he had—and I thank him most kindly for his help—and so the first phase of my work was occupied with making use of the material obtained through him. As a result, my somewhat "ideal" picture of Darby was ruined.

Through letters and the like (written by Darby or his contemporaries) it became very clear to me that Darby was, after all, very human, with faults and shortcomings. In a sense my world fell apart at this point, until I realized that it must be a poor faith I had if it hung on a single person or a group associated with him. My view of Darby became more realistic.

In the main the appearance of the biography had not outwardly changed at this point. It was then that I, more out of curiosity than anything else, began writing certain places in Ireland and England to obtain confirmation of historical facts contained in the works of others who had in the past written about Darby and the early Brethren. I was greatly surprised to find that much of what had been published was not correct, and so began a long period during which there was a constant flow of correspondence between me and librarians and historians in Ireland and England. With the Lord's help, I was able to obtain much information and now, I trust, I can present a fairly accurate picture of events. No response came from many places where I knew information to be; yet on the whole, people were really very friendly and helpful. I must have wearied many librarians with my constant inquiries, but I had "bitten" and did not want to let go until I knew what I wanted to know.

What the reader has before him now is the fruit of a work carried on over a period of seven years (on and off, not constant). I have concentrated on Darby's early years because so little is known about this time and much of what has been believed has not always been historically accurate. Secondly, this was Darby's formative period; I feel that to be able to understand what he later taught, it is of great help to know how he arrived at his thoughts.

In this biography I have striven to be fair, honest, and objective, but I know that I have not always attained this goal. The following remarks by David Bebbington are very fitting:

> The historian's history is moulded by his values, his outlook, his worldview. It is never the evidence alone that dictates what is written. The attitudes that a historian brings to evidence form an equally important element in the creation of history. The bias of a historian enters his history. . . . Historians are like others in sharing the convictions and prejudices of their time

> and place. Their outlook affects what they write far more strongly than is normally supposed. Objectivity in one sense is within their capacity, for they can treat all the evidence at their disposal with scrupulous fairness and allow it to call their prejudices and even their convictions into question. But the evidence is unlikely to modify more than a few of their assumptions. Their basic beliefs about the past, about its shape and meaning, are likely to remain and are certain to influence what they write.[1]

I should here like to thank all who in any way were a help to me in the course of my work. My special thanks goes to the following, who at different times and in different ways were a help, an encouragement, and an inspiration:

Christian Briem - Stuttgart, Germany
Dr. W. J. Ouweneel - De Bilt, Holland
Dr. D. W. Paterson - Birmingham, England
Jacob Redekop - Niagara-on-the-Lake, Canada

This is not to say that they are in favor or support of all contained in the following pages—that responsibility is mine alone.

Foreword

TO THE ENGLISH EDITION

What the reader now has is a revised version of the German edition. The foreword to the German edition, in edited form, has been included to explain my original purpose and the efforts involved in writing this biography. I should like to thank my Dutch publisher Henk Medema; staff members of Loizeaux Brothers for their help in finalizing the English edition; Albert Chapman of Buntingford, England; and especially H. H. Rowdon of London Bible College and the late F. F. Bruce, who regrettably did not live to see this biography in published form.

Since the appearance of the German edition, many have gone through the biography and I am happy to say that this "scrutiny" has not necessitated any changes of consequence in my original presentation of historical "facts." *Facts*, if understood properly, is a justifiable word, but one must keep in mind that there are no such things as brute facts alone (seen from the human perspective). All facts are interpreted facts. Nevertheless, I have striven for objectivity in my revision. Since completing my work on the German edition I have been studying church history and various schools of Bible teaching. This has been very profitable. I believe that I can now, in some better way, place the Brethren movement and teaching within the context of church history as a whole.

While working on the original German version I became aware of the Darby "myth." Since the biography's publication I have become even more aware of it. Every great servant of

God or anyone who has changed the direction of man's thoughts has a following of one sort or another. Usually these adherents have an image of the person whom they see as their leader. Once people become emotionally involved with one image, they have difficulty accepting another image, even if it has a more factual basis. I have sought to present Darby as he really was and this has pained and angered some of his following. One reaction was that my presentation of him might be quite acceptable for a historian, but not for a Christian; that is, I was seen as judging Darby and setting myself (spiritually?) above him. This was not my intention. Scripture tells us to "remember our leaders," but surely it means to remember them as they *really* were and not the images *we* have formed of them.

1
Beginnings

I have called thee by thy name; thou art mine.
Isaiah 43:1, KJV

The train pulled slowly out of the shadows of the London Waterloo Station and into the March sunshine. The old man settled back in his seat, making himself as comfortable as possible. It would take nearly four hours till he reached his planned destination. He shared his compartment with three other men who were accompanying him on his trip from London to Bournemouth. This would be his last trip.

He had made many trips in his long life. Besides traveling extensively in his native England and Ireland, he had often been to Switzerland, France, Germany, Holland, Italy, and Spain. Many times he had crossed the Atlantic, visiting Canada, the United States, and the West Indies. At one time he had traveled across America by train to the West Coast when the West was still "wild." From there he had sailed on to New Zealand and Australia. Traveling had not always been easy. The means of transportation had not always been the best and often he had gone long distances on foot. Yet in spite of all the hardships and discomforts involved, he had enjoyed the traveling, was thankful for it, and regretted none of it. He had not taken all these trips for the sake of adventure or his own pleasure. No, he had traveled in the service of One he deeply loved and to whom he had devoted his life.

His years of service had ended and his life was rapidly nearing its close. Traveling was no longer easy at the age of eighty-one, and the fall he had suffered the year before had been something like a decisive blow to his health. Now he was traveling to England's south coast where he could spend his last days in quiet and in the care of those who loved him.

Many people knew him personally. Many more knew of him. Many, from both groups, were dearly attached to him and felt themselves greatly in his debt. They looked to him as their leader. Others hated him, distrusted him, and saw in him a selfish and ambitious man seeking his own ends. He had often encountered those one would label as "enemies," those who tried to hinder or destroy the work he did and felt he had been given to do. But he had had many friends, and even now the respect and concern shown by his three traveling companions were a joy. He was thankful he was not alone.

He looked out of the window, watching the passing, ever-changing scenery. It was truly beautiful. Through quaint towns and villages, through meadows and forests, through hills and dales the train passed. His Master had shown him much of this earth's beauty. He recalled how Lake Geneva and its surroundings had so impressed him. He remembered the roaring and thundering might of Niagara Falls. He remembered the vastness, the emptiness, of the American desert. Yes, he remembered it was the beauty of creation that had brought about the great change in his life—a change that had determined all else.

Lost in memories, he saw once again the face of the woman he had loved. Theodosia! He had loved her and she had loved him, but they had not married and she had died young. He thought of his days as a clergyman; he recalled his studies in Dublin, his school days in London, his father's house, his mother. How vivid and alive it all was now. The years rushed past his mind's eye as the scenery rushed past his train window—back, back to the beginning.

Family Tree

"Birth. On Wednesday morning, Mrs. Darby, of Great George Street, Westminister, of a son." So read the small announcement in the lower right-hand corner of a page in the *London Times*. The baby, born November 18, 1800, was Mrs. Darby's sixth son and eighth child. (Her last child, a daughter, would be born in 1802).

Mrs. Darby was born a Vaughan: "Anne, daughter of Samuel Vaughan of London," as records show. Samuel Vaughan was a wealthy merchant and owned plantations in the New World. Anne married John Darby in 1784. The Darbys were an old family. Records in England go back to the fifteenth century and to Gaddesby (near Melton Mowbray in Leicestershire). The church in Gaddesby contains an altar tomb from the fifteenth century with graven figures of the knight William Darby and his wife. (See appendix A for the Darby family tree.)

The connection between the Darby family and Ireland began in the sixteenth century when a John Darby, son of Edmund Darby, served under the Earl of Sussex as a Captain of Horse in his campaigns there, either in the year 1557 or 1559. The earl besieged the castle of Leap belonging to the family of the O'Carrolls of Eile in the part of Ireland later known as "King's County" but today as Offaly.[1]

During one of the attacks on the castle John Darby was captured and held prisoner in the castle in a room measuring four by seven feet. Food was passed to him through a hole in the wall. This was the duty of O'Carroll's young and beautiful daughter Finola, and in the expected romantic tradition they fell in love with each other. When Finola discovered that her father planned to hang John Darby she helped him to escape by unbarring his door. As Darby was racing down the stone stairs to expected freedom he was confronted by Finola's brother, who sounded an alarm. Darby turned and ran back up and out onto the battlements. From there he jumped into the branches of a large yew tree and escaped. The siege of Leap Castle continued and ended in its finally being taken by the English forces. John Darby later married Finola O'Carroll, the heiress of

Leap Castle
(Commissioners of Public Works in Ireland, National Monuments Branch)

Sir Admiral Henry Darby
(1749-1823)
(National Maritime Museum, Greenwich, London)

Location of Leap Castle
(The author)

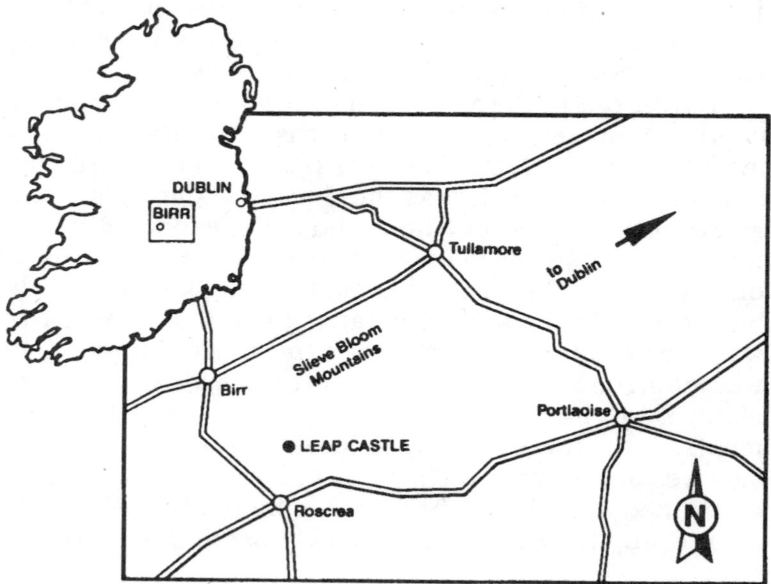

the castle, and through her acquired a part of the Leap estate.

The greater part of the estate remained in the possession of its Irish proprietor. John Darby died in 1608. The Irish portion of Leap was later confiscated for the use of the English king James I (1603-1625), but the Darby part remained in the Darby family. In the rule of Charles II (1660-1685) the confiscated portion was sold to a certain John Holland. The Darbys later bought this part from him and so the entire Leap estate passed into Darby hands.

In 1745 the owner of Leap, a Jonathan Darby (the eldest son was always named Jonathan), married a certain Susannah Lovett. In the course of their marriage they had eight sons and one daughter. Their third oldest son, Henry D'Esterre (born 1749), joined the navy and won a name for himself by his gallant conduct as the captain of the ship *Bellerophon* in the battle of the Nile in 1798. He was a very distinguished man, said to be Lord Nelson's favorite commodore. In 1819 Henry became an admiral and later received the title of "Sir." The inheritance of Leap Castle fell to him after the death of his oldest brother Jonathan (Robert, the second oldest, had died earlier, in 1764).[2]

The London Darbys—J. N. Darby's Parents

Henry's brother, three years younger and the next in line, was John Darby. He seems to have spent most of his life in England. He was a merchant and had his business at Russia Row, Milk Street, in Cheapside (London), and lived in a large house at St. John's, Cambridge Heath, Hackney (London). He was a wealthy man and possessed much land.[3]

In 1784, as we have already noted, John had married Anne, daughter of Samuel Vaughan of London. In 1800 the family, then numbering seven children, moved to a house in Westminster (London), number 9 Great George Street,[4] which they leased from the dean and chapter of Westminster Abbey. It was here on November 18, 1800, that their youngest son, John Nelson, was born.

John Nelson Darby was baptized fifteen weeks later on March 3, 1801, at St. Margaret's Church, according to the rites

William Henry Darby
(1790-1880)
(The collection of Ulrich Bister)

George Darby (1796-1878)
lived in Warbleton.
(Edward Reeves, Lewes)

Markly, Warbleton
(A. C. Fox Daries, Armorial Families, *supplied by East Sussex County Council)*

Great George Street, corner of King Street, London (1831)
(Victoria Library, City of Westminster)

St. Margaret's, London, interior (1809)
(Victoria Library, City of Westminster)

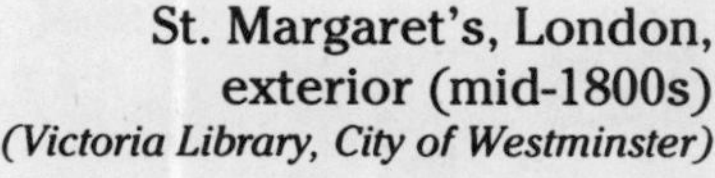

St. Margaret's, London, exterior (mid-1800s)
(Victoria Library, City of Westminster)

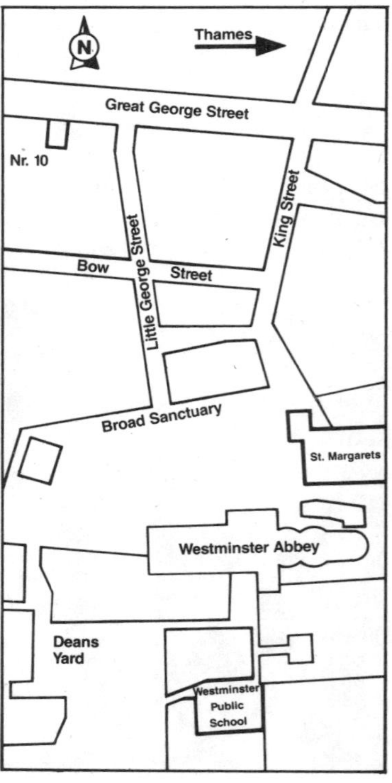

Top: Westminster Public School, London, interior
(Victoria Library, City of Westminster)
Above: Westminster Public School, London, exterior
(Victoria Library, City of Westminster)
Right: Westminster, London, city map detail, end of eighteenth century
(The author)

of the national church. In 1874 he wrote, "The circumstances of my own baptism, though done *bonâ fide*, and in the main with right intentions, were not such as I should wish, but I do not think it can be repeated."[5] (See appendix B.)

His first name, John, he received without a doubt from his father. His middle name, Nelson, certainly was given to him because of his uncle's connection with the man by that name who at the time was the active head of the navy and hero of the British people. Lord Nelson was, as has often been stated in other places, the baby's godfather. What is not true is that Nelson himself was present at the baptism. One Darby biographer goes so far as to say that Nelson held the baby over the baptismal font himself. But this is only descriptive fantasy. Besides the fact that Nelson at the time had only one arm, having lost the other at the battle of Teneriffa, history shows us that he was on his ship, the *St. George*, at Spithead on March 3, 1801; the *St. James Chronicle* reported him to have been at Yarmouth on March 4, and not in London at all. Yet this does not mean that Lord Nelson could not have been Darby's godfather. William Kelly, a close friend of J. N. Darby in later years, stated this as a fact in one of his letters dated June 22, 1899. Nelson was probably represented by a sponsor at the actual baptism, which was permitted then as it is today.

We do not know much about John Nelson Darby's parents, or the character of the atmosphere that ruled in the house. The little we know of his father does not put him in a good light. Gustav Ischebeck, in his otherwise not very reliable biography of Darby, compared J. N. Darby's father with the father of the English writer Thomas Carlyle; the elder Carlyle was said to be as hard as granite, deeply serious, and almost inflexible and pitiless in character. In this point Ischebeck appears to have been right in his comparison.

While John Darby was still living in Hackney he leased six small houses adjoining his premises "for the express purpose of not permitting improper persons to get into possession of them." He allowed a man by the name of William Griffin to live in one of these houses and asked him to collect the rent from those living in the other houses. In 1816 Mr. Griffin himself was behind in paying his rent. Even against the advice of his solicitors, Darby had this man arrested and sent to prison.

Some fifteen years later B. W. Newton was traveling with J. N. Darby and they stopped to visit Darby's father. Newton described the visit:

> About 1831 or so I rode up to London from Plymouth with [J. N.] Darby. It was cold going across in the neighbourhood of Salisbury. We reached his father's house at 6 in the morning. . . . They lived in a good house in Westminster. We two were shown into the dreary room where his sister was having her music lessons. She bowed to us, and no more notice was taken. "Well, John, where have you come from?" "From Plymouth, Sir." "And where are you going to?" "To Oxford, Sir, with Mr. Newton." And no more notice was taken.[6]

James Butler Stoney, a close friend in J. N. Darby's later years, once noted an interesting incident: "When J. N. D. was a young man, and exposing the defects of others, his father said to him: 'I say John, improve the world by one man.' "[7]

Mrs. Darby was of quite a different character from her husband. She appears to have exercised a deep and lasting influence on her youngest son, though she only had him for herself a short time.

When J. N. Darby reached the age of fifty-two, he wrote:

> I have long, I suppose, looked at the portrait of my mother, who watched over my tender years with that care which only a mother knows how to bestow. I can just form some imperfect thought of her looks, for I was early bereft of her; but her eye fixed upon me that tender love which had me for its heart's object–which could win when I could know little else–which had my confidence before I knew what confidence was–by which I learnt to love, because I felt I was loved, was the object of that love which had its joy in serving me–which I took for granted must be; for I had never known anything else at all. All that which I had learnt, but which was treasured in my heart and formed part of my nature, was linked with the features which hung before my gaze. That was my mother's picture. It

> recalled her, no longer sensibly present, to my heart.[8]

One of J. N. Darby's letters says:

> I have a charming portrait of my mother, which reminds me of her just as she was. That which is precious in it to me is my mother herself. The portrait has no value except as far as it is a good representation of her who is not there. I say, it is my mother. I could not throw it aside as a mere piece of canvas; I discern my mother in it. I cherish this portrait; I carry it with me.[9]

Affection, as Darby himself put it, begins very early in a child, and thorough confidence in his parents comes through their tender care and sacrifices for him. This was J. N. Darby's experience with his mother. As noted above, he lost his mother at an early age. We do not know exactly when. What it meant for his child's heart we can only guess, and perhaps only those who have gone through the same can truly understand the sorrow it entails. At the age of seventy-nine he wrote a letter to someone whose mother was ill. The following extract serves to give us a glimpse of what J. N. Darby's feelings were when he lost his own mother:

> I trust and pray that God may graciously spare Mrs. ______. A mother, be she ever so sick, is always an immense loss; the bond of the house or family is broken. An eye and heart are there which, even if they cannot do much, those that make up the family refer to, and run in solicitude through all. A man cannot do this in the same way, however kind a father. Still God does all things well, and can turn, however deeply felt, an evil into a real and better blessing. Still no one can be a mother but a mother, but God can be everything to us and towards us in all our cases.[10]

When Darby writes of being "bereft" of his mother, one gets the impression that she died. Many writers have asserted this, but this was not the case. In 1819 Darby's father had bought an estate called Markly in East Sussex. (His purpose was to be able to qualify for a grant of arms, which he received in 1820.) John Nelson's older brother George later lived here. The Markly estate is located in Warbleton and in the churchyard in Warbleton we find the following on a Darby grave: "In Memoriam. Anne, widow of John Darby of Leap Castle and Markly, died December 31st, 1847, aged 90."

The date of burial, January 7, 1848, is also to be found in the Warbleton church records. When Mrs. Darby first came to Warbleton is not known, but she is included in a census taken in 1841. There can be no doubt that this Anne Darby was J. N. Darby's mother. The statement made by others that J. N. Darby's mother died when he was five years old—that is, in 1806—is a mistake. It was his grandmother Susannah (Lovett) Darby, who died in that year.

Recently a large number of letters of J. N. Darby's father have been found. They are dated from 1813 to 1827 and are more of a business character. Though some of his children are mentioned in these letters, the names of John Nelson Darby and Anne Darby do not appear. From the contents of these letters, one's impression that the writer is a hard and not very pleasant man is only strengthened. Another document, still existing today, shows that in 1830 Mr. Darby was claiming that a certain amount of money from the estate of his deceased father-in-law, Samuel Vaughan, was an unpaid part of his marriage settlement with Miss Vaughan. (Mr. Vaughan had made a generous provision for Anne in his will.) Mr. Darby wanted his daughter Sarah and his son William Henry (his heir) to be plaintiffs in this suit, but they refused. This clearly shows that something had taken place within the family.

John Darby's will, dated September 25, 1832, was written in London. He began with mentioning his wife (so she was still living) and the Markly estate, which he left to her. There are several additions to this will. One, made in August 1833, was written while he was at Markly; the witnesses who signed it were from Warbleton. In another addition, bearing no date, he left the portrait of himself, which at the time hung in the house at Westminster, to his wife. Whatever led to the separation of Mr. Darby and his wife we can only guess. Stranger yet is the fact that their son, John Nelson Darby, never saw her again after his early childhood, though she died when he was forty-seven years old.[11]

School Days

On February 17, 1812, J. N. Darby entered the Westminster public school. The headmaster at the time was Dr. Carey. The school was, one might say, just around the corner and down the street from where J. N. Darby lived; yet he was a boarder there. All the sons of Mr. Darby attended this school. The classes were conducted in a large open hall, one class beside the other along the walls of the building; the students sat on terraced benches with their teachers in front of them. Westminster was one of the greatest, though not the most fashionable, of English public schools. Only children of rich parents, such as could pay the school fees, attended, though there were scholarships that provided free education for forty out of the three hundred boys attending. The instruction was given by clergymen, and the subject matter consisted almost exclusively of Latin and Greek, with some English composition. Discipline was very severe, and in keeping with the times; the boys were beaten by the headmaster with a birch rod for misbehavior.

The years that J. N. Darby spent at this school passed by uneventfully—so much so that his old schoolmaster, being questioned years later, could well recall a boy by that name, but could not think of anything worthy of special notice and actually did not know what had become of him. J. N. Darby once wrote that in a child many reflective and working abilities lie hidden and come out by being called upon. The ability to acquire knowledge may begin early, but the reflective use of what has been acquired comes later. This was to prove itself well in his own case.

In later years J. N. Darby felt that public schools trained boys for the world, with little or no fear of God.[12] He said, "My education was in my judgment not well *directed*, save by God."[13] He was not entirely opposed to education, and he believed that a Christian was free to seek the necessary improvement and cultivation for his secular work and position.[14] What he was opposed to was education for its own sake as a goal for Christians. His desire was not only to have humanity educated, but more importantly to have God made known, as he put it.[15]

Ireland

In 1815 Mr. Darby sent his youngest son to Dublin, Ireland, for further education; he entered Trinity College on July 3.

Most writers, probably following the lead given by W. G. Turner in his biography of J. N. Darby, say that at this time the entire Darby family came to reside at their ancestral castle in Ireland. This statement is not correct.

J. N. Darby's oldest sister Susannah, fifteen years his senior, married Edward Pennefather of Ireland in 1806 and moved to Dublin at that time. In 1841 Pennefather became lord chief justice of Ireland and we shall hear more of him later.

J. N. Darby's older brother Christopher Lovett also came to live in Ireland in the service of the Anglican church as rector and vicar. He must have come to Ireland sometime between 1815 and 1822. (I have been able to obtain an article written by him entitled "The Obligations of the Baptized.")

The letters of J. N. Darby's father from the years 1813 to 1827 all carry addresses from places in England, none from Ireland. The father inherited the Leap estate only in or after 1823, the year in which his brother Sir Admiral Henry Darby died. It is questionable if the father ever came to live at Leap Castle, though he is apparently buried there. J. N. Darby's connection with the family estate at Leap appears only to have been in the form of an occasional visit, if that much. There is no proof of his having been there.

Two of his other brothers, William Henry and George, were busy pursuing their careers in law in England at the time of the family's so-called return to Ireland.

When J. N. Darby left England for Ireland in 1815 he went alone. It was not easy for the young boy of fourteen to take this step. In spite of all that might have occurred at home, including the loss of his mother, home is still the center of all true feelings and leaving it was a hard thing to do. His going left a lasting impression on his young mind, for at the advanced age of sixty-nine he wrote to one who had left home, "Your very leaving home has begun the tale for you; it did once for me. I remember yet my desolation once on leaving it."[16]

The "tale" really did begin for J. N. Darby when he went to Dublin. At Trinity he began to make rapid strides, and the talent which before had lain hidden began to unfold itself. From the school records we see that he was enrolled on the same day as George Bellett (who was three years older than Darby and later a well-known and loved clergyman in the established church) and that they had the same teacher, a Mr. Singer. George's brother John Gifford (one year older) had enrolled three months previously on April 3. George probably introduced Darby to John Gifford. The two became friends, and the friendship lasted throughout their lifetimes. We shall hear more of J. G. Bellett later on.

Darby was a fellow commoner at Trinity, which meant that he came from a wealthy background, paid double fees and dined with the fellows. Although his sister and brother-in-law had their house not far away from the college, Darby lived at school and not at their home.

Trinity College was an Anglican institution and schooled many gentlemen in classical studies and mathematics.[17] On July 10, 1819, Darby graduated with a bachelor of arts degree and received the highest honors in classics: the classical gold medal. R. B. McDowell and D. A. Webb had this to say about the gold medal in Darby's time:

> Competition for the medals was restricted to students who had already proved their merit by winning a premium at a term examination; they were distinguished in the degree lists as *primarii in sua classe* and were examined at the degree examination, not only more searchingly, but on a much wider course. In both Classics and Science a respectable standard was expected, but the award of two medals, one for each subject, encouraged some degree of specialization. In Classics only a few texts additional to those of the ordinary course were prescribed (some Aristotle, a play of Aeschylus, Cicero's *De oratore,* and the *Ars poetica* of Horace), but candidates for the medal were advised to be "prepared in an extensive course of History, and should be well acquainted with the Prosody and other niceties of the Greek language, besides the nature and history of Greek drama . . . It is also requisite to possess an acquaintance with the Classical English poets, and to be practised in Latin composition at least."[18]

I have heard, from one who knew him personally, that Algernon J. Pollock, who became a well-known teacher among the English Brethren, once told the story that while he was still attending college, he had been invited to the home of a "brother" for tea. Darby had also been invited, and this was certainly the reason for the house being filled with other Brethren. Pollock, because of the lack of space, was forced to share his plate with Darby, who must have been in his seventies at the time. After hearing that Pollock was still studying, Darby playfully said, "Be sure to get the gold medal." This was the only "ministry" Pollock received from the great man.

After finishing his college studies Darby decided to become a lawyer and began to study law. This must have been a source of great joy for his brother-in-law, who in 1816 was a king's counsel, for he not only hoped that Darby would rise to the highest honors in the profession, but also that his penetrating and generalizing genius would do much to bring order into the legal chaos of the day.

Darby was admitted to Lincoln's Inn on November 9, 1819.[19] He had first been admitted to King's Inn, the legal inn in Dublin (that is, an Irish inn), and was then recommended and admitted to Lincoln's Inn (that is, an English inn of court). He did not attend Lincoln's Inn in London, but remained in Dublin and received his schooling there. Bellett, on the other hand, did go to London for this schooling period and completed his eight terms there on November 26, 1821.

Darby was called to the Irish bar on January 21, 1822. He was now a barrister. In Ireland a common citizen had to submit his complaint quietly to an attorney–today known as a solicitor–who then instructed the barrister to plead the cause in open court by legal argument.[20]

Spiritual Awakenings

Darby wrote in later years, "Before I was converted, I believed there was Christ as much as I do now."[21] On another occasion in 1853 he wrote:

> When I was a poor dark creature I remember when first awakened to serious and, in some measure, continued

> moral thought, I was reading, partly through desire of knowledge, partly alas! through the vanity which likes to possess it, Cicero's *Offices*, and I came to the passage, nearly the only one which remains to me unobliterated by an active life, "Truth Subjected as a Material to the Mind." I said to myself (or rather the divine truth flashed across my mind), "This cannot be in the case of God, for my mind must be superior to the matter which is subjected to its operations; if it be, that which is so is not God. Faith alone can put Him in His place, which, if He be God, must be above me, as God must be above man."[22]

Darby's thinking, as we shall shortly see, was later influenced by Thomas Scott (1747-1821) the Bible commentator. Scott's following remarks are of the same nature as Darby's above:

> In rejecting the doctrines evidently taught in the Bible, we must either arrogate to our own understanding a superiority above the omniscience of God, or impeach his veracity, or deny a part of the Scriptures to be a divine revelation; reserving to ourselves the infallible determination, what part is of divine authority, and what is not.[23]

It was probably this similarity of thought and reasoning that impressed Darby when he read Scott.

In another place Darby remarked, "I remember, when I was unconverted, the sense of beauty in creation made me feel I must have to say to God."[24]

In his twenty-first year, John Nelson Darby was converted to God and the entire course of his life was changed. The thought that Darby was converted at the age of eighteen is wholly unfounded. This statement was made in one of his earliest biographies[25] and has been accepted by nearly all writers since. Darby nowhere spoke of this, but rather he said repeatedly that after being under "the rod of the law" for seven years after his conversion, he was finally delivered at the end of 1827. The year of his conversion then was 1820 or 1821. His mention at the age of forty-five of having been converted twenty years ago[26] was only a rounding off, which he often did, and not an exact statement. William Kelly confirmed the correctness of the 1820/1821 date by writing in a letter[27] that Darby was converted while a barrister (or studying to be one). At first glance this may not seem so important, but we shall shortly see that it is very important in the story of Darby's life. This 1820/1821 date has been confirmed by several remarks Darby wrote down in his copy of a four-volume Greek New Testament. By 2 Timothy 3 we find the statement: "I loved Christ, I have no doubt, sincerely and growingly since June or July 1820, or 21. I forget which." (See appendix C for a complete transcript of Darby's comments.)

Yet, as hinted above, Darby did not at once have peace of soul after his conversion, for conversion (repentance) and the assurance of the forgiveness of sins are two different things. In 1874 he wrote, "In my own case, I went through deep exercise of soul before there was a trace of peace, and it was not till after six or seven years that I was delivered."[28]

During these years universal sorrow and sin pressed upon his spirit. Darby's conversion took place, as he himself testified, through the reading of God's Word alone and not with the help of man. He felt that Christ was the only Savior, but was not able to say that he possessed Him, or that he was saved by Him. He looked for proofs of regeneration in himself, something that can never give peace, and rested in the *hope* of Christ's work, but not in *faith*. He spent his time in fasting, praying, and giving alms. On Wednesdays, Fridays, and Saturdays he would eat nothing at all until evening, and then only a little bread, or nothing. If he could fast three days, he thought he could fast four; if four, then five; if five, better still six; and if six, then seven.[29] When he wanted to take the sacrament he would always go to his clergyman first, so that he might judge of the matter.

Darby may have found comfort in Thomas Scott's comments on the Lord's supper:

> But the humble trembling penitent, who would seek salvation in the crucified Saviour, by using the means which he has appointed, ought not to suspect any snare, or fear any danger in approaching the Lord's table; even though many doubts may still disquiet his

> mind, or great remaining darkness obscure his views . . . Such self-examination must always become professed Christians: not in order to find out some excuse for neglecting to obey the dying command of their loving Saviour; but in order to remember him with more fervent affection and more exalted thanksgivings. It is very useful, when we have the opportunity, to set apart some time previously to the administration of the Lord's supper, thus to re-examine ourselves, to enquire into our progress in vital godliness, and to renew in secret our cordial consent to the new covenant in the blood of Christ. Such a preparation is especially important to the new convert, when (with the instructions and prayers of ministers and pious friends), he first approaches to make this profession; and to the backslider, when he is recovered from his wanderings, and desires to renew the solemn transaction. In all cases self-examination should be considered merely as introductory to the exercise of repentance and faith, the practice of works meet for repentance, and fervent prayers for divine teaching, and grace to enable us more profitably to attend on the ordinances of God: for should any one discover, that at present he could not approach the Lord's table in a suitable manner, he ought by no means to rest satisfied with absenting himself; but should rather become more earnest in using every means of becoming an acceptable communicant. The believer, however, who habitually examines himself, and daily exercises repentance and faith, may very properly receive the Lord's supper without any further preparation, when an unexpected opportunity presents itself.[30]

In the beginning of his conversion Darby had been attracted to the church of Rome, but Hebrews 9–10 made it impossible for him to follow her. In the previously mentioned Greek New Testament Darby described this time of Roman Catholic influence on himself:

> For my mind had passed, after its own repentance, under the dark cloud of the popish system, (i.e. to look

> for the powers of Christ's agency in the visible authority of the Church), though God was with me through it all. And I used to hold up Christ to my brother as availing against the claim of men on their points, yet it prevailed so far as to prevent my mind from finding comfort in the truths I honestly urged on him, which I had found in what poor reading of Scripture I had.[31]

J. N. Darby went with the established church. It is interesting to note that part of the oath he had to take when called to the Irish Chancery Bar contained the vow to prevent the further growth of popery.

Darby fully believed in apostolic succession (the belief in the uninterrupted and continuous succession of bishops from the time of the apostles up to the present day) and held that the only channels of blessing were through them. Men such as Luther and Calvin, together with their followers, he considered for this reason to be outside of these channels, but he was (he said) not their judge and left them to the uncovenanted mercies of God. Reading the sixth chapter of Romans he could wonder at it, but did not understand it. The union of the church with the state he felt to be Babylonish (we shall shortly see a confirmation of these feelings in his reaction to an event that led in this direction). The church should govern herself; she was in bondage but was still the church.[32]

In all this scene of struggle Darby felt deeply that if the Son of God had given Himself for him, then he owed himself entirely to Him—his soul, his body, his means. The exercises of his soul were very strong at this time. He wrote of it nearly fifty years later on February 5, 1874: "I, a conservative by birth, by education and by mind; a Protestant in Ireland into the bargain; I had been moved to the very depths of my soul on seeing that everything was going to be shaken. The testimony of God made me see and feel that all should be shaken."[33]

Ordination

Darby felt that the so-called Christian world was characterized by deep ingratitude toward Christ, and he himself longed for complete devotedness to the Lord's work. And so, in search of relief from the unceasing anguish of his soul, he followed the advice of those who were more advanced in ecclesiastical things and had himself ordained in the Anglican church.[34] His decision to be ordained must have been made sometime in the year 1824, for in the Darby collection there is a receipt dated December 9, 1824, for making a clergyman's gown.

Darby wrote that he was induced to take orders. It is my firm conviction that the Reverend Robert Daly (who, along with Thomas Scott, probably had the greatest influence on Darby's spiritual life) was the one who induced him.

Daly was rector of Powerscourt and later became bishop of Cashel. During his time in Powerscourt he came into contact with many people later connected directly or indirectly with Darby. Daly was greatly involved in the Home Mission and the Bible Society. Darby received an invitation from Daly to the tenth annual Wicklow Auxiliary Bible Society in August 1823, but their acquaintance with each other is of an earlier date. Edward Pennefather sent Darby a note announcing the birth of a daughter dated May 26, 1819, with the remark, "Tell Robert Daly I am sorry I missed seeing him." George and John Bellett also knew Daly. George wrote of visiting Kilgobbin Church (the parish of the Bellett family home, ten miles out of Dublin) in 1818:

> Mr. Daly, Rector of Powerscourt, afterwards Bishop of Cashel, came often to preach there, and at that time we highly esteemed him, and his sermons were not without their effect, but they owed their success more to the intense earnestness of his manner than to anything else.[35]

Many writers have seen Darby's deliverance from inner bondage as his real reason for ordination. This is not true. In fact he did not feel drawn to take up a regular post. He became ordained in the hope of finding inner peace and not because he already possessed it.

Of this time he wrote in his Greek New Testament: "I had once had my soul brought I knew not where so deep as no . . . tongue, I suppose, could tell; others may have felt it, I know it not—hardly before I began to preach repentance."

The archbishop of Dublin (from 1822-1831), William Magee, wrote to his son, the Reverend Thomas Magee, on August 2, 1825: "This will be handed to you by Mr. Darby, a Rev. when ordained I purpose to appoint to the care of the Calary District, which is important to be attended to immediately. I trust that in his hands the duty will be faithfully discharged."[36] Archbishop Magee was as well known for his fight against the spread and influence of Roman Catholicism as Robert Daly was for his firm adherence to the authority and spread of the holy Scriptures, and Magee would play a major role in Darby's life.

Darby was ordained as a deacon on August 7, 1825, (this date is important for further calculations) by Bishop William Bissett in Raphoe Cathedral.[37] The *Christian Examiner and Church of Ireland Magazine* for October 1825 does not mention the name *Darby* among the ordinations that took place at Raphoe Cathedral on August 7. The list does include the name *Darley*, and this is a misprint for *Darby*, as *b* in written form often has the appearance of *le*.[38]

Darby's decision not only disappointed his brother-in-law Pennefather, but also called forth a violent reaction from his father. His father, it is said, not at all in agreement with his youngest son's action, disinherited him. The exact reasons for this are not known. J. N. Darby's older brother Christopher was a clergyman and this, as far as is known, was never a cause of conflict. Perhaps Mr. Darby had had great plans for this one son, in the hope of his making a splendid career in law and enhancing the Darby name–plans that were ruined by his son's entering the service of the church (he could have made a name for himself there as well, had he desired it). How far this disinheritance went, or how long it lasted, is hard to say. From other sources it is clear, as we have already seen, that when J. N. Darby was in London, he visited or stayed with his father, and that J. N. Darby was mentioned in his father's will. I was not able to find any confirming evidence that J. N. Darby was the means of his father's conversion and that they were reconciled at the father's deathbed, as stated in the German edition of *Miller's Church History* (but not in the original English edition).

J. N. Darby had not studied theology at Trinity College, and there is not the least ground for assuming that he did so between the time of his being called to the Chancery Bar in 1822 and his ordination in 1825. When writing of his conversion and the time following in his Greek New Testament, Darby did mention Thomas Scott and did note that Scott's *Essays* influenced his thinking at one time, but as we have already observed, Darby also wrote of his "poor reading of Scripture." A deacon was the lowest ranking ordained clergy in the Anglican church. Darby would only have had to convince a bishop (in his case it would seem to have been the archbishop himself) that he was a worthy candidate for ordination.

An example of this is seen in the case of Thomas Scott mentioned above; Downer wrote:

> He [Scott] called on a clergyman whom he astonished with the announcement that he intended to offer himself for Holy Orders. Being asked whether he knew anything of Latin and Greek, he translated a passage of the Greek Testament into both English and Latin; and the clergyman promised to mention him to the Archdeacon ... After one interview with the Archdeacon, whom he satisfied as to his knowledge [not Scriptural knowledge] he was encouraged to hope for success in his purpose.[39]

If being ordained was as simple as that, Darby would have had no difficulty in being accepted, having enjoyed an education Scott never had.

The German edition of *Miller's Church History* also states that Darby studied medicine a short while, though this remains without confirming evidence. Darby is still referred to as Dr. Darby in the Wicklow area of Ireland, but doctor of what, is not known.

It had been Darby's desire to work among the poor Roman Catholics in Ireland. He had a great love for Catholic believers and in later years wrote a series called "Familiar Conversations on Romanism," which were particularly aimed at helping them come to a clearer understanding of the truth and freeing them from what he believed to be the teachings of men. His field of service in the county of Wicklow, south of Dublin on the Irish east coast, was mainly populated by Roman Catholics. It was a wild and uncultivated district; the inhabitants were said to be as wild as the country itself. Before we go into Darby's work there, which lasted two years and three months, we shall take a look at the general state of the clergy in those days, as described by Turner in his biography of J. N. Darby. The contrast proves to be interesting.

The clergy were, as a whole, careless in giving out the bread of life to the flocks who had been committed to their care and keeping. At best they preached a carnal and soul-benumbing morality, and trafficked with the souls of men by receiving money for discharging the pastoral office in parishes where they did not so much as look on the faces of the people more than once a year.

The typical clergyman had no great aims or theological enthusiasm. He felt no serious alarms about the souls of the people who made up his parish, and would have considered it a waste of time to speak in a doctrinal and awakening manner to these simple folk. He would have agreed that the only healthy effects of religion possible in the minds of such people were certain dim but strong emotions, which spread themselves out as sanctifying influences over family affections and neighborly duties. He thought that the custom of baptism was more important than its doctrine, and that the religious benefits which the peasant received from the church were but slightly dependent on a clear understanding of the liturgy or the sermon. The average rector could have been called anything but an earnest man. He was more fond of church history than he was of divinity. He was neither laborious, nor self-denying, nor very liberal in almsgiving, and his theology was evidently lax.

Leaving the above dismal picture we return more directly to Darby who, in spite of his lack of peace and deliverance, stands out sharply against this dark background.

Calary

Calary, as we have seen from the archbishop's letter, was the name of the area where Darby carried out his duties; it was not legally a separate charge or a perpetual curacy until 1832, and a church was not built until 1834. Darby held services

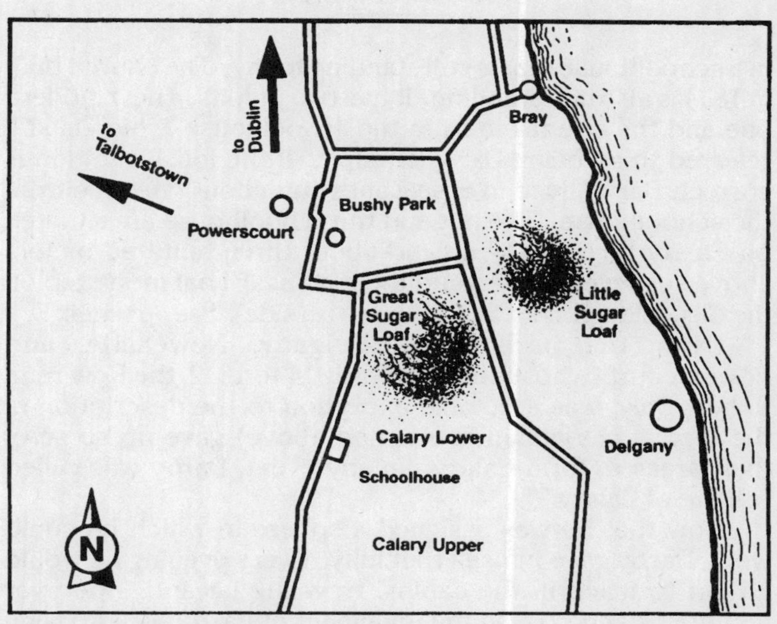

Above: Location of the schoolhouse in Calary *(The author)*
Below: Schoolhouse with Great Sugar Loaf in the background *(The author)*
Right: Entrance to schoolhouse *(The author)*

in a schoolhouse that is still standing today. The church built in 1834 is also still standing. It has two pulpits, a new modern one and the one taken from the schoolhouse, which is still referred to as being Darby's pulpit. If the local tradition is correct, Darby lived in a peasant's hut about one mile from the schoolhouse. The hut and the schoolhouse are situated on Calary bog, a lofty upland about three hundred meters above sea level just beyond the big Sugar Loaf mountain on the Glendalough side (that is, the south side). See appendix D.

Later the parishes of Delgany, Newcastle, and Powerscourt (whose rector from 1814 to 1842, the Reverend Robert Daly, was a notable exception to the description of the typical clergyman mentioned above) gave up some of their areas to form Calary. In any event, Darby was called "curate of Calary."[40]

Now that he was assigned a sphere in which he could work, Darby gave himself to it fully. Every evening he would go out to teach in the cabins, traveling far and wide over mountains and bogs in the fulfillment of his duties. Arriving back home before midnight was a rare thing. Long walks through the wild countryside and among the poor people inflicted much severe privation on him. (J. C. Philpot, who was in the same area for a short time, wrote of having "seen and talked with the poor peasants in their smoky, miserable cabins, and been almost horrified by the spectacle of Irish misery."[41]) Darby ate whatever food offered itself, food that was often tasteless and indigestible. All this served to give his frame the appearance of a monk of LaTrappe, so much had it been wasted away. The money that he had before his ordination he spent in building schools and giving alms.[42] One can be sure that such a man greatly excited the poor Romanists in the area, who looked upon him as a genuine saint of the ancient breed. The stamp of Heaven seemed clear to them in this frame so wasted by austerity, so superior to worldly pomp—in this man who shared in all their needs.[43]

And still, in spite of all this self-denial and devotion to Christ and His service, Darby had not found deliverance or peace for his own soul. He wrote of that time: "Going from cabin to cabin to speak of Christ, and with souls, if I thought to quote a text to myself it seemed a shadow and not real. I ought never to have been there. I was not set free according to Romans 8."[44] In fact, the only portion of Scripture that was of any help to him were the opening lines of Psalm 88: "Oh Lord God of my salvation." "I preached nothing but Christ and had not peace, and had no business to be in any public ministry."[45]

Though the above sounds rather negative, Darby was nevertheless a help to others spiritually. (See appendix E.) One of those who were converted through him later became well known in religious circles, as we will see.

In the autumn of 1825 Edward Pennefather came to Oxford looking for a private tutor for his sons; there he made the acquaintance of a young man by the name of Joseph Charles Philpot (1802-1869), whom he then engaged for the position of tutor. Philpot, though not leading an immoral life, was still in "his sins and without God in the world" at the time, as he himself expressed it. In the spring of 1826 he came to Ireland to take up his duties in the Pennefather home, in their country seat, not far from Dublin.[46] Philpot stayed there more than one and a half years.

From Philpot's memoirs and letters we know that in the early spring of 1827 eternal things were first introduced to his mind, and he saw himself as a poor lost sinner and was converted. In the autumn of that same year he returned to Oxford, and in 1828 he was ordained in the Church of England, from which he withdrew in the spring of 1835 because of what he felt to be the wrongness of its position. He was virtually the founder of a particular group among the strict Baptists, the Gospel Standard Strict and Particular Baptists. W. G. Turner styled him as belonging to the extreme school of hyper-Calvinistic Baptists.

Though speaking of the work of the Lord's Spirit on his soul in 1827, Philpot made no mention of the means by which this was done, referring only to a "heavy and grievous affliction" that he does not describe. (This "affliction" is revealed in *The Seceders* as his falling in love with Pennefather's daughter Anne. The feeling was mutual and the affliction existed in the fact that her parents did not approve of it and a marriage was not allowed. Philpot married later, only after Anne had died.)

We know from other sources that the one who first laid eternal things before Philpot's mind was J. N. Darby. Darby wrote, "Indeed I had been the means of the conversion of its [system of high experimental Baptists] last leader when [he was a] tutor to my nephews."[47]

Philpot knew Darby well. He was aware of Darby's deliverance from bondage before leaving Ireland. This point is very important for the confirmation of other facts, and we shall come back to it again.

On Sunday, February 19, 1826, Darby was ordained priest in Christ Church Cathedral, Dublin, by Archbishop Magee. Darby's soul was not at ease at the time, not only because he was not yet "delivered," but also because he was beginning to feel that the style of his work was not in agreement with what he read in the Bible concerning the church and Christianity. This bothered him from both a practical and spiritual point of view, but he kept trying earnestly to carry out the duties of the ministry which had been entrusted to him. But near the end of that same year something occurred that would serve to give Darby some answers to his questions, though it greatly upset him at first.

Changes

Archbishop Magee delivered a charge[48] in St. Patrick's Cathedral in Dublin on Tuesday, October 10, 1826. Magee had expressed himself at other times and in other ways that were of greater consequence in the debate over Roman Catholicism, but this charge was important in its consequences for one man—namely, J. N. Darby.

This time Magee spoke strongly against the Roman Catholic system, and in favor of the Church of England and Ireland, praising it especially for its loyalty to the state. He saw the church and the state as two aspects of the same Christian community, harmonized in the acknowledgment of the king as the supreme sovereign within the realm. The state had the right of intervention in things spiritual, though no authority to order spiritual affairs (for example, ordain ministers); the church had the right of comment on things temporal, though it acknowledged, and subjected itself to, the state. The sovereign's duty was to establish the best religion. (Contrast this with Darby regarding the union of church and state as Babylonish.)

Among other things, Magee said that the respectability, usefulness, and privileges of the clerical orders established by the state (those belonging to the Church of England and Ireland) were to be protected and the Roman Catholic influence counteracted through all means.

At this time Roman Catholics were fighting for their emancipation as, living in a land where the state religion was not Catholic, they were deprived of many rights. (This emancipation, which had long been a matter of controversy, finally came about in 1829.) Nevertheless many (apparently six to eight hundred per week) were converting to Protestantism through the vigorous efforts of the evangelical clergy.

Fearing the consequences of Catholic aggressiveness, the clergy of the archdiocese of Dublin, taking the archbishop's charge as an encouragement, came together on Thursday, February 1, 1827, at the archbishop's palace, Stephen's Green, and drew up a petition addressed to the House of Commons asking for protection.[49]

To get an idea of Darby's thoughts as to this action, it may be good to quote his friend J. G. Bellett here:

> John Darby was then a curate in the county Wicklow, and often did I visit in his mountain parish. This charge of his Diocesan greatly moved him; he could not understand the common Christianity of such a principle, as it assumed that the ministers in doing their business as witnesses against the world for a rejected Jesus should, on meeting the resistance of the enemy, turn round and seek security from the world. This greatly offended him. All this had a very decided influence on his mind, for I remember him at one time as a very exact churchman, as I may speak, but it was evident that his mind had now received a shock, and it was never again what it had been.[50]

In response to the archbishop's charge and the petition itself, Darby wrote a paper entitled "Considerations Addressed to the Archbishop of Dublin and the Clergy Who Signed the Petition to the House of Commons for Protection." However, Darby "suppressed" (as he said) this paper after writing it. Only later, after the archbishop in a sermon required oaths of allegiance for the admittance of Catholic converts to the established church, did Darby complete the paper, have it printed and send it privately to the archbishop and clergy. He called it "the first germing of the truth which has since developed itself in the Church of God."

In the paper Darby wrote of denying the protection of the church by the state, the apprehension of the believer's life as being in Heaven (at this time he saw the unity of believers as being due to a common faith in Christ; later he came to see this unity as being through the Spirit's work of baptizing all believers into the body of Christ), the church as being composed of a heavenly people, the aim of Christian ministry, the position of the clergy, and of suffering with Christ. Darby held Christ, and not the king, to be the true head of the church. The charge simply substituted the king for the pope. Darby felt that Christ's ministers should not be spared from a share, little as it might be, in the sufferings of Christ. Such suffering would affect their daily lives and stamp them with Christian character.

Darby's paper appeared but had little effect. The Reverend Robert Daly said to him after receiving a copy of the paper, "You ought to become a Dissenter." (Dissenters were those who disagreed with the doctrines or practices of the Church of England and Ireland and formed their own separate companies.) "No," Darby replied, "you have got into the wrong, and you want to put me there—but that you will not do."

Darby's mind was slowly being awakened to what he now felt to be the truth.

It is of great interest to read in Darby's notebook the entry under April 8, 1827.

> The Lord, whose I am, and whom I serve, give grace to the least and unworthiest of His servants to minister to His glory in all wisdom of the righteousness of the saints, gathering fruit unto His glory, which He has sown, and to obtain a place in the many mansions of His Father's house, through grace. Oh! for His appearing. Yet I know the love which causes Him to bear long.[51]

Elsewhere Darby wrote, "Before ever I knew about the Lord's coming, I think I loved His appearing. I knew nothing about the doctrine, but the principle of loving His appearing was in my mind, though I could not define it."[52]

Darby said that in the beginning of his ministry he preached holiness, but soon felt it was not the right way. Toward the end of his ministry in Calary he began to preach the love of God. In the previously mentioned notebook, an entry assumed to be of the same date (or near to it) reads:

> I think the Lord has shown me His service; I mean simply preaching His gospel to every creature in the power of His grace and Spirit. I believe He is teaching me *οσα δει παθειν* ("how much he must suffer," Acts 9:16), and herein I humbly bless Him, presenting under the influence of His mercies my body as a living sacrifice. But I look for ability in every thought simply as *abiding in Him*, and for direction simply to the will of God, proving it by the Spirit vouchsafed to us.

Darby also said that one part of the trial he had to pass through was facing the question of whether or not he was willing to endure all things for the sake of the elect. But his inner struggle was soon to come to an end. Seven years had already passed since his conversion. During this time he had been learning that there was no good in himself. Humiliation, he said, was the method God used with his soul from the beginning.[53] They must have been painful years, years of anguish and at times despair when, as Darby himself said, he had his head just above water. That first and vital lesson in the school of God, where one learns the awfulness of sin and one's own powerlessness over it, was now to come to a close for him.

Answers

While pursuing his duties one day in October 1827 (we arrive at this time by considering the date of his ordination as a deacon, his statement that he served or ministered two years and three months, plus other facts that we will shortly mention) Darby was violently thrown from his horse against a doorpost. He suffered severe injuries and had to be sent to

Dublin for medical treatment. The time of recuperation, which was more than three months, he spent at his brother-in-law's Dublin house at 20 Fitzwilliam Street. It was there that he found rest in the assurance of Christ's completed work:

> After I had been converted six or seven years, I learned by divine teaching what the Lord says in John 14, "In that day ye shall know . . . that ye are in Me, and I in you"—that I was one with Christ before God, and I found peace, and I have never, with many shortcomings, lost it since.[54]

Darby said that he was exercised night and day about whether or not he could rest the faith of his soul, as a living man, on the Word of God:

> I add that at the same period in which I was brought to liberty . . . I passed through the deepest possible exercise as to the authority of the Word: whether if the world and the Church (that is, as an external thing, for it yet had certain traditional power over me as such) disappeared and were annihilated, and the Word of God alone remained as an invisible thread over the abyss, my soul would trust it. After deep exercise of soul I was brought by grace to feel I could entirely. I have never found it fail me since, I have often failed; but never found it failed me.[55]
>
> As regards the gospel, I had no difficulty as to its received dogmas. Three Persons in one God, the divinity of Jesus, His work of atonement on the cross, His resurrection, His session at the right hand of God, were truths which, understood as orthodox doctrines, had long been a living reality to my soul. They were the known and felt conditions, the actualities of my relationship with God. Not only were they truths, but I knew God personally in that way; I had no other God but Him who had thus revealed Himself, and Him I had. He was the God of my life and of my worship, the God of my peace, the only true God.[56]
>
> But God is infallible, that is, cannot be mistaken or deceived. Infallibility is not simply always speaking the

> truth, but the impossibility of mistaking, or deceiving, or shortcoming. It involves not mistaking in anything, as well as not deceiving. Now this is part of my idea of God, the true God.
>
> The practical difference in my preaching when once I began to preach again was as follows: When a parson, I had preached that sin had created a great gulf between us and God, and that Christ alone was able to bridge it over; now, I preached that He *had* already finished His work. The necessity of regeneration which was always a part of my teaching, became connected more with Christ, the last Adam, and I understood better that it was a real life, entirely new, communicated by the power of the Holy Spirit; but as I have said, more in connection with the person of Christ and the power of His resurrection combining the power of a life victorious over death with a new position for man before God. This is what I understand by "deliverance."[57]

Darby's preaching after this deliverance, as noted in his quote above, we shall come back to in chapter 2. Speaking as to deliverance itself he wrote in 1872:

> No doubt, thank God, there is *deliverance*, deliverance in Another; but deliverance is not freedom, but what is granted and effected by another, because I have learned by experience under divine teaching that I am *not* free and cannot free myself. Freedom is the fruit of deliverance by Christ. We are crucified with Him, and I have life in the power of the Spirit in Christ, and then I am free.[58]

Darby believed that if one had been truly delivered from the state or condition described in Romans 7, he would never fall back into it again.[59]

His suffering under the righteous claims of the law may have been a factor contributing to his emphasis on rejecting the law as in any way applicable to the Christian. Darby (and through him the Brethren in general) was so strong in this emphasis that he tended to forget that there is a sense in which the Christian is also under "the law of freedom," "the royal law," "though not under law, yet legally subject to God."

Francis Newman

During Darby's stay at the Pennefather house he came into contact with a young man by the name of Francis Newman, who replaced Philpot as the family tutor. Philpot had left Ireland, as already mentioned, in the autumn of 1827, but not before Darby had been delivered. Newman came to the Pennefather home in the autumn of 1827 as well. Newman did not mention Darby's struggle of soul, so it would appear that he made Darby's acquaintance after Darby had found inner peace. These two incidents, Philpot's leaving and Newman's coming, seem to confirm without question Darby's own statements as to his deliverance being in 1827, and the approximate date of his riding accident.

A letter of Bellett's dated January 31, 1827, spoke of an injury Darby suffered to his knee two months previously.[60] 1827 is either a misprint for 1828 (which would be correct) or Bellett, as many of us do at the beginning of a new year, absent-mindedly wrote the old year instead of the new one.

Newman's brother was the well-known John Henry Newman, first an Anglican priest and then a Roman Catholic cardinal. Francis Newman himself had won an unusually high "double first class" at Oxford University. In the beginning, Newman was greatly influenced by Darby, but later gave way to infidelity. In 1830 Newman went to Baghdad as a missionary, but in time he denied the true and essential deity of Christ. His disillusionment with the truths in the Word of God led to his writing in 1850 *Phases of Faith*, which Darby ably answered with *The Irrationalism of Infidelity* in 1853. Sad though the above truly is, their first years of acquaintance were happier ones. The following is from Newman's well-known account of Darby in *Phases of Faith*. After the lengthy quote some of Newman's statements are explained and corrected.

> My second period is characterized, partly by the great ascendancy exercised over me by one powerful mind and still more powerful will . . . After taking my degree, I became a Fellow of Balliol College [this was in 1826] and the next year [autumn 1827, probably October] I accepted an invitation to Ireland, and there became

private tutor for fifteen months in the house of one now deceased, whose name I would gladly mention for honor and affection; but I withhold my pen. [It was Edward Pennefather. See appendix G for descriptions of the Pennefathers.] While he repaid me munificently for my services, he behaved towards me as a father, or indeed as an elder brother, and instantly made me feel as a member of his family. [Newman was 22 at the time and Pennefather either 52 or 53.] His great talents, high professional standing, nobleness of heart and unfeigned piety, would have made him a most valuable counsellor to me; but he was too gentle, too unassuming, too modest; he looked to be taught by his juniors, and sat at the feet of one whom I proceed to describe.

This was a young relative of his—a most remarkable man—who rapidly gained an immense sway over me. I shall henceforth call him "the Irish Clergyman" [that is, John Nelson Darby]. His "bodily presence" was indeed "weak"! A fallen cheek, a bloodshot eye, crippled limbs resting on crutches, a seldom shaved beard, a shabby suit of clothes and a generally neglected person, drew at first pity, with wonder to see such a figure in a drawing-room.

It was currently reported that a person in Limerick offered him a half-penny, mistaking him for a beggar; and if not true, the story was yet well invented.

This young man had taken high honors in Dublin University and had studied for the bar, where under the auspices of his eminent kinsman [Pennefather] he had excellent prospects; but his conscience would not allow him to take a brief, lest he should be selling his talents to defeat justice. With keen logical powers, he had warm sympathies, solid judgment of character, thoughtful tenderness, and total self-abandonment. He before long took Holy Orders, and became an indefatigable curate in the mountains of Wicklow . . . He did not fast on purpose.

That a dozen such men would have done more to convert all Ireland to Protestantism than the whole apparatus of the Church Establishment, was ere long my conviction, though I was first offended by his apparent affectation of a mean exterior. [It was his unworldly principle and practice, not an "affectation."] But I soon understood, that in no other way could he gain equal access to the lower and lowest orders, and that he was moved not by asceticism, nor by ostentation, but by a self-abandonment fruitful of consequences. He had practically given up all reading except that of the Bible; and no small part of his movement towards me soon took the form of dissuasion from all other voluntary study.

In fact, I had myself more and more concentrated my religious reading on this one book: still, I could not help feeling the value of a cultivated mind. Against this, my new eccentric friend, (himself having enjoyed no mean advantages of cultivation) directed his keenest attacks. I remember once saying to him, in defence of worldly station: "To desire to be rich is unchristian and absurd; but if I were the father of children, I should wish to be rich enough to secure them a good education." He replied: "If I had children, I would as soon see them break stones on the road, as do anything else, if only I could secure to them the Gospel and the grace of God." I was unable to say Amen, but I admired his unflinching consistency; for now, as always, all he said was based on texts aptly quoted and logically enforced. He more and more made me ashamed of Political Economy and Moral Philosophy, and all Science; all of which ought to be "counted dross for the excellency of the knowledge of Christ Jesus our Lord." For the first time in my life I saw a man earnestly turning into reality the principles which others confessed with their lips only. That the words of the New Testament contained the highest truth accessible to man—truth not to be taken from or added to—all good men (as I thought) confessed: never before had I seen a man so resolved that no word of it should be a dead letter to him. I once said: "But do you really think that *no* part of the New Testament may have been temporary in its object? For instance, what should we have lost, if St. Paul had never written the verse, 'The cloak which I left at Troas, bring with thee, and the books, but especially the parchments'?" He

> answered with the greatest promptitude: "*I* should certainly have lost something; for that is exactly the verse which alone saved me from selling my little library. No! every word, depend on it, is from the Spirit, and is for eternal service."
>
> In spite of the strong revulsion which I felt against some of the peculiarities of this remarkable man, I for the first time in my life found myself under the dominion of a superior. When I remember, how even those bowed down before him, who had been to him in the place of parents—accomplished and experienced minds—I cease to wonder in the retrospect that he riveted me in such a bondage. Henceforth I began to ask: What will *he* say to this and that? In *his* reply I always expected to find a higher portion of God's Spirit, than in any I could frame myself . . . Indeed, but for a few weaknesses which warned me that he might err, I could have accepted him as an apostle commissioned to reveal the mind of God.

It seems to be obvious that Darby was already staying at his brother-in-law's place when Newman arrived, for Newman's description of him at their first meeting gives us a vivid picture of Darby's appearance after his accident and during his time of recuperation. Yet their meeting may not have taken place right away. Darby was at Pennefather's Dublin house and Newman at his country house in Delgany. Darby is not mentioned in a letter written October 8, 1827, by Newman to his brother giving first impressions of the Pennefathers. Their first meeting probably took place when Newman came up from the country house to visit in Dublin.

Darby really was anything but "weak" and possessed, actually, great bodily strength. He was of massive frame and over middle height, although through some peculiarity of figure he gave many people the impression that he was short. His face was of the high and characteristic English type, with strong, well-formed, rugged features. His eye, as Newman mentioned, was a recurring problem, and Darby referred to it often in his letters. That his clothes were plain and that he wore them to shabbiness is true, but he was punctiliously clean as to his person. The story goes that while he was visiting in Limerick once, his friends took advantage of his sleep and replaced his old clothes with new ones. He put them on without a word.

He spent money received from his father in building schools and giving alms in the Wicklow area where he served as a clergyman. By the end of his time there he had almost nothing left, but he wrote, "I honestly began by giving up everything, though in point of fact my faith was never tried in that way, as an uncle left me something before I was run out, or very soon after."[61]

The uncle Darby mentioned here was Sir Admiral Henry Darby. He died, as mentioned before, in 1823 and his will was probated in 1824 by Edward Pennefather. This was before J. N. Darby entered the established church as a clergyman, but it appears, for reasons not known to me, that he received his share in his uncle's will only after leaving the church in 1827.

Some writers have sought to give J. N. Darby a special place in his uncle's affections and see this as the reason for his being mentioned in his will. Actually J. N. Darby was simply mentioned along with the other six children in his family—his youngest sister Letitia and his oldest brother Jonathan had died before this time. In fact some of the other children were mentioned more times than Darby was. Yet the sum he received was not small, and his cousins (or nephews—the accounts differ) borrowed his money at high interest, knowing his generosity, to prevent him from giving it away.[62]

Then when his father died in 1834, he received something from his will as well as from Pennefather when he died.

J. N. Darby always insisted on what he understood to be the Scriptural principle that *full*time laborers in the Lord's work should be dependent on the Lord alone for their support and not on a secular or steady income of some sort. "The workman is worthy of his hire" (this he did not apply to those only ministering part-time). Darby himself, it appears, was not dependent on the Brethren or assemblies for his support; he had inherited enough for himself. Yet money played no great role, if any, in Darby's life, except if he could help others with it. He wrote, "I am not very rich, but what I have, I hope, through the grace of our God, will be always devoted to His work."[63]

Newman's comments regarding fasting were not quite correct. After finding inner peace Darby did not fast as strenuously as before, though he did find fasting of value if done spiritually. He said to William Kelly as the two were dining together, "I should like to tell you how I live. Today I have more than usual on your account. But it is my habit to have a small hot joint on Saturday, cold on Lord's day, cold on Monday, on Tuesday, on Wednesday, on Thursday. On Friday I am not sorry to have a bit of chop or steak; then the round begins again." Darby could subsist on the most scanty and unappetizing diet. In mid-life, while trudging through France and Switzerland, he would sometimes refresh himself on the way with acorns. At other times he would be thankful to receive an egg, for, as he said, no unpleasant visitors for certain could get in there. If invited to dinner, he would freely and thankfully eat of all that was set before him. Darby was not ascetic, but he desired to please the Lord in all things, even as to necessary food.

As to Darby's reading habits William Kelly remarked, "Actually he was a diligent and critical student of Hebrew and Greek Scriptures, of the ancient versions and of anything of value bearing on revelation, he was also well versed in Church history."[64] This contrasts with what Newman noted, but he was describing an earlier period in Darby's life when the Scriptures (as Darby himself put it) acquired complete authority over him. Darby had been greatly influenced by Thomas Scott (Newman thought Scott to be "a rather dull, very unoriginal, half-educated, but honest, worthy, sensible, strong-minded man"[65]) who wrote:

> Does He (God) give us a book to guide us to happiness in this world and for ever? and shall we not study it? Does He make known to us mortals those glories which angels adore with unceasing rapture? and shall we turn away with contemptuous aversion? Has He provided for us sinners such a redemption, as sinless "angels desire to look into"? And shall we think the subject unworthy of notice? Who can presume to justify such conduct? Yet how much more pains do lawyers, physicians, and other students, who desire to excel in their professions, bestow in poring over voluminous authors,

> than men called Christians do in searching the Scriptures? Yea, how many give a decided preference to amusing and ingenious trifles, or political discussions, (not to say publications suited to corrupt their principles and morals,) above the sacred word of God! They would be ashamed not to have read some admired or popular author, though the work perhaps be wholly useless, if not worse; yet they remain year after year, unacquainted with the Holy Scriptures! "Surely in vain is the word of the Lord given to them; the pen of the scribes is in vain!"
>
> Examine *the whole* of the sacred Scripture . . . every part of the sacred oracles has its use, and throws light upon the rest . . . every word demands a measure of our attention.[66]

In later years Darby's library could no longer be designated as "little." He had books on all that touched man's relation to God, ancient and modern philosophy, science, and especially geology. Among the rare editions of Scripture which he possessed was the Complutensian Polyglott, 1514-1517, the first edition of the New Testament printed in the original Greek, and the first edition edited by Erasmus, 1516. He had the best editions of the church fathers, books on geography, archeology, travel, history, and theology, dictionaries, and so on. Darby did not mind buying expensive books if he believed they would help him in his work: "My books are quite alarming, as if I was regularly settled in the world; however, my life would hardly bear out the charge. But I use them diligently now."[67] After his death his library was sold at an auction in London on November 25, 1889. Approximately three thousand volumes brought in nine hundred pounds.

The Call

written in 1832

What powerful, mighty Voice, so near,
Calls me from earth apart -
Reaches, with tones so still, so clear,
From th' unseen world, my heart?

'Tis solemn, yet it draws with power
And sweetness yet unknown;
It speaks the language of an hour
When earth's forever gone.

It soothes, yet solemnizes all;
What yet of nature is
Lies silent, through the heavenly call;
No earthly voice like this!

'Tis His. Yes, yes; no other sound
Could move my heart like this;
The voice of Him that earlier bound
Through grace that heart to His -

In other accents now, 'tis true,
Than once my spirit woke,
To life and peace, through which it grew
Under His gracious yoke.

Blest Lord, Thou speak'st! 'Twas erst Thy voice
That led my heart to Thee;
That drew me to that better choice
Where grace has set me free.

Then would'st Thou that I should rejoice,
And walk by faith below;
Enough, that I had heard Thy voice,
And learnt thy love's deep woe -

Thy glory, Lord. This living waste
Thenceforth no rest could give;
My path was on with earnest haste,
Lord, in Thy rest to live.

Yes, then 'twas faith - Thy word; but now
Thyself my soul draw'st nigh,
My soul with nearer thoughts to bow
Of brighter worlds on high.[68]

J. N. Darby

2
A Great Recovery

I being in the way, the Lord led me
to the house of my master's brethren.
Genesis 24:27, KJV

Darby's deliverance from the law, and his joy to discover that he was really one with Christ before God, was not the only outcome of his riding accident and the following time alone with God and His Word; this time of recuperation was of the utmost importance for him personally and would serve as the foundation of all that would shortly follow. Years later, at the age of sixty-three, he summed things up in this way:

> I am daily more struck with the connection of the great principles on which my mind was exercised by and with God, when I found salvation and peace, and the questions agitated and agitating the world at the present day: the absolute, divine authority and certainty of the Word, as a divine link between us and God, if everything (Church and world) went; personal assurance of salvation in a new condition by being in Christ; the Church as His body, Christ coming to receive us to Himself; and collaterally with that, the setting up of a

> new earthly dispensation, from Isaiah 32 (more particularly the end): all this was when laid aside at E. Pennefather's in 1827.[1]

We see from the above that there were actually five things occupying Darby's thoughts and heart while recuperating from his accident. The first two we have already touched upon in our previous chapter (namely, the new standing in Christ and the authority of God's Word); the last two (the Lord's coming and the setting up of an earthly dispensation) are more the topics of our next chapter. The church as the body of Christ and Christian ministry are the subjects of our present chapter.

Before we begin we should not think that Darby was able to put all his views in their respective places or arrange them in order then as he could in later years. It was Darby's thought that even though the whole truth is given to us, we apprehend it in part only. Because we apprehend truth in detail, we never have the whole at once; the character of our knowledge is such that it lays hold of different truths singly. As we lay hold of one truth it flows into the understanding of the next and so on.

Recognition of the Church's True Character

While Darby was still laboring as a clergyman in Calary he had been honestly searching for an understanding of what the true church is, but the concept remained obscure to him. Now, realizing his union with a glorified Christ in Heaven, and seeing that Christ's place there represented his own, it became clear to him that the church of God, could only consist of such who were united in the same way. The descent of the Holy Spirit at Pentecost had formed believers into one body, uniting the members to their Head in Heaven and to each other, and acting in them according to His own will. He saw that membership in Scripture was not membership of an association organized and formed by man (even if all members of such an association were true children of God), but membership of Christ—a hand, a foot, etc. (1 Corinthians 12:18,20). For him the body of Christ, the true church, was composed of those who were united by the Holy Spirit to the Head: Christ in Heaven (Ephesians 1:22). External Christendom was in reality the world, and could not be considered as the church at all, except for the responsibility attached to the position it professed to occupy. Carefully reading the Acts of the Apostles, particularly chapters 2 and 4, Darby saw a practical picture of the early church and realized how far she had fallen away from that first state. (The church as God's house was an aspect that he came to see later on.)

Where was Darby to find the true church, or rather its expression, he was seeking? Where was he to find the unity of believers with their Head in Heaven and amongst themselves? He wrote:

> When I looked around to find unity I found it nowhere; if I joined one set of Christians I did not belong to another. The Church, God's Church, was broken up and the members scattered among various self-formed bodies.[2]
>
> Nationalism was associated with the world; in its bosom some believers were merged in the very world from which Jesus had separated them; they were besides, separated from one another, while Jesus had united them. The Lord's Supper, symbol of the unity of the body had become a symbol of the union of this latter with the world; that is to say, exactly the contrary of what Christ had established. Dissent had, no doubt, had the effect of making the true children of God more manifest but here they were united on principles quite different from the unity of the body of Christ. If I joined myself to these I separated myself from others everywhere. The disunion of the body of Christ was everywhere apparent rather than its unity.[3]

It was the apprehension of what Darby believed the true church to be in God's eyes that led him to leave his ecclesiastical position. He probably never did this formally, and he could probably have resumed his ministry in the Church of Ireland at any time, had he wanted to, by simply subscribing to the Thirty-Nine Articles. William Kelly in one or two places said that Darby left the church in 1827. Some church records also give this year. Other writers have sought, for various reasons, to place the date of his leaving much later. I do not believe it would have been possible for Darby to return to his former ministry in the Church of Ireland after recovering from his accident and coming to his new views on the character of the church and Christian ministry. It is true that the external church still exercised a certain traditional power over him at the time, and he said, "I remember the text alarming me on quitting the Establishment: 'They went out from us because they were not of us,' till I said: To be sure, because I was not of them; that is just the truth, and I would not be."[4] And so he left.

In the Greek Testament already referred to in chapter 1 Darby wrote of preaching the gospel in its simple power for a *short* time at Calary after his recovery. Whether this was still as an ordained clergyman in the Church of Ireland is questionable. Outwardly it may have appeared to be so, because he never left it formally as we noted above, but inwardly he was separated from it. He said that he did not believe his work as a clergyman was the task the Lord had appointed him to. His returning to those he had previously worked among and his feeling a responsibility to them are quite understandable. He had been delivered and had come to see the gospel of God more clearly. He surely would have liked to share his discoveries with those to whom he had ministered before. He said that he preached not only that there was no other salvation but in Christ as before—previously his preaching had dealt more exclusively with abstract principles—but also that Christ was the active power of divine love leading to salvation. The difference, he said, was felt. The Word plowed much deeper than before. He dealt more fully, more practically with souls. But these statements do *not* support the thought that he remained a clergyman for a longer period of time. Darby's parishioners sent him a letter dated March 28, 1829, thanking him for his service among them (see appendix H), so he had given up his clerical position at this date the latest.

Writing on September 21, 1876, Darby said, "In a few days it will be fifty years since I left the camp."[5] It could be that he mistook the year here (for fifty years ago would be 1826, not 1827), but "in a few days" seems to confirm the month of his riding accident: namely, October 1827 (the year he means).

In another place he spoke of having left the establishment forty-five years ago; in 1873 that would be 1828.[6] These two dates are further examples of his rounding off the year of an event, as seen already in chapter 1.

Darby said, "It was the unity of the assembly of God, of those who are united to Christ by the Holy Ghost, which forced me to leave the Anglican Church and prevented me from joining any other." When Daly heard of Darby's leaving he asked him, "Well, John? You have left us; what Church have you joined?" Darby replied, "None whatever. I have nothing to do with the Dissenters, and am as yet my own Church." He wrote of this time:

> At first, when I left the Episcopal Church, there was no one with whom I could walk; I was led on and guided simply by the Word of God.[7]
>
> What was I to do? Such was the question which presented itself to me without any other idea than that of satisfying my conscience according to the light of the Word of God. A word in Matthew 18 furnished the solution of my trouble: "Where two or three are gathered together in My name, there am I in the midst of them." This was just what I wanted; the presence of Jesus was assured at such worship; it is there He has recorded His name, as He had done of old in the temple at Jerusalem for those who were called to resort there.[8]

It is important to notice here that Darby came to the realization of these points alone, without the influence of other men such as Bellett or A. N. Groves. In another place[9] he said that 1 Corinthians 10–12 formed the basis of the conclusions he reached; Matthew 18 provided the practical application of the principles later.

Darby's views, when fully developed later, would prove to be in many points contrary to the ones normally accepted by the church at large. Darby, as we noted, had been greatly occupied with the early church as described in Acts. What he saw around him he did not like. His views which then developed were "new"—that is, different from those of his contemporaries. He defended his views as being the "original" ones that the church very early in her history had lost sight of. This ties in with his thoughts on the "ruin" of the church, which we shall deal with in a separate section. Also the question of the "originality" of his views will be addressed later.

Darby, still hindered by the effects of his riding accident, had to use crutches to move about for a while and was thus not able to make his convictions publicly known. If he was alone in the beginning, then he was not to remain so for very long.

Others Led by the Spirit

We shall leave Darby for a short while now and take a look at three other men who were occupied along similar lines: J. G. Bellett, A. N. Groves, and Edward Cronin.

While Darby was still laboring as a clergyman he often had contact with Bellett. Darby introduced Bellett to another young man by the name of Francis Hutchinson, son of the archdeacon Sir Samuel Synge (Samuel Synge assumed the added surname Hutchinson after succeeding his uncle to the title of Sir in 1813).[10] Bellett and Hutchinson soon became close friends and had much in common as regarded the Lord and spiritual things.

Bellett, after studying at Trinity, went to London to study law, but returned to Dublin in 1821. He was called to the bar while there, but it seems that he did not practice much, though it is said that his name is to be found in several court cases that are still extant. He was financially well off and had no real need to practice. He was more interested in religious matters, and he gave his time to these in whatever ways were open to him as a layman. Bellett wrote of his time with Hutchinson:

> Dissatisfied as I was, we went occasionally to the dissenting chapels together, but we had not much sympathy with the tone prevalent. The sermons we heard had generally, perhaps, less of the sympathy of Christ in them than what we had in the pulpits of the Established Church, and the things of God were dealt with more for the intellect and by the intellect man, as we judged, suited the proper cravings of the renewed and spiritual mind. I believe I may say this for him as well as for

> myself; so we held on (loosely though it was) by the Established Church still.[11]
>
> In the summer of 1829 [read 1827][12] our family was at Kingston and dear Hutchinson at Bray [summer resort towns on the seacoast, southeast of Dublin]. We saw each other occasionally and spoke on the things of the Lord, but where he went on a Sunday at that time I cannot tell. I attended the Scotch Church at Kingston, where all who were understood to be new-born were welcome. But returning to Dublin, in the November of that year [the year would have been, according to the correction, 1827; the reader is sure to notice how this fits in with the time when Darby had his riding accident and was recuperating at his brother-in-law's place] F. Hutchinson was quite prepared for communion in the name of the Lord, with all, whosoever they might be, who loved Him in sincerity, and proposed to have a room in Fitzwilliam Square [notice "Square" not "Street"; Darby was at 20 Fitzwilliam Street; Hutchinson's house was at 9 Fitzwilliam Square West][13] for that purpose. He did so, designing however so to have it that if any were disposed to attend the services in the Parish Church or Dissenting chapels they might not be hindered; and he also prescribed a certain line of things, as to the service of prayer, singing and teaching, that should be found amongst us each day.[14]

According to most recent writers all of Bellett's account quoted above took place, as he mistakenly said, in 1829—that is, two years after Darby's riding accident, and thus two years after meeting him and breaking bread with him. To remove the difficulties that arise with this presentation of events, the writers conclude that Darby, after arriving at his view of the church, returned to his county parish and worked for the Church of Ireland, at least till the end of 1829.[15]

Some thought that Bellett and Hutchinson, after learning of Darby's views, attended services in other churches as well until 1829! William Kelly wrote:

> Mr. J. G. Bellett also was slow in breaking off his old connections. There may have been others of similar

> feeling. But these remarks are quite inapplicable even to those who preceded Mr. Darby, (that is, Cronin) as well as to himself. The late Dr. Cronin has named to me his distinct abandonment of his ecclesiastical associations at an earlier date than is here set down [that is, 1826] before he saw his liberty to remember Christ in the breaking of bread. Probably the hearty welcome of such as still frequented their churches or chapels might easily lead to the notion that none for a time saw further. It is, however, a positive error; for those who began to meet together were far from wishing to attend ordinary services. That they originally meant meetings of a subsidiary character is the dream of one—perhaps of more—who always wished something of the sort.[16]

Bellett's and Hutchinson's visiting other churches took place before their first meeting for the breaking of bread with Darby. If the first breaking of bread took place in Hutchinson's house in 1827, why does Bellett speak of it again in 1829 as being a completely new thing? In these notes I have gone ahead of the events as we have them thus far in our story, but I have done this only in the hope of showing the reader how the main text is supported in the picture it attempts to show.

Anthony Norris Groves was also an early friend of Bellett's. Groves had been a dentist but gave up his practice since he desired to become a missionary. He began studying so that he could be ordained and fulfill his wishes. While studying he came to the conclusion that human ordination is not necessary to heed the Lord's call to service. Now it is not with the least thought of calling into question Groves' love and devotion to Christ, or with the wish to throw a bad light on his missionary zeal, that it must be said that he was neither founder nor father of what came to be known as the Brethren movement, as some writers have tried to prove. William Kelly said, "Mr. A. N. Groves, so far as suggesting any distinctive truth or practice only dropped in among them [the early Brethren] and always remained as a 'free lance'; he never shared their decided convictions, but retained to the last a link with the ordinary ways of Christendom."[17]

The place others have given Groves in their accounts of the history of the Brethren is partly due to his connection and friendship with Bellett. Groves sailed on his first missionary journey to Baghdad in June 1829. The fact that in September 1830 several of the early Brethren went to join him may also have led to the thought that he took a prominent place among them. Francis Newman, as mentioned in chapter 1, was one of those who joined Groves in 1830. Bellett recorded that the group that left to join Groves in Baghdad did so in 1831, while evidence is conclusive that it was in 1830—further proof of Bellett's undependability in naming dates.

Groves lived in Exeter, and he traveled to Dublin to take the quarterly exams at Trinity College; these were the studies mentioned above. In 1826 Henry Craik (who was to play no small role in the Brethren movement) came to Exeter to read the classics with Groves—coaching him for his exams, one might say—and to teach his two sons. He later tutored in the house of John Synge, whom we noted in connection with Hutchinson.[18] It was through the repeated visits to Dublin that Groves came into contact with Bellett and even stayed at his house.[19] Craik's diary and letters serve as a good source for determining Groves' movements. For example, from them we learn that Groves was in Dublin from October 10, 1826, to the beginning of November 1826.[20] Bellett is well known for this remark:

> Groves has just been telling me, that it appeared to him from Scripture, that believers, meeting together as disciples of Christ, were free to break bread together, as their Lord had admonished them; and that, in as far as the practice of the apostles could be a guide, every Lord's day should be set apart for thus remembering the Lord's death, and obeying his parting command.[21]

Groves may have had this insight, but, as we shall see, Edward Cronin was already putting the idea into practice.

This conversation between Bellett and Groves took place during one of Groves' Dublin visits before August 1827 (and never as late as 1829). This date is easily ascertained from the Groves memoirs. A Miss Bessy Paget had accompanied Groves to Dublin on this visit.[22] Groves noted that on returning with Bessy she proposed to him to take charge of a group at Poltimore.[23] Groves was at first reluctant, but later, in a letter dated August 8, 1827,[24] Groves wrote that he was leading the flock at Poltimore, so the Dublin visit in question was *before* this date.

It is my firm conviction that Groves did not influence the Brethren movement as much as he influenced or prepared Bellett to be open and receptive for the views later called *Brethren* in character. Bellett was very careful and cautious, as accounts of the early years show, and needed encouraging.[25]

Craik mentioned that Groves was absent from Exeter for some time in October 1827.[26] Bellett wrote that Groves was in Dublin at the end of the year 1828.[27] It is my belief that here, once again, Bellett mistook the year, and that the date mentioned by Craik is correct. Groves did not complete his studies at Trinity, for he came to see that man's ordination was not necessary to do the Lord's work. When did he stop attending classes? Records at Trinity College would be helpful in determining this, but I am informed that none exists (perhaps because Groves did not graduate); yet H. H. Rowdon mentioned October 16, 1826, as the date of Groves' entering Trinity College,[28] apparently quoting from the *Alumni Dublinenses*; he also suggested that Groves stopped attending Trinity College in the summer of 1827. If Rowdon's date is correct, it would fit in with Bellett's account when we change the year from 1828 to 1827. Bellett wrote, "In the close of 1828 [read 1827] he visited Dublin, *though he had seceded from the College.*"[29] Perhaps Groves had gone to Dublin at this time to close his connection with Trinity College officially. Bellett wrote further:

> Walking one day with him [Groves], as we were passing down Lower Pembroke Street[30] he said to me: "This, I doubt not, is the mind of God concerning us, that we should come together in all simplicity as disciples, not waiting on any pulpit or minister, but trusting that the Lord would edify us together, by ministering as He pleased and saw good from the midst of ourselves."[31]

Groves said that he mentioned this idea to Bellett on his "last" visit to Dublin.[32] Groves' words helped prepare Bellett to accept Darby's proposal to break bread a short time later

(Bellett never attended Cronin's meetings it seems). Groves was never mentioned as being at the first breaking of bread with which the movement, so to speak, officially began, and he is not mentioned in connection with any of the events directly following, which can be explained by the date of his last visit to Dublin. All the important events occurred after that. (Supporters for a 1829 date might find their view sustained in the fact that Groves had left for Petersburg in June of 1829,[33] and that is why he was not in Dublin.)

Bellett's wife had a cousin by the name of Edward Cronin (later Doctor Cronin). He had been born in Cork, Ireland, and raised as a Roman Catholic, but later in life he turned Protestant. Cronin had been sent to Dublin for his health (in 1825?) and as a visitor there he was able to take part in the communion service with all the dissenting congregations. This continued until it was discovered that he had become a resident in Dublin. He was then informed that he would not be able to break bread any more with any one of them until he had special membership with one of them. This was the beginning of his coming to see the church of God as one; he saw that all were members of one body, so he firmly refused special fellowship. Because of this refusal, he was denounced from one of the pulpits of these dissenting chapels on York Street. A deacon by the name of Edward Wilson protested as to this denouncement and left the congregation. Thus separated, in 1825 or 1826 the two began to meet together for the breaking of bread at the home of Mr. Wilson in the Bible society's office, of which he was the assistant secretary, on Upper Sackville Street, Dublin.

After Mr. Wilson had to leave for England, the meeting place moved to the home of Mr. Cronin, where he broke bread with Mr. Timms, a bookseller, and two cousins—sisters of Mrs. Bellett, the Misses Drury, members of the same church. These four met in the back parlor of Cronin's house at 13 Lower Pembroke Street. Bellett must have known what his wife's cousin was doing, as Cronin lived just down the street from him at 5 Upper Pembroke Street, and the Misses Drury lived next-door to him.[34]

Bellett wrote of Cronin's doings as follows: "In a private room he [Cronin] had the Lord's Supper with, I believe, three others, while I was going still to Sandford Chapel and J. N. Darby was still in county Wicklow as a clergyman."[35] This then was before Darby's riding accident. Cronin's account is as follows:

> Thus separated we two [he and Wilson] met for breaking of bread and prayer in one of his [Wilson's] rooms until his departure for England. I was not alone. The two Miss Drurys, my cousins, were led in the same path, and also left Mr. Cooper's chapel [the one who had denounced him] where they were members (and also Mr. Timms, bookseller in Grafton Street) and met with us in the back parlour of my house in Lower Pembroke Street.
>
> It then became noised abroad, and one and another became affected by the same truth, which really was the Oneness of the Body and the presence of the Holy Spirit, also seen by us very clearly. At this time, dear J. G. Bellett and J. N. Darby [the inclusion of Darby's name here is a mistake, as we shall shortly see; these remarks are applicable only to Bellett] were more or less affected by the general state of things in the religious world, but were unprepared to come into entire separation, and looked suspiciously at our movements, feeling still able to attend and minister in the Church of England as well as to come occasionally to our little assembly.[36]

These remarks tie in with what we have previously noted about Bellett and Hutchinson more than Darby.

It was perhaps through Bellett that Hutchinson heard of Cronin and his doings, for Cronin wrote: "Mr. Hutchinson found us out and offered the use of his large room in Fitzwilliam Square." This would go along with Bellett's account of the matter, for after writing of Hutchinson's proposal to provide a room for the purpose of communion, Bellett added: "Edward Cronin was prepared for this fully. I joined, but not I think at all with the same liberty and decision of mind."

Results

We have now all the men together who formed the nucleus of a movement that would in time affect many of the Lord's own the world over. It is also interesting to see how close they were geographically to one another: Fitzwilliam Street (Upper and Lower), where Darby was, runs parallel to Pembroke Street (Upper and Lower), where Bellett and Cronin were. Between these two streets lies Fitzwilliam Square, where Hutchinson was. Certainly these locations played a role in further developments.

We have seen Darby greatly exercised as to coming to a true view of the church and then arriving at what he believed to be a right understanding of her character. We have seen Bellett and Hutchinson disappointed as to how things were in the established church and the various dissenting bodies. We have seen Cronin barred from all communion and coming together with a few friends to break bread in private. Hutchinson wanted to set aside a room in his house where believers could come together for communion. Hearing of Cronin, Hutchinson offered Cronin this room, but before this offer was taken advantage of, Cronin and Bellett visited Darby at Fitzwilliam Street. How do these three accounts fit together? Darby wrote:

> I have heard since [that is, since their first meeting to break bread at Fitzwilliam Square] that Cronin had already met with Wilson and some others, but they had broken up [that is, after beginning at Fitzwilliam Square]. Of that I knew nothing.[37]
>
> Four persons [they were Cronin, Bellett, Hutchinson, and a Mr. Brooke; it is of interest to note the relatively young ages of these men at the time: Cronin 26, Bellett 32, Hutchinson 25, and Darby just turned 27] who were pretty much in the same state of soul as myself came together to my lodging; we spoke together about these things and I proposed to them to break bread the following Sunday, which we did.[38] [This may have been Darby's reason for writing years later, "I was myself the beginning of what the world calls 'Plymouth Brethren.'"][39]
>
> We began to meet in Dublin, Ireland, 1827-28. I found that wherever two or three were met in Christ's name, He would be in our midst, and acted on the promise with three other brethren [Mr. Brooke did not come to the actual breaking of bread] and the wife of

9 Fitzwilliam Square, Dublin
(Beattie's Brethren, the Story of a Great Recovery, *John Ritchie, Ltd.)*

9 Fitzwilliam Square, Dublin
(Veitch's The Story of the Brethren Movement, *Pickering & Inglis)*

Dublin, city map detail
(The author)

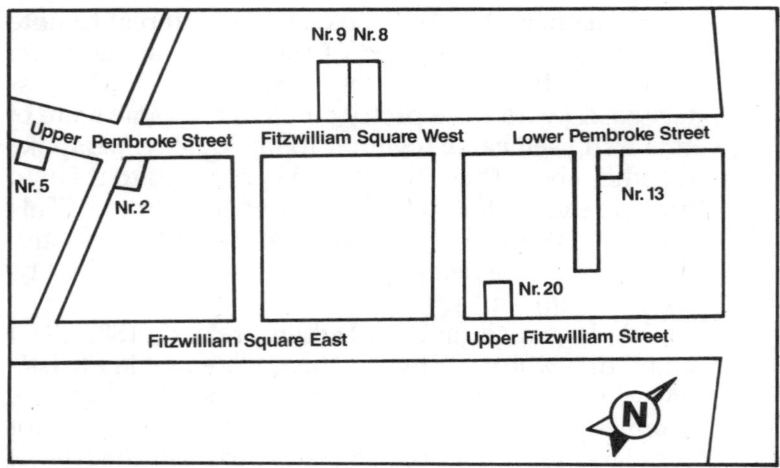

> one of them [this may have been Mrs. Hutchinson, the sister of the Earl of Donoughmore].[40] [I take it that the first breaking of bread took place in February 1828.]
>
> The Word declares to us that where two or three are gathered to the name of Jesus, He will be in their midst, Matt. 18:20. This is what we have done. There were only four of us to do it at the first, not I hope, in a spirit of pride or presumption, but deeply grieved at seeing the state of that which surrounded us, praying for all Christians and recognizing all those who possessed the Spirit of God, every true Christian wherever he might be found ecclesiastically as members of the body of Christ. We have thus found the presence of the Lord.[41]
>
> We never thought to go beyond thus meeting the need of our consciences and hearts according to the Word. God was doing a work I had no idea of myself, and it spread over the world.[42]

Leaving the established church and beginning a separate group was not unique at the time we are here considering. The group around John Walker, gathered early in 1804 in Dublin, is an interesting case in point. There were many parallels, but also great differences between Walkerites and the Brethren.[43]

It is almost impossible to believe that Darby did not know anything of what Cronin had been doing, especially as Darby was aware of the activities of other groups (see appendix I) and was closely connected with the people involved with Cronin. One explanation might be that Bellett, still not sure of what to make of the whole business, did not mention anything to Darby.

The question of Darby's originality comes up. Darby was later known as the most prominent propagator of ideas or views for which he claimed direct or indirect originality. When examined closer one finds that these ideas were already in existence in Darby's surroundings in one form or another—ideas dealing with both Christian fellowship and prophetic questions. The case can probably be made that he shaped existing ideas, giving them a new and stabler form, with more concrete directions and consequences.

Darby became well known for his thoughts on the ruin of

the church, but these can be found in a somewhat different form in earlier sources such as William Cave (died 1713) and Gottfried Arnold (1666-1714) and even John Wesley, though with a more optimistic view of the future. Scott's *Essays* have already been mentioned as an important factor in shaping Darby's early thought. Darby also had Scott's Old and New Testament commentaries. I have not been able to obtain copies of them, but it would be worth the effort to study them to ascertain (if possible) how much and in what way they influenced Darby.

Nevertheless there was a difference between Darby and other dissenters, even if it was only in understanding. It would seem that the others had left the churches, dissenting or established, not so much from principle as from dissatisfaction with their ways, whereas Darby was motivated by his idea of the church: one by its union with Christ. Cronin, next to Darby, may have understood this more than the rest, but he said, "With the strong impression on my soul, though with little intelligence about it, that the Church of God was one, and that all that believed were members of that one Body."[44] Of himself Darby said:

> It was not dissatisfaction with the apostolic succession of the English national episcopal body. I had found peace to my own soul by finding my oneness with Christ, that it was no longer myself as in the flesh before God, but that I was in Christ, accepted in the Beloved and sitting in heavenly places in Him. This led me directly to the apprehension of what the true Church of God was—those that were united to Christ in heaven; I at once felt that all the parish was not that.[45]

Kelly remarked, "Mr. Darby was, I think, the only one who saw the Church at all clearly in early days." (And Kelly knew Cronin well and had spoken with him about the early days.) This would clearly prove itself in later years with the Bethesda troubles. He was then accused of having changed the principles held in earlier days.

Perhaps the views held by others may be seen in the expression used by Bellett and Hutchinson: "Where all who were understood to be newborn were welcome"—that is, that common life is a ground of communion and fellowship. When the meetings began to take place on Aungier Street, about two and a half years later, Darby asked those who had gathered what principles they were acting on.[46] They answered that they were meeting on the ground of being children of one God and the possessors of one life. (This was also Groves' viewpoint.)[47] That this was true for them individually was one thing, but Darby pointed out to them that the assembly of God was not set up on that ground and that if they should continue to think so, they would have no true basis on which to refuse association with evildoers.

Why was Darby accused of having changed his first principles in later years? Had he changed them? The following quotations may be helpful.

> I believe at my deliverance from bondage in 1827-28, God opened up certain truths needed for the church. I believe that, though holding and seeking to help souls by them, for what was called peace and union I swamped them, had not faith to make them good in service.[48] I blame myself as unfaithful in passing over many truths for the sake of what is called peace.[49]

What does he mean by "swamping" truths for the sake of peace? Darby wrote, "For a year or two at the beginning I preached everywhere they let me . . . though the trumpet gave an uncertain sound, it resulted in bringing out, even if the gospel only were fully preached. Now the question is fully raised and the testimony has to be clear."[50] Darby was asked, "Then is it wrong or not to go on with Christians in denominations for the furtherance of the Lord's work?" He replied, "Well, I did for a little while, but I found the trumpet gave an uncertain sound."[51]

Darby, with his view of the church's true character, went about preaching this wherever he could. These views regarding the Church were just coming out and needed to be made known to others. Through this Darby was brought into contact with many. Some contacts and associations he later felt forced to break. Once the truth had been presented to all, he felt the testimony had to be kept clear. There could be no association with such who, knowing of these truths, refused to follow the path marked out so clearly, as Darby thought, in God's Word. While the door was open for the opportunity of making his views known to others, Darby made good use of it. But after defenses had been built up and the views resisted, he no longer had the liberty as before. Writing in 1877 Darby explained the path he had chosen:

> I am deeply convinced that it is a testimony which God Himself has raised up for these last days. I have been walking in this way for fifty years [a further confirmation for the year 1827]; I have seen weakness in myself, and mistakes, I do not doubt, in the way of walking; but never doubted for a moment that it is the work of God. But it is needful that each one should be convinced of this himself by the Word of God. It is a path of faith, and faith only can sustain the soul in this path; but I know that the peace, the approval of God are there; and those who walk in it by faith are made happy by them; I hope that my love for the brethren with whom I cannot walk will be always increasing. We cannot realize the blessings which belong to us if we do not comprehend all the saints in our Christian affections (Eph. 3:18). Not to walk with them in a path that is not according to the Word is not saying that one does not love them, but just the contrary.[52]

In 1844 Darby wrote to an acquaintance:

> Alas, my brother, weak indeed as I am—and I am more and more feeling my weakness, and my entire dependence on grace, and I hope always to feel it, more and more—for these seventeen years I have had to undergo the consequences, painful and trying to my heart, of the convictions and of the faith that God Himself has wrought in my heart by His Word. I have suffered from it, and greatly; but while making sometimes humiliating experience of my weakness, I have a recompense—I could not tell you how abundant—even here below.[53]

Darby's father died in 1834, but Darby did not attend the funeral because of the clerical system maintained there, a system contrary to what J. N. Darby saw as the truth of God.[54] He thought his presence at the funeral would give the impression of his acknowledging the system there. This is perhaps the clearest proof of the stand Darby had taken, and contradicts the opinion of some who say that he first took such a position in the early and mid-1840s. Reminiscent of the unwillingness of some to accept the facts mentioned in chapter 1 concerning Darby's mother, Darby's not attending his father's funeral has been called into question. It is argued that Darby wrote "I would not" and not "I did not," but this kind of subtlety cannot change the facts. Knowing what we do of Darby's character, when he said he *would* not we can be certain he *did* not.

Ruin and Separation

To be able to understand Darby's view of the church's true place today, and the Christian's responsibility in it, we must look at two very important words for him: *ruin* and *separation*.

Newton wrote, "The only person who had any apprehension of all this ruin was Darby; and I felt it so too, *that* was why I so clung to him. He seemed to realize the general breakdown of the whole scene around us."[55]

Cave, Arnold, and Wesley have been mentioned as such who also saw the church as very early falling into unfaithfulness, but their difference from Darby, at least in Wesley's case (who was postmillennial), was that they saw the failure of the church, though beginning early and lasting long, as not necessarily irreparable.

Darby's view is evident in the following quotation from his lecture in Geneva in 1840 on the "Progress of Evil on the Earth":

> What we are about to consider will tend to shew that, instead of permitting ourselves to hope for a continued progress of good, we must expect a progress of evil; and that the hope of the earth being filled with the knowledge of the Lord before the exercise of His judgment, and the consummation of this judgment on the

> earth, is delusive. We are to expect evil, until it becomes so flagrant that it will be necessary for the Lord to judge it. . . . I am afraid that many a cherished feeling, dear to the children of God, has been shocked this evening; I mean, their hope that the gospel will spread by itself over the whole earth, during the actual dispensation.[56]

Darby saw that in every new dealing of God with man, man's failure in responsibility quickly followed. This was the case with our first parents in the garden of Eden, and with Israel in connection with receiving the law. In the church Darby saw this failure as developing very fast. Hardly had the last apostle been called home (and even before then the decline had set in) when a great change took place among those professing the name of Christ. Human authority and human direction took the place of the guidance of the Holy Spirit and of the authority of God's Word. Doctrines that had been so blessedly set forth, more particularly those found in the writings of the apostle Paul, were soon set aside. Leadership positions were soon acquired by men of corrupt minds, and these men began to oppress those who were true to Christ. Corruption and violence abounded.

The Reformation was seen as a great light in this growing darkness, and most certainly a work of God in which the truth of justification by faith alone shone brightly. Yet Darby thought the movement overlooked much Scriptural teaching regarding the church and substituted the opinions and the preferences of the leaders of the time. These leaders sought the favor and protection of the world, while Roman Catholicism had always sought to control the world.

The church, seen in her outward testimony here on earth, had fallen from her first place and was in ruins. Darby wrote of this ruin:

> As to the ruin of the Church, the theory came for me after the consciousness of it, and even now, the theory is but a small thing to my mind; it is the burden one bears.[57] Some years after the conversion of my soul I looked around to find where the Church was, but I could not find it. I could find plenty of saints better

> than myself, but not the Church as it was set up with power on the earth. Then I say the Church as thus set up is ruined, and I cannot find a better word for it.[58]

Darby came to this view of ruin in an early stage, at a time when his knowledge of church history and awareness of the church's present state of affairs were limited. He had not yet been outside of Ireland or England and he was still living, relatively secluded, in Wicklow. His view was obviously rooted in what he thought to be the teaching of Scripture and in what he intuitively felt was the reality of the present state of the church. His conclusions were, therefore, not a result of much personal experience and learning. His later experiences confirmed his initial thoughts; or, if you will, his early ideas colored his way of viewing later experiences.

Darby can be rightly called the father of modern dispensationalism, for his view of dispensations was different from views previously expressed:

> God has always begun by placing His creatures in a good position, but by infidelity the creature has invariably abandoned the position in which it has been placed by God. After long sufferance, God never reestablishes anyone in the position from which he has fallen. It is no part of His ways to restore something that has been spoilt; He removes it and brings in something entirely new, and much better than what had gone before.

Believers had often seen God as dealing differently with man in different dispensations (one example among many: William Cave's distinctions among the patriarchal, Mosaic, and evangelical dispensations). But these dispensations were seen as a natural process or unfolding of God's plan, culminating in the church of the New Testament. Darby saw each dispensation as a distinctive period (perhaps not with clearly defined transitions) involving a new testing of man and man's invariable failure. This required the introduction of another dispensation with different conditions that man again failed to meet. In fact all dispensations would end in failure (from man's viewpoint), even the long-awaited millennial kingdom.

Though Darby was the originator of this form of dispensationalism, he never had any clearly defined arrangement of successive dispensations like the seven or eight distinct periods made so popular today by, among other things, the Scofield Bible.

The principle of non-restoration seemed important to Darby. He felt that many Christians had thoughts concerning the church, but they were thoughts of the church in power and splendor. Many were seeking to restore old things for the service of God, instead of being broken down before Him because they saw the ruin of the church and their own unfaithfulness.

The house, the church seen in her outward testimony here on earth, had been ruined. An earthquake had destroyed her foundations. It mattered little how others tried to make the house an agreeable dwelling place afterwards. They had forgotten that the way to true peace and blessing is to be found in openly confessing what we are in the presence of what God is. If only two or three did this, they could be assured that God would be with them. If it be true that we have only a "little strength," the important thing is to keep His Word and not deny His name.[59] But Darby also had a warning for those who comprehended the ruin:

> Do they say all is in ruins? Well, do they take part in it as Daniel did, or do they fancy they are going to be something out of it, and so deny that it is so? The ruin is our ruin if we are identified with Christ's glory in the world.[60]
>
> Wherever an assembly, or those within the assembly set out to be a testimony, they will only be a testimony to their own weakness and inefficiency; because the object of their walk cannot be one which efficiently forms a Christian. When they have the proper object, they will be a testimony; but to be one is never the first object. Whenever Christians set up to be a testimony, they get full of themselves and do not even realize it and think it is having much of Christ.[61]
>
> The first sign of weakness is, the *gathering* itself becoming the object of attention, instead of Christ. The activity and zeal will be for the system.

Darby viewed the church from two aspects. First, he saw the church as a divine institution, founded by the redemptive work, resurrection, and ascension of Christ, who thus became its Head after the Holy Spirit's descent at Pentecost. In the church the saints are united to each other and to their Head, the ascended Christ in Heaven. The saints are seen as the body and bride of Christ. The body is built up and assembled by God Himself. The church cannot fall away from the position it has been given, or lose any of the promises it has received. The church is composed only of true believers—those who have laid hold of grace, have received the forgiveness of sins, have been saved, and have the Holy Spirit dwelling in them.

Darby also saw the church as the house of God, where He dwells. When God is at work building this house, all is perfect (Matthew 16:18; Ephesians 2:19-22; 1 Peter 2:5), but when man has a part in the building, failure is possible (1 Corinthians 3:10-15).[62]

The unity of the church is God-given; it is the work of the Holy Spirit and is therefore perfect and indestructible. On the other hand, the outward expression of this unity has been entrusted to man, and one look at the state of Christendom is enough to see that men have failed; the ruin cannot be undone and no human effort can repair it. Yet the church is one, and there can be no question of an invisible unity; the church is to be a light in the world and how can a light be invisible?

The church should have allowed herself to have been guided entirely by the direction of the Holy Spirit, but she did not do so. The Holy Spirit was soon replaced by human organization. Because of this independent spirit and lack of faith, disagreements, quarrels, heresies, and the like arose. This process of ruin has continued from the time of the apostles, Darby believed, to the present day. Compromise with temporal powers and bringing people who had no personal faith in Christ into the professing church added to the sad state of affairs. The church would remain the house of God as long as it did not deny its faith (the apostasy after the true church is gone was also foreseen), but it is now the "great house" of 2 Timothy 2:20.

> Division and disunity. The Church is filled with conflicting ideologies and principles which dissipate the

> glory of Christ. The Church—once beautiful, united, heavenly—has lost its character, is hidden in the world; and the Christians themselves are worldly, covetous, eager for riches, honor, power—like the children of the ages.[63]

Christendom now appeared as a set of human ecclesiastical systems, all of which had no right to claim to be *the* church of God, because there were true Christians in all of them. To try to bring about a union as is being attempted today—that is, along ecumenical lines—would be wrong. In attempting to bring all the separated groups together one only denies the true and already existing unity of the church of God.

To seek to restore the church to its primitive outward unity and spirituality would also be wrong, for God, as Darby saw it, does not restore that which is fallen. Yet, in all God's dealings with man, in spite of man's failure, there has always been a faithful remnant, a remnant that has separated itself from the evil around (for example, 1 Kings 19:18).

Darby felt that believers today should separate themselves from the various bodies around them. Believers should simply gather to the Lord's name alone (not around a teacher or a creed) on the basis of the unity of the body of Christ (1 Corinthians 10:17) with those who call upon the Lord out of a pure heart (2 Timothy 2:22). Such gathering is the only testimony of the unity of Christians there can be in this day of ruin. The thought was not to seek to be a church alongside many other churches, nor to assume to be *the* church, but the thought was to give expression to an already existing unity, the only one God recognizes, the unity of the body of Christ, the one true church.

This unity was expressed by the breaking of bread at the Lord's supper, at His table (1 Corinthians 10:17). But in this unity, separation was also seen—separation from evil, whether moral evil, doctrinal evil, schism, or evil resulting from human organization. If believers have separated themselves from the above-mentioned evils, these evils cannot be tolerated among themselves either. Separation from evil involves discipline, an example of which we have in 1 Corinthians 5.[64]

Believers who gathered in this way we have just been

considering have been called *Brethren*, but this is a Scriptural name (Matthew 23:8) and applies just as much to every true believer in Christ. Darby wrote:

> We have not to promote "brethrenism," but the interest of every soul we meet with, just where its need is. I can honestly say I never thought of "brethren" with a single soul I ever met with—never—but what that soul wanted from God, as far as I was able.[65] I never asked a person to come among brethren in my life, nor ever would.[66] I do not ask any one to join or own brethren, as they speak, but I do look to their full submission to the yoke of Christ.[67] I am sure more faith might walk more *powerfully* in this path, but the path is a right one. There I walk with God's help. I have seen many swerve and seek ease, I have seen my own failure and feebleness in it, but the path is Christ's, and I desire to walk there still. I did not enter into this path for its success, but for its truth, because I believed it Christ's. I walk in it still for the same reason. I did not enter into it for brethren, or brethrenism: there were none to join. I did so because the Spirit and the Word showed me it, and that it was following Christ. It has not ceased to be so; and now that many have left for a broader, and I think more worldly one, I still prefer the narrow one. I did not choose it for them; I do not leave it because they have left it.[68]

Darby felt that it would be better to seek to present Christ to others rather than to begin by speaking of the ways of meeting and so on. He would present Christ (1)as dead and risen (justification through the death and resurrection of Christ); (2)as ascended and seated on high (formation of the church in connection with Christ ascended and the Holy Spirit sent down from Heaven); and (3)as coming again (to receive the saints and judge the world). He said that the Reformation did not go beyond point one, and that most Christians do not clearly see points two and three. It is important that they should understand these great truths.[69] The intention was not to urge others to become part of a special group and to bow to certain views of Scripture, but rather to exhort them to be obedient to the Word of God, to be in harmony with His thoughts, and to bow to the Lord's authority.

In December 1877 Darby wrote:

> I have the fullest persuasion that the testimony we have is God's testimony for the last days—the gospel Paul preached—what I never suspected when I began in this city [Dublin] just fifty years ago now. I sought to walk for my own conscience as the Word taught me. Jeremiah 15:19 laid hold of me in starting as a guiding verse [this also would support his not returning to the service of the Church of Ireland after recovering from his riding accident]. I admit in the fullest way, the ruin of the Church in the world, but this is no reason for continuing in the evil that brought it in, and into which it has led.[70]

In the books of Ezra and Nehemiah Darby and the Brethren saw a type of this ruin of the church, her being carried away into Babylon because of her unfaithfulness (Babylon portraying for them the worldly and idolatrous system of the church). During this period of captivity there were no offerings brought to Jehovah in Jerusalem, the place He had made His dwelling. There was no temple, no altar there in all this time, though there were Israelites scattered everywhere over the world. There may have been, and were, many faithful individuals among the Lord's people of old—for example, Daniel—but there was no longer a united testimony. After the seventy years of captivity a small weak remnant returned to Jerusalem (notice: to Jerusalem, the place of God's dwelling, where He had put His name forever; not Bethel, or Bethlehem, or any other such place). In the return of the remnant Darby and the Brethren saw the return of such who had been for so long imprisoned in the systems and organizations of men to the simple obedience and authority of the Word of God (Matthew 18:20).

The Brethren once again set up the altar (Ezra 3:2)—for us, the Lord's table (1 Corinthians 10). The temple was once again built up on its foundations—the recognition of the whole house of God (1 Timothy 3:15). It was very important for them to notice here that the glory of the temple they built at their return could not be compared to the glory of the first one (compare Ezra 3:12 with Haggai 2:3). After the temple had been built the city walls were raised (Ezra 9:9, though the actual building of the city walls we find in Nehemiah). The walls implied separation (compare Ezekiel 42:20 with Haggai 2:12-13).

The buildings of the temple were viewed as representing the state of Christianity today and the entire complex of buildings and court as typifying professing Christianity. The shrine was viewed as representing all true believers, those born of God (Ephesians 4:4), and the court as typifying those carrying the name of Christ but not having His life (Ephesians 4:5). That which lies outside of the temple compound was viewed as representing the world (Ephesians 4:6).

The altar was set up first; then the temple was built. It is interesting that Darby first saw the significance of the altar and later the significance of the house of God. The order was the same. Afterward the walls were raised.

Writing in 1879 Darby said:

> It was this [the truth of the unity of the body] more than fifty years ago, brought me out of the establishment: nor have I any other principle now. In the last days we are called on to distinguish those who "call on the name of the Lord *out of a pure heart,*" which at the first was not called for.[71] The first [Brethren] were a testimony for separation;[72] that brought in many. Are they so now? is the question; not speculating about Philadelphia. But I trust the Lord. But brethren's work has spread out far and wide beyond them as an effect, and these products of it are a hindrance. At the beginning it was faith acting on the Word—conscience; now it is looking to see the state and effect.[73]

Darby saw instruction for the Christian of today in the conduct of Zerubbabel in the book of Ezra. He was heir to the place that Solomon had once occupied in days of glory and prosperity, but Zerubbabel did not speak of his birth, nor of the rights that were thus his. He was faithful in the whole path of separation he had to walk, faithful in the midst of sorrow and conflicts. For the believer today it should be the same. The church began in power and glory, but that is no longer the case. As the men of Issachar "had understanding of the times, to know what Israel ought to do" (1 Chronicles 12:32, KJV), so should the believer be able to discern the times and his responsibility in them. Today is a day of ruin, and not the time for Christians to be seeking a place for themselves. They should much rather recognize their state and take their place there accordingly; that is, with their faces in the dust, with true sorrow of heart, realizing the ruin caused by man. This would be the rightful place, but also the place of blessing.

> What I felt from the beginning, and began with, was this: the Holy Spirit remains, and therefore, the essential principle of unity with His presence for (the fact we are now concerned in) *wherever* two or three are gathered in My name, there I am in the midst of them. When this is really sought, there will certainly be blessing by His presence. When there is an attempt at displaying the position and the unity, there will always be a mess and failure. God will not take such a place with us. We must get into the place of His mind to get His strength; that is now, the failure of the Church. But there He will be with us. I have said we are the witnesses of the weakness and low state of the Church. We are not stronger or better than others, dissenters, etc; but we only own our bad and lost state, and *therefore* can find blessing. I do not limit what the blessed Spirit can do for us in this low estate, but I take my place where He can do it.[74]

Having now considered the two terms *ruin* and *separation* (see appendix J for Darby's summary on the church) we can return to the more historical, chronological order of events in our story.

The Movement Spreads

After Darby had recovered from his riding accident he did not stay in Dublin very long, but went off to other parts of Ireland to preach the Word of God. The first place he visited was Limerick in the southwestern part of Ireland. There he met a Mr. Thomas Maunsell, and the work began.

Darby's life was at times in danger. In a letter dated February 2, 1829, a Captain Rock Darby accused J. N. Darby of disturbing the people of Corosin by his preaching and advised him to leave the country or fear for his life.[75]

Bible reading meetings were held and many clergymen and people of the upper classes came. There was also open-air evangelism in the roughest places: fairs, markets, races, and regattas. Gatherings began to grow.

The Brethren, and Darby in particular, were accused of simply seeking to proselyte believers from other Christian groups. Their critics claimed that not many came to them from out of the world—that not many had been saved through their gospel efforts. It was said that the Brethren were less concerned about the salvation of souls than about others accepting their views. Darby answered this as follows:

> The account in the _____ might lead to suppose, that the work known under the name of brethren was a mere abstraction of persons, already believers, from other bodies; whereas, in England, the greater number are converted to God from a state of worldliness, and abroad nearly all have been so.[76]

Of Darby's work at this time his friend Bellett wrote:

> He visited different places, amongst them Cork and Limerick, ministering wherever he might the truth which God had given him from His Word. I doubt not, from what I remember, he found in all these places evidence of the independent work of the Spirit of God on the hearts and consciences. In Limerick and Cork, occasionally preaching in pulpits of the Established Church, he also met Christians in private houses, and the influence of his ministry was greatly blessed. Light and refreshment visited many a soul, and that too, of an order to which they had before been strangers.[77]

When Bellett spoke of Darby's preaching in pulpits of the

established church he did not mean that Darby was in the service of the church; he was just an invited guest. Kelly, referring to Darby, made this clear:

> After he left the Anglican Establishment he preached occasionally at the call of godly clergymen who urged it; but he only appeared for the discourse and was not present at the previous service. So in France afterwards he preached for pious ministers of the Reformed Church; nor did he refuse the black gown as an academical dress; but when they brought the bands, "Oh! no," said he: "I put on no more."

Edward Pennefather's nephew William, later well known in evangelical circles, received the following letter dated March 14, 1835, from his sister:

> Mr. [Darby] is in Dublin, and we have the enjoyment of seeing him sometimes. He calls here occasionally, and seems to communicate the joy in heavenly things which he feels. He presses *rejoicing* on believers very much, because he says, "Christ not only died, but is risen, and had purchased everything for us, and believers are children and heirs." This joy in believing, he thinks, is the surest way of bringing about deadness to the world. I believe that you know his views, about the Church of England: he wishes to draw believers out of it, although he admits there is salvation in it. On this subject he has not spoken to any of us. Surely we may be living as risen with Christ, whether connected with the Church of England or not. Many real Christians on this ground do not like to associate with Mr. [Darby]; but this I cannot enter into, when there are so many delightful spots of common meeting. He appears to be engaged from morning till night preaching, expounding, visiting, &c.: he now seems ready to go anywhere, either to dine or call, *always premising, "If you will allow me to preach"*; and he never goes anywhere unless about his Master's business. He says he feels his office principally lies in urging believers to walk worthy of their high and holy calling.[78]

Newton noted: "It was strange he [Darby] never would use the prayers in the Prayerbook, but yet would preach in Churches."[79]

In 1828 Darby authored a pamphlet entitled "Considerations on the Nature and Unity of the Church of Christ." The following was written in response to Darby's pamphlet, probably by William Kelly:

> It would be impossible for any godly soul who accepted that paper as a just application of divine truth to the actual state of Christendom, to continue a churchman or a dissenter. And in fact neither the writer [Darby] nor those who felt with him as to this remained at that date [1828] in the denominations of which they had previously been members or ministers.[80]

Darby said he published the pamphlet when he left the establishment.[81] Many found help in this paper[82] and came to a clearer apprehension of God's truth regarding His church. As Bellett saw it, God was working the same way on the hearts of believers in many different places, and Darby was apparently the one the Lord used to give this work its proper direction. Darby wrote:

> One person may not have enough spiritual discernment to discover what is right; but the moment another shows it to him, he understands that it is truth. All are not engineers, but a simple waggoner knows a good road when once it is made.[83] So men taught in the word may point out a path which the mass of brethren would not have discovered, but which they see to be scriptural when suggested.[84]

In our first chapter we mentioned that Darby had not been happy with his style of work as a clergyman; he felt it to be in disagreement with the teachings of the Bible. After leaving the establishment he preached the truth of God everywhere. It is obvious that he had come to a clearer grasp of what he later came to see as true Christian ministry. He wrote:

> At the time I was occupied with these things, [truths

> regarding the Church], the person with whom I was in Christian relation locally, as a minister was an excellent Christian, worthy of all respect, and one for whom I have always had a great affection [it was the Reverend Robert Daly]. It was however the principles, and not the persons, which acted on my conscience, for I had already given up, out of love to the Saviour all that the world could offer. I said to myself, If the apostle Paul were to come here now, he would not, according to the established system, be even allowed to preach, not being legally ordained, but if a worker of Satan, who by his doctrine denied the Saviour, came here, he could freely preach, and my Christian friend would be obliged to consider him as a fellow labourer; whereas he would be unable to recognize the most powerful instrument of the Spirit of God, however much blessed in his work of leading multitudes of souls to the Lord, if he had not been ordained according to the system. All this, said I to myself, is false. This is not mere abuse, such as may be found everywhere; it is the *principle* of the system that is at fault. Ministry is of the Spirit, but the system is founded on an opposite principle; consequently it seemed impossible to remain in it any longer.[85]

Could Darby have remained in the service of the established church with such thoughts?

Ministry

The following may be considered as a short summary of Darby's views regarding true Christian ministry.

Ministry is characteristic of, and also essential to, the church. A minister, or one who ministers in the church, is one who speaks as the oracle of God. A minister does not argue for the Scriptures, but from them. There are two main aspects of ministry: first, the presentation of the gospel of salvation to sinners who need Christ as their Savior; and second, the edification of the church—those who have already accepted Christ. Ministry involves presenting Christ to man through the holy Scriptures, which are the revelation of God and His thoughts; the Scriptures can bring man into immediate and direct contact with God.

Ministry is different from worship, for that is pure privilege and involves the giving of honor, thanks, and adoration to God for what He has done and for what He Himself is. Worship is more important than ministry because when man worships, God receives His due. God gives to man through ministry, but good ministry should lead a soul to worship with more spiritual intelligence.

Gifts are the basis of all true ministry. (Priesthood is the portion of all believers and is the basis of worship.) In a certain sense each Christian has some gift by which he can contribute to the functioning of the whole church, but only a few have a gift for direct ministry, in the more exact meaning of the term. Darby's view was that a person cannot study for the ministry. Either he is called by God for this, and is thus already fitted by God for the ministry he has to do, needing no special secular training, or he is not. A believer who has a gift is responsible to the Lord, and to Him alone, to make use of it for the benefit and blessing of others (2 Timothy 1:6).

Gifts can be considered in two ways. The believer receives a gift from the Holy Spirit (1 Corinthians 12:11), and this believer is at the same time himself a gift of the risen and glorified Christ to His church, for the edification of the body—that is, the whole church of God (Ephesians 4:11). Gifts and their exercise are to be distinguished from offices in the church, such as elders or deacons. Offices are of a local character and do not necessitate a gift in the same sense.

There are three prominent gifts that have remained in the church until today. *First is the evangelist.* He is one who announces the glad tidings, the gospel. He continues his outreach until those hearing the gospel accept Christ and the remission of sins. His work takes place outside of the church, among the unsaved, but is the means by which the church grows. Darby considered this gift to be the most privileged. He often spoke of his love for evangelism, and his "envy" of those who were called to this ministry, but he himself felt more called to serve those who were already saved.

> I feel it of all importance that we should evangelize. I quite recognize the difference of gifts, and we cannot

> appropriate what is not given; still there is a love to souls, the love of Christ constraining us, which is an important element in our own state. I feel it as to myself. I do not doubt I fail in everything, but in a certain sense my heart is filled with the desire of the blessing of the Church, of Christ's glory in it, for that I could spend myself with His grace; but love to sinners' souls—I could not say I have none, and I anxiously evangelize when I can; but it does not press on my spirit like the other; yet I constantly see that a meeting goes on well when the love of souls is there.[86]
>
> I am not satisfied with myself as to my love to souls. I bow to filling up the little niche I may have been allotted, but still envy (not with an ill feeling) more active evangelists, and sometimes ask myself whether cowardice and want of zeal does not hinder one. Fully occupied and labouring, the question is whether a simpler love to souls would not put me in another place. I am content with—and thankful for—any the Lord will allow me to have, unworthy as I am of any. I ask if the exposition of Scripture is the task allotted me. I see the Church's need as to it, and I am content with anything, but I have ever loved evangelisation. I have gone out on that work. The Church is at my heart, perhaps more than souls: yet I trust I love them. But Christ's glory must connect itself with evangelising for me.[87]

Darby said that evangelism characterized the Brethren in the beginning[88] and that he would be sorry to see this work among souls given up through stressing peculiar principles of the Brethren (though the gathering of saints was not to be de-emphasized either).[89] He felt that if the Brethren ceased to be an evangelizing group of Christians they would become sectarian—if not theoretically, then practically.

Darby was happy for every soul truly saved, though he could not accept all the means used in evangelizing. He was against too much emphasis on feelings (though recognizing that emotions were involved) rather than the exercise of conscience. Those who are converted in an atmosphere of excitement, levity, and activity would want this atmosphere to continue; they would not be interested in quiet submission to

Christ. And there are those who are never really converted, but simply act on impulse or as a part of a mass emotional response.

> I think the more we get back to the old manner of preaching the better, especially in Acts—preaching Jesus and the resurrection. I am satisfied, the more we insist on the fact, the more real power there would be to set people free.[90]
>
> I believe we ought to preach the love of God to sinners, and appeal to them more than we do. All I look for is that the teaching should be such that it should convict of sin, and the impossibility of sin and God going together, so that it should be well understood that there is need of *reconciling*. And here Christ at once comes in, and atonement and righteousness. Holiness precluded all sin from God, righteousness judges it. This I believe the sinner should understand, so that he should know *what love applies to*, yet that love should be fully preached. It does itself often convict of sin, for the conscience has often its wants already, and this draws them out, so that men find consciously where they are. But conviction of sin under righteousness is a very useful thing if grace be fully preached with it, and both unite in Christ.
>
> I think its very important that preachers should go to the world, especially now, with a message of distinct love to them. All I desire is that it should be love manifested in Christ, so as to bring out the sinner's condition to himself; that it should not be mere easiness as to sin; that it is a gracious love of sinners—grace abounding over sin—grace reigning through righteousness, than which nothing is more perfectly grace. Sometimes I think the love of God is so preached as if it were a kind of boon of the sinner to accept it. It is God's joy. Still, as a sinner, his being a debtor to God ought to be before his soul.[91]

Darby also saw a danger in the evangelist's becoming popular and being exalted more than Christ. "It is God's work, and man should be hidden—though he be the servant—and God glorified. Publicity in the Lord's things is not good."

In a letter Darby wrote:

> One thing that you relate gave me much to think of, as indeed it has been a subject of thought pretty often for a long while, nor am I sure that I have the Lord's mind clear upon it. I think evangelizing the greatest privilege of any in respect to gifts, though I am not an evangelist, only when I can doing the work of one as well as I can. This is not my difficulty, but what you say, that the evangelization has enfeebled the teaching the saints. The gifts are clearly distinct; but I do not see that one should enfeeble the other. Paul assuredly evangelized, and as surely taught, and taught in evangelizing. Witness the Thessalonians; and if he did not look for, he certainly found, present fruit. He distinguished being a minister of the gospel, and a minister of the church, to fulfil (complete) the word of God. This is not in the Thessalonians: all is personal, not corporate. We must be with God for each, as called of Him to it; and then I do not see why power should not be for both.
>
> But a certain salvationism, instead of Christianity, I think, has to say to it which God may bless, but which carries its effect with it. Few carry in their mind, I endure all things for the elect's sake. It is a general idea that God is love, and would have all men to be saved, which is blessedly true; but thus it ends in being saved—man's safety. There is no purpose of God in it—no glory of Christ—all called upon to bow to and own Him. Hence, as to the preacher's state of mind, when he has got the person saved, and this confessed, he is content, going no farther. God's interest in His own is lost, which leads on to building up. If we were with God about them, the heart would soon be drawn out in testimony to them.
>
> There is another thing—glory to Christ in His church. This, I confess, greatly absorbs my spirit, though I be a poor hand for this work too. But this leads us to prayer for saints, so also to testimony to them. The evil is not earnest devotedness to evangelizing, which is itself the way of blessing to an assembly, or rather God working in one by His presence

> builds up the other; it is being absorbed by it. But this affects the evangelizing itself; there is less of Christ in it, more of man's importance, and when pursued in a revival way, more of delusive work; it never gives a solid foundation to build upon.
>
> I should be most loath to weaken evangelization; I believe God is blessing it, especially for gathering out in these last days; and it is healthful for an assembly that their hearts are engaged in it. At the very beginning it characterized Brethren, and I trust still does, though it be more common now on all hands. The love exercised in it binds also saints together; but God is in a great professing body, awakening them to their state, and this has its importance also. The cry that awoke the virgins was not the gospel, ordinarily so called. Finally, the hand cannot say to the foot, I have no need of thee. I do not reject the joy of counting converts, but we must not lean upon it. "When ye have done all things, say, we are unprofitable servants, we have done that which it was our duty to do." The bond of service to Christ is kept up, and this is of great importance. It is not referring the effect to our work, but our work and heart to Him. I am sure, if we were near Christ, we should do both well, assuming of course that Christ has called us to do it. Do not be content to put one in place of the other, but see what Christ means by it. Be with Christ about the saints when you have to say to them. Be with Christ as to both, and then see what is the result. The question in general has long pressed upon me in connection with the spiritual activities of the day. I have never been allowed to see much fruit, and have been more blessed in bringing to peace than awakening. There is One, I thank God, who is above all, and does all: let us look to Him. The Lord be abundantly with you, and guide you both in heart and work, and keep you in much enjoyment of Him, as well as for Him.[92]

The second gift is the pastor. He deals with Christians—believers—in their personal and spiritual needs. This gift is based on teaching, though it goes beyond that since it applies the teaching to the individual conscience and private life. The pastor's purpose is to guard against evil and heresy and encourage saints to live more spiritual and devoted lives. He is the shepherd caring for the sheep. The work of the pastor takes place chiefly in private. The pastor applies the truth that has been taught in the assembly meetings; he looks to the state of the heart of the individual who has heard the truth; he makes sure that use is made of the spiritual food that has been offered. A pastor's work involves finding out how the saints are coming along publicly, socially, privately, spiritually, and morally. He is familiar with their doctrine and their relationships. He can share the sorrows and needs of a fellow saint, carrying them on his own heart (not talking with others about them, confidence and trust being very essential) and going to the Lord with them. How greatly do we need true pastors in this our day!

Darby considered this gift to be the most difficult to exercise and the one requiring the most maturity. "I hear from dear______, who is anxious about a certain change in himself from evangelist to pastor. I covet evangelizing, but the latter gift is more."[93]

The work of a pastor necessarily involves visiting the saints in their homes.

> I think the visiting part myself, quite as important, if not the most important part of the work: it is said, "publicly, and from house to house." In these days, when there is a good deal of general testimony, though feeble and mixed perhaps, the latter assumes more than its primary relative importance. The clock, of course, strikes the hours, and avails to the passers by, but the works inside make the good clock, and make the striking and the hands right. I think it should be your substantive work, and take all else as it comes; indeed, I do not believe any can minister well without it. The springs of love, and the use and application of doctrine are fed there, minds are understood, the Spirit is led to apply truth to need spiritually understood and entered into; we are apt to get essays else, theories or thoughts. The Holy Ghost, I believe, teaches people while it teaches truth, and suits the truth to conscience and its known state; and it is good for our own souls besides. I

> dread much public testimony, and altogether so, if there be not private work.[94]

If Darby did not consider himself as having the gift of an evangelist (though he felt the call, as we all should feel it, to do the "work of an evangelist"), he had without doubt the gift of a pastor.

Darby's normal day was divided up as follows: mornings were devoted to his personal study and reading of God's Word (he usually got up at seven); afternoons were spent visiting the poor and the sick; and in the evening he attended meetings or preached the Word (he usually retired at eleven).

When the poor are mentioned, we have to think of them as they were in nineteenth-century England, particularly London, where it was said that there were thirty thousand filthy, naked, lawless, deserted young children in 1848. Adolf Brennecke wrote:

> In the 1880's it was reported that per year the number of infants, which had been wrapped in rags or newspaper and then thrown away were in the thousands! The children sold matches, flowers or cheap fruit to earn some little bit of money. Some worked twelve or more hours in the day in coal mines, dragging waggons of coal behind them on their hands and knees—and that as young as five years of age! Women worked in factories from morning till night under, often, hard foremen and received terribly low wages. The men worked in factories or on the docks and at the markets. If anyone walked through the poor part of the city where these people lived he would have found drunkenness, immorality and despair. Thousands lived together in decaying houses which contained almost next to no furniture, without heating and where the sun and fresh air never entered. A terrible state![95]

Darby visited the poor. We are now more occupied with visiting believers and the above has described more the state of the lost, though there were certainly believers among the poor. Darby visited both believers and the lost—wherever there was need. He wrote in 1870:

> Many Christians are labouring in the scene of the [German-French] war; large sums of money have been sent to them. All this does not attract me. God be praised that so many poor creatures have been relieved; but I would rather see the brethren penetrating the lanes of the city, and seeking the poor where they are found every day. There is far more self-abnegation, more hidden service in such work.[96]

We know much, relatively speaking, concerning Darby's work as a teacher and expounder of God's Word, but we know next to nothing about his work as a pastor, about his visiting. Why? It is, as he said, a more hidden service. One account gives us a glimpse into his manner and way. An old woman asked to come into fellowship with the Brethren. She was visited first by two young men and then by an older brother. She said afterward that the first visitors were very learned but she had not been able to understand them; she got along well, however, with the simple old gentleman who had come later. The "simple old gentleman" was J. N. Darby. Darby wrote:

> I love not only to preach, but to be in direct communication with souls as to their relation with God—saints, and sinners yet more.[97]
>
> How many needs, hidden even in the most degraded souls, would confess themselves . . . if a love, a goodness, which could give them confidence were presented to them . . . How many souls are whirling in pleasure, in order to silence the moral griefs which torment them. Divine love not only answers needs, it makes them speak.[98]

William Pennefather noted about Darby:

> My sister has told you that Mr. [Darby] is now in Dublin: he has kindly called on me several times, and his visits I have greatly enjoyed. He, happily, has never touched on those points on which I cannot agree with him, and which would only disturb us both. I know of no one more calculated to deal with sincere but desponding Christians. The privileges of believers and

> the enjoyments of heaven are placed by him before the mind with all the vividness of reality.[99]

The third gift is the teacher. He is concerned mainly with doctrine. His work is the explanation of the Scriptures, giving their meaning and significance, and instructing others from them. Prophecy is closely tied to this gift (1 Corinthians 14); the teacher does not foretell the future or give new revelations, but he preaches the mind of God in a way that not only instructs, but also edifies, encourages, and comforts its hearers. He applies the mind of God to the need of the moment. The gift of teacher can also be connected, in one person, with the gift of pastor. When there is such a combination, the gift of pastor can be exercised with immense moral power and the gift of teacher can be exercised with an affectionate tenderness. Darby felt that the pastor should also have the ability to teach.

To summarize these three gifts: the evangelist brings in; the pastor guides those brought in; the teacher unfolds the Word for those who have been brought in (the pastor also makes sure that this teaching has been understood). Related to the gift of teacher is the prophet who applies the Word in power.

Ministry, then, involves gifts. These gifts cannot be obtained from man, but are given directly by God. One in possession of a gift is responsible to the Lord to use it and does not require the ordination of man. The sphere for exercising a gift (except for the evangelist) is the whole church of God, and not a particular body or group.

Further Developments

While Darby was away from Dublin ministering the Word in other places in Ireland, the little meeting in the house of Francis Hutchinson was steadily growing. Many who came were of the poorer class and felt themselves ill at ease in the house of a wealthy man, and so in the spring of 1830 (Darby was probably at this time in England) they moved to a larger place, an auction room, which they hired for Sundays. The address was 11 Aungier Street. (This street runs perpendicular to York Street, the location of the church that had excommunicated Cronin.) This move had been suggested by John Parnell (the later Lord Congleton), who also felt that the Lord's table in their midst should be more of a testimony to the world outside.[100]

The brethren came together on Saturday evenings to move the auction furniture out of the way and to set up the table with bread and wine for the following morning. These times left very many precious memories in the hearts of those involved. They felt the Lord's presence and smile in all that they did. The room was later on bought for their sole use and they continued to meet there for a few years, until they moved to Brunswick Street.

J. G. Bellett was uneasy about the step from Fitzwilliam Square to Aungier Street. He wrote, "The publicity of it was too much for me. I instinctively shrank. Mr. Hutchinson, as I remember, would also have continued in the private house, so that I believe I did not join them for one or two Sundays, and I am not sure that he did, but the others were there at once."[101] J. G. Bellett gave the following description of the gathering there after he began to attend it:

> It was poor material we had, and we had one or two solemn and awful cases of backsliding. There was but little spiritual energy, and much that was poor treasure for a living temple, but we held together in the Lord's mercy and care, I believe advancing in the knowledge of His mind. The settled order of worship that we had in Fitzwilliam Square gave place gradually. Teaching and exhortation were first and common duties and services, while prayer was restricted under the care of two or three who were regarded as elders, but gradually all this yielded. In a little while no appointed or recognized eldership was understood to be in the midst of us, and all service was of a free character, the presence of God through the Spirit being more simply believed and used.[102]

The move to Aungier Street coincided approximately with J. G. Bellett's formally leaving the established church. His brother wrote:

> It was also somewhat about this time [that is, 1831] that we were both a good deal tried by the secession of dear John and Mary from the Church of England—they joined the Plymouth Brethren. I am quite uncertain about the exact date. It ought not to have been unlooked for, as his associations had long been with persons who either were not in connection with the Church, or whose attachment to her was very loose and uncertain. Nevertheless, his actual separation from the Church greatly distressed us, though the love and sweetness of his spirit tended to soften the pain it produced.
>
> Meanwhile, dear Tom and I became stronger in our allegiance to the Church and further advanced in what are termed Church principles. Besides, the new friends with whom John became associated were not congenial to me—either to my natural tastes, or my religious feelings. I was fastidious, which John was not. He had too much real excellence for that, and their opposition to the amenities of life, as well as their rigid Calvinism, grated more on me than they should have done had I valued as much as he did "the root of the matter" which was in them.[103]

Darby, except for the warning we noted previously, gave a brighter account of the Aungier Street meeting: "The brethren who meet in Aungier Street are going on in much unity and sweetness of spirit amongst each other. I should only fear their getting too comfortable amongst themselves, and sitting quietly down, but they all labour in the Lord as far as I know."[104]

England

After Francis Newman had completed his fifteen months as a private tutor in the Pennefather home he returned to Oxford, England. Darby came to Oxford in May of 1830 and met several people there, among them Newman's friend Benjamin Wills Newton. Newton, who was a young man of twenty-three at the time, had been elected a fellow of Exeter College and taken a first-class degree. Though it might not have appeared possible at the time, he would one day be the cause of great sorrow for Darby and for the movement that was beginning to grow so rapidly. Newman described Darby's time at Oxford as follows:

> Most striking was it to see how instantaneously he assumed the place of universal father-confessor, as if he had been a known and long trusted friend. His insight into character, and tenderness pervading his austerity, so opened men's hearts, that day after day there was no end of secret closetings with him.

The reason for Darby's being able to win the hearts and confidence of others might be explained in a few words from J. G. Bellett's "The Moral Glory of the Lord Jesus": "It is always a sign of moral power, when confidence of another is won, without having sought it; then in such a case the heart has recognized the reality of love." Darby's own views were:

> When a person is owned, the heart, the conscience, the affections, and respect are engaged; it is *a bond,* a bond formed by the exercise of the gift, in the heart of such who have profited thereby. The heart that has received blessing responds to the action of the Holy Spirit, which has taken place by means of the brother who has been its instrument, and thus the heart attaches itself to that instrument, and owns God in him; it is God's will that it should be so, and He binds together the members of the body by those mutual helps.[105]

Darby also made the acquaintance of George Vicesimus Wigram.[106] He was also a friend of Newton's and twenty-five at the time. Wigram came from a wealthy family and was his father's twentieth child, as his middle name implies. He had served in the Guards, but after his conversion he entered Queen's College with the purpose of taking ecclesiastical orders. He would prove to be one of Darby's most loyal and faithful friends until Wigram's death in 1879.

Newton invited Darby to visit him at his home in Plymouth (where Wigram had apparently already settled) sometime in 1831. At Plymouth they met Captain Percy Francis Hall, a young man of twenty-six who had, after attaining the rank of a naval commander, resigned his commission and sold his possessions and spent his time preaching in the villages. The meeting at Plymouth may have begun in a small house on King Street, but in any case on December 2, 1831, Wigram bought a chapel (for 750 pounds) on Raleigh Street, known as the Providence Chapel. (In 1840, because of the increasing number of believers attending, a new chapel was built on Ebrington Street.)

The work had great success in Plymouth and it was said that there was not one household there without at least one representative attending the meetings. In fact, the theater had to be closed for three years because no one seemed to be interested in this sort of amusement or entertainment anymore. The general desire among many was to live in separation from the world. Contrary to what might have been expected, the owner of the theater, who had suffered great external loss, did not become embittered but joined the others who had chosen this path of separation and devotion to the Lord.

The greatest number of believers who ever attended the meeting at Plymouth at one time was seven hundred according to Darby, though he himself was not at all in favor of numbering believers or making a list of meetings, as the following quote clearly shows:

> I never liked it [a list of meetings]. It was the principle; and the gravest things often come from very small ones when a principle is in it. But I never wished to make any fuss or bother about it. It is of course very convenient. Still such motives as that lead to many things. My objection was, that it was making a list—numbering the people—and of brethren a distinct sect; as Congregationalists or Baptists might count their churches. This was my grand difficulty; but there has been another. The names put in . . . [confer] a kind of position as elders. Now this may lead, not to the influence of those who are pillars, which I find in Scripture, but soon to a recognized place.[107]

Darby said that he liked small meetings, provided that they were really in the unity of the Spirit.[108]

Among the believers gathered together at Plymouth there was great freshness of heart, simplicity, devotedness to Christ, love, and union. They parted with all that was considered worldly, and made freewill offerings of their clothes, books, and furniture. The quantity collected was so great that it had to be sold at an auction that lasted three days. The only desire of the saints was to express their indifference to the world, their separation to Christ, and their waiting for His return. A brother who was among those gathered at Plymouth left the following account:

> All was happiness and peace, unruffled by personal questions, and undisturbed by jealousies or ambitions. The distinctions between rich and poor were lessened by holy, loving fellowship and unity which characterized their intercourse. Their dress was plain, their habits simple and their walk distinguished by separation from the world. The meetings of the assembly were calm, peaceful and hallowed; their singing was soft, slow and thoughtful; their worship evinced the nearness of their communion with the Lord; their prayers were earnest for an increased knowledge of God, and their deep searching of the Scriptures under the guidance of the Holy Spirit, while the exercise of the varied ministry, under the power of the Spirit, testified to the blessedness of the teaching of God's Word on each important subject.
>
> I breathed what appeared to me the pure element of love, I was in the enjoyment of the liberty of home. I was enlightened by its teaching, cheered by its joys, comforted by its hallowed fellowship, strengthened by godly companionship and encouraged by those who were over me in the Lord. Those were delightful times, so sweet for their simplicity. The fruits of the Spirit were in evidence.[109]

These believers also lived a great deal in each other's houses and company, so that there was no such thing as domestic privacy among them. One of their contemporaries

Francis William Newman
(University of London Library)

Benjamin Willis Newton
(Veitch's The Story of the Brethren Movement, *Pickering & Inglis)*

George Vicesimus Wigram
(The collection of Ulrich Bister)

James Butler Stoney
(The collection of Ulrich Bister)

who did not join them described the meeting at Plymouth as "that slough of love." Darby wrote:

> Plymouth, I assure you, has altered the face of Christianity to me, from finding brethren, and they acting together.[110] The order and peace of Plymouth is one of my comforts here . . . I do pray He may make them all a pattern of believers.[111] Various portions of light and truth might be furnished by different brethren, and supposing difference or mistake, they dwelt together in unity and were glad to communicate to each other their thoughts even that they might be corrected; and progress was made in the truth.[112]

However, Darby warned, "I fear knowledge has too much prominence at Plymouth, though it be precious." Yet Darby's greatest fear for believers at all times, and not just at Plymouth, was not so much evil teaching and false doctrine coming in, but worldliness. He mentioned this fear repeatedly:

> I have long said, brethren began by practical separation from the world. Though certain great truths for the last days were there, still what the world saw was that they were not of it. Is there going to be this testimony now? It was so in houses, ways, conduct—many faults, I doubt not, but there was that stamped upon them and characteristic of them.[113]

The origin of the name *Brethren* we have already considered. The designation *Plymouth Brethren,* so well known today, came from the fact that the believers in Plymouth had no name, did not belong to any particular denomination, and so they were spoken of by others as brethren from Plymouth; this led naturally to Plymouth Brethren. Also it was in Plymouth that the movement first came into public notice.

Darby did not remain long in Plymouth. He visited Oxford several times in the next two years and also went to London and Row in Scotland. The purpose of his visit to Scotland was to investigate what had been called a renewed outpouring of the Holy Spirit, accompanied by gifts of healing and speaking in tongues. Darby's verdict was negative. In the early church, he felt, sign gifts—including healing, miracles, and speaking in tongues—were given so that the world could see a demonstration of God's power and blessing upon Christianity (1 Corinthians 14:22). Miracles were linked to the original establishment of a new testimony of God and were meant to be temporary. What would be their value today when, according to his view, the church was in ruins?

Percy F. Hall went to Hereford where a new gathering was formed, and Wigram to London where a gathering began as well. Writing in 1871 Darby mentioned there being about three thousand saints in London.[114] The number of meetings at that time numbered about twenty-six or thirty.

Newton, of the original four, was left alone at Plymouth, where he soon exercised a great influence. As a teacher he was very attractive and convincing, possessing great natural gifts. The striking appearance of his eagle-like face only added to his impressiveness. This all proved to be a danger to him and Darby wrote to him, "The influence of your mind and the love of influence has always been your snare . . . It is the snare of every strong mind, as yours is in many respects, to like a circle of persons round itself, who receive its views and statements."[115] In the beginning this danger was not so apparent, but in time Newton would turn against the teaching of the Brethren; he later held and taught fundamentally false doctrine as to the person of Christ. See appendix K.

In 1835 Samuel Prideaux Tregelles, who would become so well known as a Biblical textual critic, joined the company at Plymouth, which at the time numbered about eighty persons (though it increased rapidly, soon attaining the seven hundred mentioned by Darby). Tregelles assisted Wigram in the early stages of his work on the Englishman's Greek (1839) and Hebrew (1843) concordances. Wigram himself provided the money for this work, a sum of fifty thousand pounds, and spoke of it as simply passing through his hands. In this work he rendered an eminent service to the whole church of God; these volumes are still being reprinted and used to this day by many. He also introduced a new hymnbook entitled *A Few Hymns and Some Spiritual Songs, selected 1856, for the Little Flock.* The first one, *The Christian Hymn Book,* had been published sometime before 1836.

Other men who came to Plymouth and were well known

later on were Sir Edward Denny[116] and James George Deck, writers of Christian poems and hymns. William Trotter, best known for his books *Plain Papers on Prophetic Subjects* and *Five Letters on Worship and Ministry,* was also at Plymouth.

The first Brethren periodical appeared in 1834. Published every three months, it was entitled *The Christian Witness.* After the death of the first editor, it was edited by James Lampden Harris until it was discontinued in 1841. Wigram started a new periodical called *The Present Testimony.* Henry William Soltau started the first Bible and tract depot in 1838. He was best known for his *The Vessels and Furniture of the Tabernacle* and *Tabernacle, Priesthood and Offerings.*

William Kelly wrote of one of Darby's early visits to London:

> It was, if I err not, before 1830 [it was probably in 1830] that, filled with the sense of the Christian's union with Christ, J. N. D. visited London, and laid it before one regarded as among the most mature of the Evangelical clergy. But his own indifference to worldly appearances seemed to render that precious but little understood truth a dead letter to this divine, who confounded it with the new birth, as ill-taught saints commonly do. His tone was pompous and self-complacent. He evidently regarded his visitor as a poor curate airing as a wonder what all knew. But the well-appointed carriage from Westminster, with coachman and footman, came to take Mr. Darby to his father's house, and happened to catch the clergyman's eye, when his manner changed to servility. This disgusted my friend, who could make allowance for ignorance, but was pained by a worldly spirit in a Christian, especially in a Christian minister. He well enough knew that the clergyman was of humble extraction: but this was nothing in his eyes if there had been spiritual feeling. Nor did the clergyman grow in grace any more than truth, when he became a bishop, and a metropolitan one. There was a worm at the root of his theology; for he betrayed unsoundness as to Divine inspiration, both before his elevation to the episcopal throne, and after it. Such men cannot be expected to have ears to hear.[117]

In 1832 Darby also visited Bristol, a seaport town one hundred miles northeast of Plymouth. He met, perhaps for the first time, Henry Craik (whom we have already mentioned in connection with Groves) and George Müller.[118] These were two young preachers who had taken charge of Christian congregations in Bethesda and Gideon chapels, and were conducting them on modified Baptist principles. God had richly blessed the preaching of these two men and souls had been saved. Before long a bond of Christian love and affection sprang up between the believers at Bristol and those in Plymouth and the two came into fellowship with one another. Darby wrote:

> The Lord sent us a blessing, and disposed the hearts of the saints much toward us at Bristol, and many also to hear. We preached in both chapels [Bethesda and Gideon]. The Lord is doing a very marked work there, in which I hope our dear brothers Müller and Craik may be abundantly blessed, but I should wish a little more principle of largeness of communion. I dread narrowness of heart more than anything for the Church of Christ, *especially now.*[119]

In October of 1832, Darby set out on a tour of Ireland and visited some of the little bodies of believers he had heard had come into existence. He visited two or three different places a day. At Limerick weekly Scripture reading meetings were set up; a little body for communion formed and it soon grew larger.

What was the reason for the "success" of the Brethren movement? Why did it survive its origins and spread worldwide when other groups, formed around the same time, did not? Other groups were in some ways very similar to the Brethren. To one who sees the movement as originating from the Lord Himself and being a work of the Holy Spirit the reasons will seem obvious. The truth working on the hearts of believers brings results. Whether we see the movement this way or not, there are some practical factors and human aspects to be considered.

One of the great appeals of the movement, or of Darby in particular, was the assertion that this "new" teaching was in actuality the simple and plain teaching of Scripture—not hampered by human (even if well-meant) views and opinions or additions. It was a teaching that, if one were spiritual and open to the Lord's leading, could be grasped if the reader simply let Scripture speak to him. It was a returning to Scripture. Many believers were distressed as to the general low state of Christian life and teaching of their day and so the great respect shown by the Brethren for the Word and its authority worked like a strong magnet.

There was also a longing for fellowship among true children of God; there was a desire for unity and a doing away with artificial, unnecessary, denominational separations among Christians in general. The Brethren's view (Darby's view) gave all these inclinations a firm basis and direction.

Prophecy was a subject of great interest at the time and the view presented by the Brethren, though quite novel, seemed to have the right answers and confirm the feelings of many believers.

But a fourth factor is also of great importance: Darby's own personality. The above characteristics, in some form or another, were true of other groups of believers, but they had no outstanding personality who could synthesize their teachings and present them in a complete unit and in an attractive way.

Bellett, Groves, or Cronin, in spite of all their devotedness, did not have the attractiveness Darby did—even his enemies had to admit that. One cannot imagine the movement prospering the way it did if either Bellett, Groves, or Cronin had been the spokesman. In fact it didn't flourish until Darby arrived.

During Darby's lifetime there were few who could, as it were, compete with him, an "advantage" that was enhanced by the fact that Darby traveled far more than other leaders. Other notable Brethren, such as William Kelly and F. W. Grant, with all due respect to their learning and originality, never had such a big impact as Darby had. Darby, regardless if he wanted it to be so or not, eventually became the pacemaker, the dominating factor in the movement.

It was in 1833 that James Butler Stoney, then a young man of nineteen, first came into contact with the Brethren in Dublin. He had studied at Trinity College and had hoped to make a career of law, but after his conversion at the age of seventeen he gave up this ambition. He joined the divinity class at Trinity and his desire was to be ordained. His family was greatly upset, as they felt he was throwing away his fine talents and opportunities, and his uncle would no longer have anything to do with him. Stoney's first visit with the Brethren did not appear to be very promising, but his attitude later changed:

> I at first very reluctantly went to hear at Aungier Street, but my "chum" in college, a Mr. Clarke, was a constant attendant. I was eventually much interested in the teaching there. I partially remember Mr. Darby on being "Accepted in the Beloved," and Mr. Bellett on Mark 5; but I did not think of joining them—I was expecting great things from Mr. Irving. Mr. Bellett brought Mr. Benjamin Newton to see me in my rooms in college, in order to disabuse my mind of Irvingism. I was constantly hearing of J. N. D., and at length heard him on Joshua 7: "Wherefore liest thou upon the ground? Up, sanctify the people." Get rid of the evil first, God cannot be with us until we are separated from the evil. I was broken down. I felt for the first time the immense step of leaving the Established order [the movement to which Irving belonged advocated remaining in the church system] for the unsightly few in Aungier Street. This was in June, 1834.[120]

Stoney, although fourteen years younger, would become one of Darby's closest friends. Stoney was with Darby several weeks before he passed away.

The Irving whom Stoney mentioned above was Edward Irving. He was a man who preached the second coming of Christ and believed that the last days would see a restoration of the church as it was in the days of the apostles. This restoration would also include the gifts of the Spirit and the offices and ministries found in those days. He was associated with the beginnings of the Catholic Apostolic Church, a movement with a college of twelve apostles, prophets, elders, assistants, deacons and sub-deacons. He was named "angel" of his church in London. In him and his company we find the first manifestations of what today is called Pentecostalism, though there is no historical connection. Irving taught the blasphemous idea that the Lord's humanity was capable of sinning but that His divine nature triumphed.

Some have tried to connect Irving's thoughts and Darby's thoughts regarding the Lord's coming. There is no connection possible, though Irving and Darby arose out of the same milieu, because their thoughts on this subject conflict just as their views on the church differ. In the next chapter we shall consider how Darby came to his views of the Lord's coming.

God in the Wilderness
written in 1837

Rise, my soul, thy God directs thee;
Stranger hands no more impede;
Pass thou on, His hand protects thee—
Strength that has the captive freed.

Is the wilderness before thee—
Desert lands where drought abides?
Heavenly springs shall there restore thee,
Fresh from God's exhaustless tides.

Light divine surrounds thy going,
God Himself shall mark thy way;
Secret blessings, richly flowing,
Lead to everlasting day.

God, thine everlasting portion,
Feeds thee with the mighty's meat;
Price of Egypt's hard extortion,
Egypt's food no more to eat.[121]

J. N. Darby

3

Prophecy and a Lady

And at midnight there was a cry made,
Behold, the bridegroom cometh;
go ye out to meet him.
Matthew 25:6, KJV

Powerscourt

I do think it among the most painful of the Lord's dispensations to sinners: to be the means of crushing one who loves you—for the happiness or misery of one dear to you, to hang upon your yes or no, and yet to have to pronounce no, and thus leave an impression of ingratitude and unkindness—to know there is *one* in this wilderness whose every thought is yours, miserable on your account, and yet not able even to attempt to administer comfort—it is very painful, especially when to this is added a long *never.*[1]

The above words were those of a young lady who was once engaged to John Nelson Darby. The letter was written to someone other than Darby, but it was he she may have been thinking of.

Theodosia Anne Powerscourt, known by all as Lady Powerscourt, was the daughter of the Honorable Hugh

Left: Wingfield/ Powerscourt family memorial in the Powerscourt church
(The author)

Below: Memorial detail
(The author)

Bottom: Powerscourt estate, approximately 1838
(Mrs. G. M. Slazenger of Powerscourt estate)

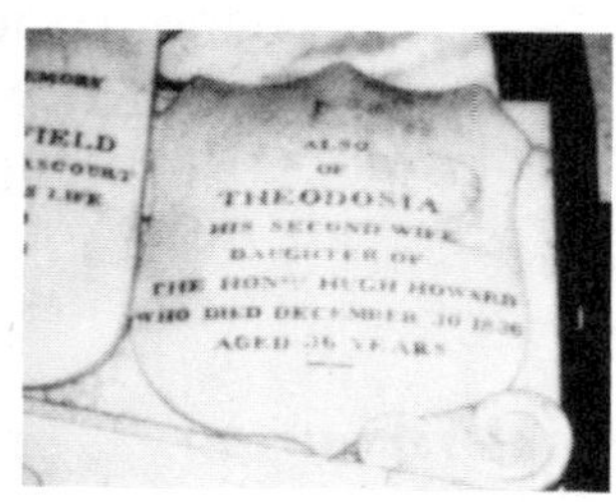

Howard of Bushy Park, County Wicklow. She was born in the year 1800. Her cousin, Francis Theodosia Bligh, was married to Richard Wingfield, the fifth Viscount Powerscourt.

Powerscourt is one of the great gardens of Europe, and lies just south of Dublin. It has a one-thousand-year history, and was originally church land. This land was the site of a royal castle in the reign of Edward I (1272-1307) and was held by a Norman knight, from whose name Powerscourt was derived. In 1609 the Wingfield family, who were Saxons, received the estate.

Powerscourt House was designed in 1730 and incorporated the original smaller castle with walls about 2.5 meters thick. The house is rectangular and is built of hewn granite. There are over one hundred rooms. King George IV (1820-1830) was entertained in the ballroom in 1821.

The parish of Powerscourt has been called a "parish of mountains, glens, valleys, and waterfalls," and is truly a beautiful place.

The Lady

Francis Powerscourt died in May 1820. During Francis's last illness her cousin Theodosia Howard was converted to God in 1819. The Reverend Robert Daly, the rector of Powerscourt, seems to have played a role in her conversion, and she was always greatly indebted to him. He wrote of her conversion, "I can testify that a great change took place in her views, in her tastes, in her life, in her conversation."[2]

Daly also said that Theodosia had "the strongest mind that I ever met in any woman" and noted her "uncommon masculine strength, combined with the extremest feminine gentleness."[3] After meeting Theodosia, Henry Craik wrote, "Felt united to Lady Powerscourt, who seems a dear, humble saint."[4] Groves wrote of "dear Lady Powerscourt."[5] William Pennefather, the nephew of Lord Chief Justice Pennefather, wrote of Lady Powerscourt on the occasion of her death in 1836: "I have not seen her for many years, yet I felt as if I knew and loved her. She was one whose soul had been panting after the fulness of Him who filleth all in all, and therefore surely felt that this was not her rest."[6]

Of those who knew Theodosia, only Newton seems to have had a critical opinion of her. He saw a side of her the others overlooked:

> A lady who never apprehended the force of an argument.[7] I never saw a person so devoted and pious and so unfit for discriminating as to what was to be taught [in divine things].[8]
>
> Lady Powerscourt once said to me: O that I had guidance from God! O that I could see God and He would direct me in the way I should walk! I replied to her: O Lady Powerscourt, if I could see you only giving heed to Scripture![9]

On June 29, 1822, Theodosia was married to Richard Wingfield, the husband of her departed cousin, and thus became Lady Powerscourt. Richard Wingfield is said to have been a very earnest Christian, and both he and Theodosia were deeply influenced by Daly.[10] But their earthly joy and happiness were to be short, for Viscount Powerscourt died on August 9, 1823, just over a year after their marriage. Theodosia wrote, and she most certainly meant the death of her husband:

> I am not ignorant of what it is to give up an object tenderly beloved, but I can only say, I am not ignorant of the peace which follows, when the lacerated soul is at length able to surrender itself, with a subdued and unruffled heart, into the arms of everlasting love, saying: "Undertake for me."[11]

After her husband's death Theodosia wrote a poem called "Divine Sympathy," the opening verse of which is as follows:

> Jesus, my sorrow lies too deep
> For human ministry;
> It knows not how to tell itself
> To any but to Thee.[12]

Theodosia resided at Powerscourt House until her stepson reached adulthood. She spent her life in doing good and was truly a remarkable woman, pious and warmhearted, with more than a touch of the mystic (which probably was the cause of Newton's negative remarks). It seemed as if she lived in Heaven and barely touched the earth. Daly said:

> She, of all the Christians I have been privileged to know, came nearest to that which she has, in such strong, uncommon terms, stated to be her idea of a Christian: "Not one who looks up from earth to heaven, but one who looks down from heaven on earth." She appears to have ascended a high and holy eminence, and from thence to have looked down upon those earthly scenes, with which too many are entirely engrossed; living up to that high and spiritual requirement of the apostle: "Set your affections on things above, not on things on the earth; for you are dead, and your life is hid with Christ in God."[13]

The early part of the nineteenth century was marked by an increased interest among Christians in the subject of prophecy. This interest was largely a result of the French Revolution and the thought of some that Napoleon was the coming antichrist.

Lady Powerscourt was interested in prophecy and she attended the prophetic meetings first held in 1826 at Albury Park in Surrey, England, in the residence of the well-known banker and member of Parliament, Henry Drummond. She was so impressed by these meetings that she began to hold some of her own at Powerscourt House. Previously every other Tuesday evening had been set aside for the study of prophecy at Powerscourt, where all who were interested were invited to come, and where Lady Powerscourt "proved" Daly with hard questions. Now she invited men from all over England, Scotland, and Ireland to her house and entertained them for a week, during which time meetings were held morning and evening, and everyone in the neighborhood was invited to attend. Daly presided over these meetings, which turned into the annual Powerscourt conferences starting in 1831. Many so-called Brethren attended, including John N. Darby. He emphasized the Lord's coming for His own (the so-called rapture) before a seven-year period of tribulation on earth.

Daly was not present at the 1833 conference, as he had in

the meantime become bishop of Cashel; also he felt that the views being expressed were extremely anti-church. Daly remained in the established church and could not go along with the views of his friend Darby on the state of the church and the need for separation. Synge presided over the conferences after Daly left.

After 1833 the conferences were no longer held at Powerscourt, but were moved, at Darby's suggestion, to a hotel in Dublin. The reason was that Lady Powerscourt's stepson, who was now of age and heir to the title, came to reside there and she no longer felt it to be her house. She left it for a more humble dwelling. The last conference was held in 1836.

After Lady Powerscourt left Powerscourt she lived in Dublin. William Pennefather's sister wrote in 1835:

> Lady Powerscourt is living at present in Dublin; through a mutual friend, S. and I were invited to attend a meeting for reading the Scriptures, which she has established once a week: we were there at one reading, and are going again to-day. I found it very profitable, and so did Susan; every one is allowed to give an opinion, or to ask questions. Mr. [Darby] and two or three clergymen were present. The former read 1 John 1, and spoke beautifully on the Christian's hopes and present comforts. Others said but little; the ladies were silent, with the exception of two or three questions. Lady P. only asked one, which I could not hear. She is a lovely-looking creature, pale, elegant, dignified, and retiring; her face looks as if she were much in prayer and communion with God. We were introduced to her, and her address is very pleasing. Mr. [Darby] and Lady Harberton kept up an interesting conversation, he urging rejoicing, she seeming to fear presumption.[14]

Of all those who attended the conferences from the Powerscourt parish, Lady Powerscourt was the only one who left the established church to join the small company of those who professed to be gathered to the Lord's name alone. She spent the night in tears when she made her decision, feeling especially what it would mean to Daly, but he left the following striking testimony as to her decision:

> What she thought, that she did with a single eye, regarding neither the censure nor the praise of men. In the only step she took which we could not but disapprove, and which could not but grieve us, we feel no hesitation in saying, we are assured she had a single eye to God. In quitting the communion of the Church of England, and separating herself from those in connection with whom her soul had received life and strength and comfort, we feel assured that she was only actuated by a desire after more holiness, more perfect purity. She did it with much pain, much personal suffering and struggle, and never in a spirit to lessen her love to those whom she valued as fellow-disciples of Jesus.

Prophecy

We shall leave Lady Powerscourt now, to return to her and her connection with Darby a little later on, and occupy ourselves more directly with the subject of prophecy and Darby's understanding of it. We will take a closer look at how Darby came to the thoughts he later expressed at the Powerscourt conferences and elsewhere.

We have already mentioned the increased attention to prophecy in the early 1800s, particularly in England. Among those whose interest was awakened were Henry Drummond and Edward Irving. From J. G. Bellett we have the following:

> In the beginning of 1828 I had occasion to go to London [this date is probably correct] and then I met in private and heard in public those who were warm and alive on prophetic truth, having had their minds freshly illuminated by it. In my letters to J. N. D. at this time, I told him I had been hearing things that he and I had never yet talked of, and I further told him on my return to Dublin what they were. Full of this subject as I was, I found him quite prepared for it also, and his mind and soul had travelled rapidly in the direction which had thus been given to it.[15]

Similarly, Darby wrote, "J. G. Bellett came up and said they were teaching some new thing in England. 'I have it!' I said."[16] This was during Darby's recuperation from his riding accident, as is seen by his saying, "At the time I was ill with my knee," in the same article.

From this we see that Bellett's visit to, and return from, London must have been *very* early in the year 1828, for Darby did not remain in Dublin after his convalescence, which, as we noted in chapter 2, lasted three months. In Bellett's letter (dated January 31) referred to in chapter 1, he spoke of hoping to be able to visit Darby. This might be the meeting that both Bellett and Darby referred to in the quotes above, and it probably took place near the end of February or beginning of March.

But what was this "new" thing Bellett spoke of, and Darby already knew of (without the influence of others)? Darby wrote:

> Isaiah 32 it was that taught me about the new dispensation. I saw there would be a David reign, and did not know whether the Church might not be removed before 40 years time. At that time I was ill with my knee. It gave me peace to see what the Church was. I saw that I, poor, wretched, and sinful J. N. D., knowing too much yet not enough about himself was left behind, and let go, but I was united to Christ in heaven. Then what was I waiting for?[17]
>
> In my retreat [at the Pennefathers] the 32nd chapter of Isaiah taught me clearly, on God's behalf, that there was still an economy to come, of His ordering; a state of things in no way established as yet.[18]
>
> The coming of the Lord was the other truth which was brought to my mind from the Word, as that which, if sitting in heavenly places *in* Christ, was alone to be waited for, that I might sit in heavenly places *with* Him. Isaiah 32 brought me to the earthly consequences of the same truth, though other passages might seem perhaps more striking to me now; but I saw an evident change of dispensation in that chapter, when the Spirit would be poured out on the Jewish nation, and a king reign in righteousness.[19]
>
> But I must, though without comment, direct attention to chapter 32 of the same prophet [Isaiah] which I do the rather, because in this it was the Lord was

> pleased, without man's teaching, first to open my eyes on this subject, that I might learn His will concerning it throughout—not by the first blessed truths stated in it, but the latter part, when there shall be a complete change in the dispensation, the wilderness becoming the fruitful field of God's fruit and glory, and that which had been so being counted a forest, at a time when the Lord's judgment should come down, even great hail, upon this forest; and the city even of pride be utterly abased.[20]

This then was the conclusion at which Darby arrived: there was a future for God's ancient people of Israel, independent of the Christian one. After having come to the views on the church mentioned in the previous chapter, he came to see a distinction between Israel and the church. (Darby was not as influenced by the news Bellett brought as it might seem, for Darby testified that he received his thoughts from the Lord alone.) What was so important in coming to this distinction? Today it is no longer new for many, but at the time it was.

Darby said, "The Church, a lowly heavenly body, has no portion on earth at all, as it was at the beginning—suffering as its Head did, unknown and well known—an unearthly witness of heavenly things on earth." Darby believed that soon after the death of the apostles, believers began wrongly to take Old Testament prophecies and promises and apply them to themselves. They had rightly seen that God had put His earthly people aside, and that they, the Christian company (one new man in Christ, out of Jews and Gentiles, Ephesians 2:15) were now *the* "people of God," but Darby concluded that they had made the mistake of thinking that Israel would no longer have a future. But what was to be done with Old Testament promises and (in part) unfulfilled prophecies? They must now apply to us, was their thought. Darby saw in this the loss of the church's true hope and character, which is a heavenly one, and the substitution of an earthly one. He made the distinction between two people of God, the earthly and the heavenly, with two different destinies.

Darby was fully convinced that the Old Testament deals with, and is for, an earthly people. His thought was that prophecy always deals with the earth. The church is never mentioned in the Old Testament, and was never an object of prophecy, being heavenly in nature. It was the mystery hidden in God (see Romans 16:25; 1 Corinthians 2:7-10; Ephesians 3:2-11; 5:32; Colossians 1:25-27; 2:2-3). The fact that now, after the teaching of the New Testament, one can see the church in types, or the fact that the Old Testament is "for" the Christian in the sense of Romans 15:4 and 1 Corinthians 10:6,11, he saw as quite another thing.

But as the church took up Jewish hopes (and practices) she lost her one true hope: the Lord's coming for her. The apostles had taught the saints to expect the Lord's soon coming to take them to be with Himself (1 Thessalonians 1:10). But that which the Lord spoke of in Matthew 25:1-13 soon took place: true believers and mere professors "fell asleep" as regards this hope.

A very simplified view of prophecy and the church (as presented, for example, by R. A. Huebner and F. B. Gill), but one that seems to reflect the thinking of Darby and the Brethren in general is as follows: Many church fathers prior to the council of Nice in A.D. 325 (called ante-Nicene fathers) expected Christ to come and set up His millennial kingdom, but they thought that they would have to pass through the tribulation mentioned in prophecy first, and that they would have to face the antichrist. They thought that a certain number of events would have to precede and accompany Christ's coming, namely those described in the prophetic books of the Bible.

After Constantine made Christianity a state religion, the teaching known as amillennialism arose. This is the idea that Christ is reigning now, over and through the church. It was thought that the year 1000 would bring the final judgment, but when it passed and nothing occurred the number 1,000 was spiritualized. The reformers were amillennialists and believed that the pope was antichrist. They were too absorbed in contending for justification by faith alone and fighting against popery to study prophecy or the church. (This, of course, is much too simplified. The Puritans, notably, *did* concentrate on prophecy, especially the question of the future of the Jews.)

When interest in prophecy was revived in the beginning

of the nineteenth century, believers returned to the view held by the ante-Nicene fathers. Some Protestants also changed the literal "days" of prophecy into years, and sought to figure out the date of the Lord's coming and other prophetic events (Revelation 12:6, for example). They did not think of the Lord coming first for His own (which is how the Brethren interpreted the rapture) and then returning with them later in glory (defined as the appearing and distinct from the rapture) to set up a kingdom on earth. They deduced from the Old Testament that a people, a remnant, would have to pass through the tribulation before entering the kingdom. They thought *themselves* to be this people. Darby saw the consequences of this view as follows:

> In denying a distinct Jewish remnant, having Jewish faith, Jewish hopes, and resting on Jewish promises during the tribulation [all this Christians applied to themselves] it reduces the Church to the level of these [by putting the Church in the position of the Jewish remnant] and the value and power of spiritual blessings in heavenly places in Christ, and the place of Christ's body in union with Him, is denied and lost.[21]

As the church, according to Darby's view, became more and more Jewish in her outward character—for example, the system of priesthood—and took up Jewish hopes, she also took up the Jewish belief in what might be called a general resurrection in which good and evil ones would all be raised from the dead at the same time—the evil ones to go into everlasting destruction, and the good into everlasting bliss. We see this belief clearly expressed in Martha's words to the Lord in John 11:24. The fact that the Old Testament saints believed in a resurrection is clear from Job 19:25-26, which also shows that they believed in a bodily resurrection. The whole Christian faith rests on belief in a bodily resurrection, as the apostle Paul, through the Holy Spirit, so clearly attested in 1 Corinthians 15.

But Darby felt a resurrection "out from among the dead" was a completely new thought. The disciples did not understand their Lord when He spoke of His own resurrection being of this nature (Mark 9:9-10). Darby stressed that the disciples were puzzled by the *phrase* Jesus used but were not surprised that their Lord expected to die. A resurrection "from among the dead" is one in which only a few, not all, are raised and the rest remain where they are. Darby saw in this a sign of God's special favor and His acceptance of those thus raised. The resurrection is a central theme in the Acts of the Apostles, and there the apostles spoke of it as "from among the dead" as exemplified by the Lord Himself (Acts 4:2).

> The resurrection of the saints is like Christ's resurrection—out from amongst the dead. When the Lord told the disciples not to speak of what they had seen until He was risen *from among* the dead, they began discussing what that meant. Martha, too, says, "I know that he shall rise again in the resurrection at the last day." But *from among* was a new thing to them.[22]

The thought of our resurrection being like the Lord's was seen in Romans 6:5 (KJV): "If we have been planted together in the likeness of his death, we shall be also in the likeness of his resurrection." The saints who have died shall also be raised "from among the dead." There will be no general resurrection; yet the church from the days of the ante-Nicene fathers until the beginning of the nineteenth century believed in a general resurrection. They only knew the Lord was coming to exercise judgment at the last judgment.

The Thessalonians were new converts and young in the faith and had been taught to look for the Lord's coming at any moment; they were perplexed about those of their number who had died in the meantime.

> Meanwhile, He has gone to prepare a place for us, and He says that He will come again and receive us unto Himself. When it is a question of those who have fallen asleep in Christ, you see another thing. The Thessalonians had got hold of the idea so fully, and were so looking for Christ's coming, that if a person fell asleep, they thought he would not be there to meet Christ at His coming; and that was a grand mistake. Paul would not have them to be ignorant about it; he comforts them with this, that God would bring such

> with Jesus. "If we believe that Jesus died and rose again, such also that die will rise again; and when the Lord comes in glory, God will bring them with Him."[23]

The passage of Scripture that Darby is referring to in the above quote is the well-known one in 1 Thessalonians 4:13-18. Here the apostle Paul showed that the departed saints would not miss out on anything, which is the main point of the passage. Christ would come, and the ones who had fallen asleep would be raised from the dead; after that the living would be changed (all occurring in the twinkling of an eye, 1 Corinthians 15:52). Both would be caught up together to meet the Lord in the air and they would be forever with the Lord. Then the Lord, according to Darby's view, would resume His dealings here on earth with His ancient people and the tribulation would take place. After the tribulation the Lord would visibly return from Heaven in glory to execute judgment and set up His kingdom. He would bring with Him His own whom He had called up before (1 Thessalonians 4:14).

Seen in this way the Lord's coming for His own required no events to occur beforehand; it was an "any moment" expectation. Before the Lord comes to exercise judgment, there will be signs and events that will point to His soon coming. The Old Testament is full of warnings of the coming judgment, which is called the day of the Lord. According to Darby the mix-up of the Lord's coming for His own and His coming for judgment is what caused Paul to write his second letter to the Thessalonians. Before the Lord would come to judge, the man of sin had to be revealed, the antichrist; and he could not come until the church and the Holy Spirit who dwells in her were removed from the earth (2 Thessalonians 2:6-7).

Christians who see themselves to be the remnant found in the prophecy of the Old Testament believe they will pass through the tribulation. They wait for things to happen before the Lord's appearing and, according to Darby's view, lose the proper Christian hope for the coming of the Lord for them at any moment. Instead of being in a state of expectancy waiting for Him, they wait for a certain number of events to take place first.

> To me the Lord's coming is not a question of prophecy, but my present hope. Events before His judging the

> quick [Matthew 25:31-46] are the subject of prophecy; His coming to receive the Church is our present hope. There is no event between me and *heaven*.[24] Those who have not the hope of the Lord's return cannot apprehend what is the true path of a Christian; they may have life, of course, in one sense, but they have not the proper stamp of heavenly life in their daily practice down here. If I am waiting for someone to come and take me up out of it [the world] what then is the world to me? What comes of its plans, and its running after money, and all that kind of thing?[25] [The Lord's return] was to run like a thread through the whole framework of Christian thoughts and feelings. It teaches us how to walk, in looking for glory.[26]

Darby probably was thinking of principles when writing the above, and not denying real godly motives in anybody. Taken in itself his statement is very black-and-white. It implies that all men of God before Darby's time (as this view of "the hope" originated with him) did not have the stamp of Heaven in their lives and did not understand the Christian path. In this context we need to take into consideration how long Darby himself struggled with coming to a definite teaching on "the hope." The above extract also implies one of the main reasons why the Brethren in general do not involve themselves with "earthly" or "worldly" issues—for example, politics, government, the arts, and so on.

Darby felt that as the church lost sight of her true character, she lost sight of her true hope as well. She was governed not only by Jewish principles, but also by worldly ones. She became like the evil servant who said, "My lord delayeth his coming; And [began] to smite his fellowservants, and to eat and drink with the drunken" (Matthew 24:48, KJV).

> It is this conviction, that the Church is properly heavenly, in its calling and relationship with Christ, forming no part of the course of events of the earth, which makes its rapture so simple and clear; and on the other hand, it shows how the denial of its rapture brings down the Church to an earthly position, and destroys its whole spiritual character and position. Our calling

> is on high. Events are on earth. Prophecy does not relate to heaven. The Christian's hope is not a prophetic subject at all.[27]
>
> Those who believe in the rapture of the Church before the appearing of Christ hold that the Church has a special and peculiar character and connection with Christ . . . The Church's joining Christ has nothing to do with Christ's appearing or coming to earth. Her place is elsewhere. She sits in Him already in heavenly places. She has to be brought there as to bodily presence . . . The thing she has to expect for herself is not . . . Christ's appearing, but her being taken up where He is.[28]

The apostle Paul, according to Darby's view, is the only writer in the New Testament who spoke of the church; he is the one whom the Lord used to make known the truth of the mystery, and he alone spoke of the rapture. When other New Testament writers spoke of the Lord's coming (except for John 14:3) they spoke of His coming for judgment, "the appearing." Whenever they (or Paul) referred to the appearing, they always connected it somehow with responsibility and reward, for the Christian will first receive his reward in connection with the kingdom. However, when Paul spoke of the rapture, there were no conditional clauses, for all is grace. "You never find the 'assembly' nor the rapture, except in Paul (the mere name is used in 2 John). Others speak of His appearing, but that has to do with the government of this world."[29]

From this we see clearly how for Darby the truth as to the church and the truth as to her true hope (the rapture) are tied together; they are inseparable. To lose one truth was to lose the other.

The Lord's coming for His own was always presented as momentary, without other events having to take place first: "At, and from the beginning, the Lord's coming was presented as the immediate expectation and hope of the believer; while in no case is the thought of the coming of Christ put beyond the life of those who were living then."[30]

Darby, and the Brethren after him, saw this clearly in the Gospels in the parable of the servants and in the parable of the wise and foolish virgins. (In the Gospels things are presented in a general way so that there is instruction for the

Christian and for the godly Jew in a coming day.) Those servants entrusted with something were the same ones who awoke. The good seed sown in Matthew 13:24 was the seed from which the harvest came—one harvest, not many harvests. Even those passages that have a future fulfillment in no way delayed the hope of the Lord's coming for His own.

The seven churches in Revelation 2 and 3 were seen as giving a prophetic history of the church. (This was not seen to clash with what has been said before: that the church being heavenly in nature and calling is not a subject of prophecy. The chapters in Revelation are said to deal with a testimony on earth, and its development as connected with man's responsibility, and not with the true nature of the church as such.) Had the believers of John's day been told that the seven letters to the churches were a prophetic map and a literal history of the church, they would have ceased to wait for Christ's soon coming. But the seven churches all existed as the apostle wrote, so this hope was apparently not hindered in any way. "The history of the Church is not given as a thing that is to continue, but it is all brought out in churches that then existed."[31]

The longer the church remained on the earth, the meaning of these letters would become more and more obvious. Points not seen before would become clear. Nothing was written that would hinder the hope of Christ's coming, but with the delay, the promise would be better understood.

Neither did coming evils dim the hope of the Lord's coming. When Paul spoke of "the last days" in 2 Timothy 3, some of the conditions he described already existed, and from these evils one was to "turn away." When John spoke of the antichrist he said, "Even now are there many antichrists; whereby we know that it is the last time" (1 John 2:18, KJV). These evils were described as already present in the letters of the apostles.

When Paul spoke of the Lord's coming and the living saints being caught up to meet Him, he said "we." Then he expected the Lord to come in his lifetime. In 2 Timothy he spoke of the fact that he would die before the Lord came, but not long before His coming.

Peter was told by the Lord (John 21) that he would die, but we do not know if the disciples understood what the Lord said (as they misunderstood the meaning of His words concerning John). Peter spoke of his death only toward the end of his life (2 Peter 1:14). Believers did not postpone their hope of the Lord's coming until Peter died. The Gospel of John is perhaps the last part of the New Testament to be recorded; it was written long after Peter died. So reading the Gospel of John could not have deferred the hope in any way, for the Lord's words to Peter had already been fulfilled.

It was then also a logical conclusion that if there are no events which must first be fulfilled before the Lord comes for His own, then there are also no possible means by which Christians may be able to calculate the date of His coming, as so many have tried to do.

> People who attempt to fix time are wholly mistaken. The Father has kept that in His own power. Not that we may not discern the times; the Lord says, "How is it that ye do not discern this time?" There are moral elements around us that a spiritual mind discerns at once; but the fixing of dates is a mistake.[32]

If world conditions become more and more like those the prophets said would precede the tribulation and the coming of the Lord to execute judgment, the Lord's coming for the church must be very near, for He must have the church with Himself before the tribulation on earth can begin.

Some might find it difficult to see a difference between the rapture and the appearing, but for Darby it was simply a question of bowing to God's Word.

> It is no mistake to be always expecting the Lord to return. The object of the conversion of the Thessalonians was to wait for God's Son from heaven. People fancy that the truth of the Lord's return is a bit of knowledge at the top of the tree; but instead of that, it is what the Thessalonians were converted for, and meanwhile they are to serve God.[33]
>
> It is not a matter of spiritual judgment, whether or not we are to look for the Lord; but it is linked up with all that characterises the Christian, instead of being just a bit of knowledge to be specially attained.[34]

> Are our hearts really waiting for God's Son from heaven? I do not talk of understanding the prophecies—very blessed in their place—but the Morning Star is what belongs to us, a heavenly Christ who has given His life for us. As, then, we are found looking to be with and like Christ for ever, this helps us to go through this world. The character attaching to the Christian is, then, that of watching. It is not understanding prophecy, but it is attachment to Christ as having got the promise that He is coming so that we are waiting for Him. Such have found Christ precious to them, and they say, "Oh, that He would come!" Are we Christians, then, as men that wait for their Lord? If the Lord were to come tonight, would He be able to say of each one of us, "*There* is a blessed servant"? Remember He is waiting more truly than we are.[35]

There is another reason for the Lord's coming for His own, besides the fact that it is the answer to the longing of His heart to have them with Him and it is their desire to be with Him: He can no longer recognize the church as a testimony to Himself and the truth, since she has failed in outward testimony here on earth.

> We insist on the fact that the house has been ruined, its ordinances perverted, its orders and all its arrangements forsaken or destroyed; that human ordinances, a human order, have been substituted for them; and, what merits all attention of faith, we insist that the Lord . . . is coming soon in His power and glory to judge all this state of things.[36]

After the true church is gone from this earth—all those who had known Christ as their Lord and Savior and had life in Him—there will be a lifeless, professing church here that will undergo the Lord's judgment. Darby understood the apostle Paul's warning in Romans 11:16-21 in this way. Apostate Christendom is judged in Revelation 17. The kingdom and the heavenly glory will then take the place of the corrupt church. As in the days when the Christian testimony first began and God put the Jewish system fully aside and judged it in the destruction of Jerusalem in A.D. 70, so will it be in the case of the church. Before Jerusalem was destroyed the Lord called all His own to leave it, so that when the city was destroyed there was not a single Christian in it. When the system of Christendom is judged there will not be a single true believer left in it, for the Lord will have called them all to Himself.

For Darby the Lord's coming was a living and real hope: "If we were really waiting for Christ, would we be heaping up money and property here? Would we be really glad if Christ came to-night, I mean as to the state of our hearts?"[37]

We return now to considering how Darby arrived at his beliefs. He did not have clearness as to all points involved in his particular view of the rapture at once. For a while he also held the theory that days in prophecy were meant to be understood as years, as did many other Christians occupied then with the study of prophecy, but this soon changed. For a while he also thought that some three-and-a-half-year periods mentioned in prophecy (see Revelation 11:2-3) referred to the first half of Daniel's last week in Daniel 9; but later he saw references such as this as applying only to the second half. Yet in spite of these steps in the development of his understanding of prophetic Scriptures, we are safe in saying that, on the united testimony of B. W. Newton and William Kelly, Darby came to understand the rapture in the early 1830s. The only question about which Darby had doubts for a while was whether the rapture would be secret or not—that is, whether or not the rapture would be seen by the world.

Francis Newman also left a testimony regarding Darby's view of the Lord's coming at the time he made his acquaintance at the Pennefather house. Newman, at the time, saw the Lord's coming connected with judgment, as shown in the following quote. Darby might not have been in agreement with all the particulars of Newman's representation but it is quoted here as being of interest.

> My study of the New Testament at this time had made it impossible for me to overlook that the apostles held it to be a duty of all disciples to expect a near and sudden destruction of the earth by fire, and constantly to be expecting the *return of the Lord from heaven.* [This was ante-Nicene thinking.] The importance of this doctrine is, that *it totally forbids all working for earthly*

> *objects distant in time;* and here the Irish clergyman [Darby] threw into the same scale the entire weight of his character. For instance, if a youth had a natural aptitude for mathematics, and he asked, ought he to give himself to the study, in the hope that he might diffuse a serviceable knowledge of it, or possibly even enlarge the boundaries of the science? my friend would have replied, that such a purpose was very proper, if entertained by a worldly man. Let the dead bury their dead; and *let the world study the things of the world* . . . But such studies cannot be eagerly followed by the Christian, except when he yields to unbelief. In fact, what would it avail even to become a second La Place after thirty years study, if in five and thirty years the Lord descended from heaven, snatched up all His saints to meet Him, and burned to ashes all the works of the earth?[38] However the hold which the apostolic belief then took of me, subjected my conscience to the exhortations of the Irish clergyman, whenever he inculcated that the highest Christian must necessarily decline the pursuit of science, knowledge, art, history—except so far as any of these things might be useful tools for immediate spiritual results.[39]

While at the Pennefathers' Darby believed that there would be a new earthly dispensation set up, having to do with restored Israel. Even if he arrived at his view of the rapture several years later, still Darby would not have had such a thought as Newman's that the earth would be destroyed by fire at the Lord's coming, for Darby expected a new dispensation on this earth, and not its immediate destruction. Newman's statement of the moral implications of the belief that the Lord is coming soon does coincide with the position Darby held in later years of non-involvement in worldly or earthly affairs.

Darby, as we mentioned before, stated expressly that it was *not* through man's teaching that he came to see the distinction between Israel and the church. His apprehension of the rapture was different. In 1850 he wrote, "It was this passage [2 Thessalonians 2:1-2] which, twenty years ago, made me understand the rapture of the saints before—perhaps a considerable time before—the day of the Lord (that is before the judgment of the living, Matthew 25:31-46)."[40] These two verses helped Darby to see the rapture as we have been considering it. But someone else directed Darby's attention to them.

William Kelly wrote an article entitled "The Rapture of the Saints: who suggested it, or rather on what Scripture?" in which he spoke of Darby's arriving at this view.[41] B. W. Newton had told Kelly in 1845 that many years ago Darby had written a letter to him in which he mentioned the influence of a certain Mr. T. Tweedy.[42] Tweedy had suggested the passage in 2 Thessalonians to Darby as a decisive Scriptural proof that the rapture would take place before the day of the Lord, and this cleared up for him difficulties he had previously felt on this point. Kelly's account has been confirmed by a discovery in Newton's reminiscences where he spoke of the same thing and dated Darby's letter as 1832 or 1833. At the 1833 Powerscourt conference the teaching as to the rapture was openly presented by Darby.[43]

Love

We return now to Lady Powerscourt. When she first met Mr. Darby is not at all certain, but it is very probable that it was before the Powerscourt conferences which Darby attended. (There the teachings we have been considering were publicly introduced.) Two facts point to a meeting earlier than the conferences. First, Daly was a close friend of Darby's, and Daly was also the man through whom Lady Powerscourt was led to the Lord; through this connection an acquaintance was possible. Secondly, as was mentioned, the schoolhouse in which Darby held his services while still in the established church in all probability belonged to the Powerscourt estate; this connection could also have served as a point of contact. In any case we do know that they *did* meet each other, and they fell in love and became engaged.

The story goes that when the Brethren in Dublin heard of Darby's engagement they prayed that the Lord might dissolve it and hinder a marriage; they felt that the Lord was using Darby mightily for His work and they feared that a wife would only hinder him in his service. When Darby heard of this reaction, he no longer felt at liberty to go on with the engagement.

It is said that the engagement was mutually broken. Whether it is true that the letters that they wrote one another in which they both spoke of breaking the engagement crossed in the mail is hard to say. In any case William Kelly wrote in a letter dated September 8, 1897, that a certain brother by the name of Hargreaves, and others, sought to convince Darby to abandon the thought of marriage. The quotation from Lady Powerscourt's letter at the beginning of this chapter implies that she took more of the leading role in breaking the engagement; it broke her heart to do so, but it seems she saw it would be better for Darby not to marry. Years later Darby said, "I turned down a marriage and broke a heart by doing so." But he was not spared any pain in the matter either. When he was eighty-one he wrote to a young brother just married, "You have a helpmeet, and *I have trod it alone; but all is lost,* so to speak, in His grace and faithfulness" (italics added).

The following quotation does not necessarily apply to Darby's breaking his engagement to Lady Powerscourt, but the words do show the motivation involved: "Did I look, as I once did, even unconsciously to anything here, I should be dismayed and overwhelmed; but I do feel the heavenward path and my home there everyday more simply mine."[44]

Lady Powerscourt believed she saw the way in which the Lord would be more honored, and she went this way at a very high price to herself. She died at the age of thirty-six on December 30, 1836. It is said she died of grief and a broken heart. Darby was already very active before this time, but in the following year Darby traveled to Switzerland; this was the first of many trips and the beginning of a great work there.

Both were motivated by the principle, "Seek ye first the kingdom of God," as they understood it. No other lady would have been a better helpmeet for Darby than Lady Powerscourt. Whether their decision was right or wrong we will not be able to say definitely this side of Heaven. Considering Lady Powerscourt's early death, she would *not* have been a hindrance to Darby.

Summary

In the beginning of chapter 2 we took a quick look at the Scriptural subjects that Darby studied while he was recovering from his accident. Through coming to understand his true position in Christ Darby saw what he believed to be the true character of the church of God. His new understanding of the church led Darby to believe that there was a distinction between the church and the Lord's earthly people Israel. He believed that there was still a future for Israel; some prophecy was yet to be fulfilled. But the church had a future as well, not here on earth, but in Heaven; and through the help of another he came to see the rapture (in his interpretation of it) as the true hope of the Christian. His understanding progressed step by step.

Darby's view was that the church had lost her true hope, and this made him feel that he had to retrace it. So he set out on a quest for the church's hope and essential character.

The Soul's Desire
written in 1881

I'm waiting for Thee, Lord,
Thyself then to see, Lord;
I'm waiting for Thee,
At Thy coming again.
Thy glory'll be great, Lord,
In heavenly state, Lord;
Thy glory'll be great
At Thy coming again.

Caught up in the air, Lord,
That glory we'll share, Lord;
Each saint will be there,
At Thy coming again.
How glorious the grace, Lord,
That gave such a place, Lord;
It's nearing apace,
At Thy coming again.[45]

J. N. Darby

4

Character and Personal Traits

To me to live is Christ.
Philippians 1:21, KJV

As Christians we all belong to the body and bride of Christ, to the family of God. We are not individually the body or the bride of Christ, or the family of God (though each one of us does have a personal relationship to God). We only make up a part of what forms the whole.

Yet we are individuals and have our own individual characteristics. First Corinthians 15:42-44 confirms the thought of individuality being maintained: it is sown, it is raised. In Heaven, as now, we will not be all one mass poured out into one form (though here we are not referring to differences in position).

Each person has some good characteristics and some bad. Even the exemplary young man in Mark 10:21 lacked Christlike love. His natural goodness was not enough. He did not know himself; he did not judge himself before God as a lost sinner; he did not follow the Lord. All man's goodness has been marred through sin.

When someone is converted, a certain change in his character takes place—in some cases a notable change. But the individual is still the same; he is not a different person (in the sense we are now considering) even if he has put off the old man and put on the new and is now in Christ. He is a new creation; yes, that is certainly true. But he still has traits that distinguish him from others. He retains his personal characteristics.[1]

God is a God of variety. Psalm 104:24 (KJV) says, "O Lord, how manifold are thy works! in wisdom hast thou made them all: the earth is full of thy riches." We also read that "the Lord hath made all things for himself" (Proverbs 16:4, KJV). We have only to look at ourselves as Christians. There is probably not one conversion like another, and each one of us has spiritual experiences and development that are unique. How beautiful it is to see, in each of our brothers and sisters, a personal trait that reminds us of the person of Christ. We are all together the epistle of Christ. One brother or one sister does not exhibit all in him/herself. Each has his own particular part. All are necessary.

We often hear Hebrews 13:7 quoted in reference to men of God who have taken a leading role among Christians. What we sometimes forget is that the verse says to imitate their faith, not to imitate their peculiarities and habits. These habits may be good or bad—perhaps good for the leading brother, but bad for the one trying to imitate him. If we know a spiritual brother we usually think that we are spiritual too when we imitate his habits. That thought is totally false and such imitation is not true spirituality at all. I heard of a group of Brethren who, while praying, had the habit of clearing their throats repeatedly because brother Darby apparently used to do so! Is this what the Lord wants? It is important to see the difference between imitating a person's characteristics and habits and imitating his faith. Darby told the following story:

> A straw shows which way the wind blows; they used to put up texts on the walls, and at first they were in black and white, but now they have all kinds of beautiful things, and so on. We ought to be careful about such things. Though only a personal matter, I name it to

show what I mean: I had slipped in Canada and broken my spectacles, and someone kindly gave me a gold pair of glasses. I took them and thought no more about them, for one does not look a gift horse in the mouth, as the saying is. But in Barbados the brethren meet in rather a dark place, and I used my glasses there. Well, the other day, I got a letter from dear S______ telling me he had spoken to a brother about the rings on his fingers—as they are apt to wear them, for they are naturally full of vanity—and at once he answered, "Oh, they are not a bit worse than Darby's spectacles." Got another pair since! This is very practical truth.[2]

Do we not often justify things we do by taking a spiritual brother as our standard? We think that if such a spiritual brother can do this or that, we can too. Darby did not think twice about the glasses being gold, but the other brother thought he was therefore justified in wearing rings. Thus the gold glasses were a stumbling block that Satan was eager to take advantage of. If the other brother had imitated Darby's *faith,* he would have acted very differently, for Darby saw such things as rings as a hindrance and an indulgence of the flesh.

We shall now take a look at some of Darby's characteristics. At the same time we will see evidence of his faith and much worth imitating.

Descriptions by Critics and Friends

Many of Darby's critics, past and present, have described him as being jealous of his ecclesiastical authority. They have portrayed him as antagonistic, tyrannical, domineering, arrogant, vain, peremptory, and haughty. They have said he used his friends to further his personal ambitions.

Darby was a man just like us. To present him as faultless would be nonsense. He did have faults, shortcomings, and weaknesses. But it was his greatness that gave prominence to his weaknesses. People who knew Darby better than some of his opponents did, have given the following testimonies.

William Kelly, Darby's personal friend for almost forty

years, said, "I have never regarded J. N. D. otherwise as a great and good man; and the terms rarely go together."[3]

Julius Anton von Poseck, who worked with Darby on the German translation of the New Testament and knew him for about thirty years, wrote:

> You could not be in his presence more than a few minutes without soon feeling that you were in the presence of a great man and ever greater servant of God... I have often wondered at God's grace in J. N. Darby, which was able to sustain him in such healthy, spiritual simplicity for so many years in spite of the increasing amount of human praise surrounding him.[4]

Walter Scott, best known for his *Handbook to the Bible* and *Exposition of the Revelation of Jesus Christ,* wrote in connection with Darby's death:

> It has been the experience of most men brought into personal contact with Mr. Darby, that the influence exercised over them was overwhelming. His marvellous power in grappling with principles and tracing their applications to their legitimate results; his simple and unaffected piety; combined with the ripest scholarship and unequalled ability in expounding the Word of God, accompanied by a generous appreciation of the good and excellent outside the ecclesiastical sphere in which he moved, fitted him to become, as he undoubtedly was, a recognized leader in the Church of God.[5]

A modern writer on the history of the Brethren spoke of Darby as being winsome and deeply sympathetic and having a personality that could enslave by its sheer attractiveness.[6]

W. G. Turner, in his biography of Darby, described him thus:

> The tender devotion of a St. Bernard of Clairvaux, linked with the fiery dominant personality of a St. Dominic in his zeal for the truth and hatred of heresy; the mystic engrossed in the heavenlies, and yet so truly the ecclesiastic, that as one remarked in a strain of pleasantry, "He always had his surplice in his pocket";

> a leader of matchless sagacity, yet with an impetuous impulsiveness that was occasionally a source of embarrassment to other leading brethren, his life resembles a landscape with its towering rocks and solitudes; its verdant meads and meandering streams; its rushing torrents and calm lakes; each of which in turn stand out upon the canvas as the arresting feature of the picture. As a man, as a Christian, and as a scholar he was and is held in the highest respect by all who knew him, save indeed those who permit themselves to be blinded by prejudice or invincible party feeling. His unchallenged consistency, sincerity and unwearied service to the faith to which his soul was yielded in his early years commands the reverence and admiration of those who recognized in him a spiritual guide. But there is always need for caution lest this admiration of a Christian leader's intellect and spiritual qualities should be allowed to pass (unconsciously perhaps at first) into an unwarranted and dangerous deference to his authority, or even into a passive acquiescence in all his teachings, as though it were impossible for such a man to err in any point of faith or practice.[7]

The last sentence of the above quote should be taken to heart, and Darby himself would not have had it otherwise, for he always taught that Christians should test everything with the Word of God itself. He never claimed infallibility for himself.

F. Cuendet included the following character sketch in his Darby biography:

> Darby possessed a noble simplicity in his habits and ways. In addition he had a fine poetical feeling, to which his many poems bear witness . . . He had missed a womanly influence [through his mother's absence] and was fitted with a spontaneous determinism and lively spirit of the Irish and in this way he fought his battles with a swing he was accused of . . . Darby wasn't a feminist. You could say that the sisters in England have the tendency to form small groups around their favourite brother. As a sister once remarked to Darby, after a meeting: Oh, Mr. Darby, what a wonderful hour

> we have just had! he shot back: The devil has told me that already as well.[8]

Darby had a very strong character and personality. Darby's followers spoke almost exclusively of his positive traits,[9] his enemies almost exclusively of his negative traits. Who was right? After years of studying Darby and his life I must answer, both. Darby's personality was not only strong; it was also complicated. At times he could show the deepest humility and the most tender concern and understanding; at other times the more negative qualities would surface and a shadow of his father's character would become noticeable.

Von Poseck wrote, "Mr. Darby had, as many men of great natural mental abilities, a strong, indomitable natural will and an untamable energy."[10]

Kelly noted the "extravagance of acrimony and abuse" in writings of Darby[11] and of his "influencing too often."[12]

B. W. Newton wrote:

> J. N. Darby was a very subtle man. He had been a lawyer, or at least educated for the law. Once he wanted his Archbishop to pursue a certain course, when he (J. N. D.) was a curate in his diocese. He wrote a letter, therefore, saying he had been educated for the law, knew what the legal course would properly be; and then having written that clearly, he mystified the remainder of the letter both in word and in handwriting, and ended up by saying: You see, my Lord, such being the legal aspect of the case it would unquestionably be the best course for you to pursue, etc. And the Archbishop couldn't make out the legal part, but rested on Darby's word and did as he advised. Darby afterwards laughed over it, and indeed he showed a copy of the letter to Tregelles. This is not mentioned in the Archbishop's biography, but in it is the fact that he spoke of Darby as "the most subtle man in my diocese."[13]

William Henry Darby called his brother "potted arrogance" and remarked that "gift" would not edify or energize the church of God, but that grace, in the teacher and the hearers, would.[14]

Turner recorded some negative incidents in his biography as well as positive ones:

> A London surgeon told the writer a story of a Bible Reading which Darby was giving in the States. A number of ministers were present paying great attention to him. One of them, Rev. Dr. G. F. Pentecost broke in with a question as the meeting proceeded. Darby replied briefly, but his questioner not quite grasping the relevance of the reply, asked him to kindly repeat it. This he did, but Pentecost remarking that he still could not clearly see the point, asked for a third and more detailed explanation. Arrested by this in the full flow of a most interesting argument, Darby rather spoiled things by very tartly retorting, "I am here to supply exposition not brains," or words to that effect.
>
> It is interesting, too, to know that while in Chicago on one occasion Mr. Darby was invited by D. L. Moody to give a series of Bible Readings in Farwell Hall. These were attended by many lovers of the Word of God, but unfortunately suddenly came to an abrupt end as the two clashed over the question of the freedom of the will. Mr. Darby held to what Mr. Moody considered extreme Calvinism on this point, affirming that so perverted was man's will he could not "will" even to be saved, and he based his contention largely on the texts "Which were born not out . . . of the will of the flesh . . . but of God" and "It is not of him that willeth . . . but of God that sheweth mercy." Mr. Moody insisted that man as a responsible person was appealed to by God to turn to Him and would be condemned if he did not. "Ye will not come to me that ye might have life," said Jesus to those who refused His message. "Whosoever will," is the great gospel invitation. The controversy became so heated one day that Mr. Darby suddenly closed his Bible and refused to go on, thus losing one of the great opportunities of his life, as will seem to many.
>
> Separating from Mr. Moody, Darby did not hesitate to condemn Mr. Moody's work in his characteristic way. In his letters he warned his followers against it as likely to bring a great increase of worldliness into the

> Church. It is a striking instance of how prejudice can blind and mislead an otherwise great man . . .
>
> Another American leader whom Mr. Darby met was Dr. Daniel Steele, the great Methodist divine, and advocate of Wesleyan perfectionism. He was at first greatly delighted with Mr. Darby's downright earnestness of purpose and vast knowledge of the Word and attended many of his readings in Boston. But he could not accept the doctrines of grace and considered Mr. Darby's teaching on the two natures and the believer's eternal security utterly false. One day when Darby was expounding 1 John 1:7 showing that the subject dwelt on there is "*where* you walk, not *how,*" Dr. Steele interrupted with the question, "But, Brother Darby, suppose a real Christian turned his back on the light, what then?" "Then," replied Darby, "the light would shine on his back!"
>
> Mr. Darby, however, had the greatest patience with the poor, unlettered, simple believers, and at Bible Readings was frequently known to help an uneducated brother out with his questions, and to go patiently over the same ground again until the difficulty was cleared up. Occasionally, but rarely, his stock of patience ran out with those of another class whom he thought were inclined to temporize with the truth under consideration.[15]

The Reverend Sir Charles Brenton was not all that wrong when he commented that he never knew a man in whom the two Adams were so strong as they were in Darby.[16] The negative side of Darby's character is undeniable and it would not be honest to try to play it down. The question is whether it was the dominating factor.

Darby was an Englishman by birth and upbringing. His background was Irish and he spent formative years in Ireland. It is interesting to note what he had to say of the English and the Irish.

Of the English: They "cannot bend or adapt themselves in general to those amongst whom they are, but must bend them to their ways; this is a mistake."[17] If this description can rightly be applied to Darby, then it is only fair to notice that he saw this attitude as a mistake, and, if aware of it in himself, he must have fought against it; that he was not always successful is another thing.

Of the Irish: "All Irishmen whom grace has not total mastery of" have "an amazing confidence in" themselves.[18] As a Christian Darby professed to have no confidence in himself, or any other man, but in Christ alone. He sought always to let grace have total mastery of him. That he did not always succeed, as none of us do, is obvious. Does this disappoint us? Only One was perfect, and Darby's faults show him to be only one of us, and this is, in a certain sense, an encouragement.

Darby rightly maintained, "I am no more either Jew or Gentile, or a man living on the earth; I am a Christian."[19] Yet he realized as well that "the Thessalonians were not the Ephesians, nor were the Corinthians Philippians."[20] The people of each land do have certain characteristics. A negative example of this is found in Titus 1:12-13. Darby bore characteristics of his background as we all do, but as a Christian he sought to bring the negative ones under Christ.

The Lord Jesus was Darby's one and all. He gave up all for Him, and he held fast to all he considered true, regardless of the cost. Because this truth was so real and important to him, he would not back down from his beliefs. He tried to convince others of the truth as he saw it. At times he got in his own way, but predominantly the ruling and guiding principle in his life was Christ. "The man with one object is the energetic man. The Christian's object is Christ."[21]

It was after Darby had gone to be with the Lord that Kelly, fully knowing his faults, spoke of him as great and good. It was a sober intelligent judgment.[22]

Regardless of what we might think of Darby, we have to consider the testimonies of people who really knew him, both friend and foe alike. The statements made by men like Groves, Newman, and others are generally not accepted as valid by people who consider Darby as an important leader in the church of God. Of course one would be very skeptical of their opinions as being biased and unfair. But we must realize that the opinions of Bellett, Kelly, and others are biased as well, even if in the other direction. Both testimonies must be filtered and weighed. Both considered together give a truer picture. Some of William Kelly's more critical comments on Darby, few though they be, coincide considerably with the negative remarks of opponents. There was light and shade. It is naive to believe one extreme view or the other.

Self-appraisal

In many of his letters Darby spoke of himself as being a coward and not having enough faith and courage. Yet J. C. Philpot said of him that he was "possessed of more than martyr courage."[23] Darby also regarded himself as being cold and undemonstrative,[24] but one has only to read some of his many letters to the bereaved to see the warmth and concern flowing out of his heart in the effort to administer comfort in some way. Demonstrative he was not, for he hated anything like show.

If we find evidence proving the contrary of what Darby thought of himself, we should not jump to the conclusion that his humility was false and pretended. He had a proper and healthy spiritual attitude. However, one should not be occupied with his own shortcomings except when self-judgment is necessary (this is only occupation with self in another form), but rather with Christ alone.

> There is a danger of being too much occupied with evil; it does not refresh, does not help the soul on. "Abstain from every form of evil," but be occupied ourselves and occupy others with Christ. The evil itself becomes not less evil, but less in comparison with the power of good where the soul dwells.[25]

We have the admonition in Scripture that one should not "think of himself more highly than he ought to think" (Romans 12:3, KJV).

> When we are occupied with Jesus the littleness of all that one is, or of all that one has done, remains in the shade, and Jesus Himself alone stands out in relief. . . . Our prayers, our praises and our services are so poor and worthless, and yet we are proud of them. We seek praise from our fellowmen for the very things we have to confess as tainted with sin before God. What need,

> therefore, to bare our hearts and say, "See if there be any wicked way in me, and lead me in the way everlasting."[26]

Darby's humility was genuine, and his selflessness as well. The following is a quote from Anna M. Loizeaux's "Sketches for My Grandchildren":[27]

> Mons. Ponge was a quiet, elderly French gentleman. He was very much attached to Mr. Darby and often went about with him. The brethren, knowing this, always left the chair next to Mr. Darby's for Mons. Ponge. One day, the latter was late; coming in and seeing the chair unoccupied, he felt embarrassed, and began to say to Mr. Darby: "Really I am ashamed to have this seat." "There! There! Ponge; it is too late to be ashamed of me," Mr. Darby quickly replied. The humour of it was only for those, however, who understood French, in which it was said.
>
> All who knew Mr. Darby honored him, yet the lowliest might feel at home in his presence. But woe to anyone who, filled with pride, made a show of learning in opposition to the truth.
>
> An Irishman, working in the field nearby, came to see Mr. Darby, about whom he had heard much in his own country. He was barefoot, but not ashamed. "And are you the great John Darby I heard so much about in Ireland?" And, continuing, he made quite a little speech—evidently prepared for the occasion. Mr. Darby replied not a word. Looking at him, he said quietly, "Tell me, is Christ in you?" As quickly as possible, the man turned and went away.

Many think of Darby as being very strict and stiff—traditional is perhaps the word, used in a negative sense. The following story, told by Neatby[28] and confirmed by Kelly[29] with a slight correction, might serve to show a lighter side of Darby's nature.

Andrew Miller (well known for his history of the church in general and of the Brethren in particular) and his wife had just come into fellowship with the Brethren and received their first visit from Mr. Darby. After supper they knelt down to pray, Darby very close to the table. Darby offered up a prayer with which his hearers were greatly impressed. But Mrs. Miller was uneasy; she was distracted by the unmistakable sound of the family cat eating the remains of the supper. It was only her awe for Mr. Darby that prevented her from getting up and scaring the cat away while he was praying. When they got up from their knees she quickly glanced at the table. Darby noticed this and said, "It's all right. I saw that she got nothing but the bones."

If Darby had a weakness or fault, it was his gullibility. He said, "I know I am very slow in discerning people and evil. Certainly I have the kind of charity which thinks no evil, though it is in danger of being spoiled in a long life."[30]

Someone once ventured to say that Darby was the most gullible man in all of England. Kelly thought this statement was much too exaggerated, but he did say that Darby often made mistakes in trusting men quite unworthy of his trust, especially if he believed that they had suffered for Christ and the truth. Darby was too easily deceived.[31] On one occasion he said, "Strange thing, that my pets should turn out scamps."

Darby had the habit of believing the first person who came to him with a story. The danger in this is that it is usually the light and party-spirited Christian who spreads stories and seeks to gain the support or influence of spiritual leaders. The more faithful saints are slow in spreading bad reports. Kelly used to pray that the first report to reach Darby might be the true one.

Darby was very straightforward in his ways, making many people uncomfortable. To one who had the habit of putting on airs he said, "Come, not so much of the gentleman."

Darby knew a brother who had been very useful to the Lord but then married a worldly-minded lady. He caused Darby some grief in that he began speaking ill of some of the saints. Darby saw through it all and said, "Ah! It is not the brethren but the wife." Because of this remark the wife never allowed the breach in their relationship with him to be healed.

To another Darby said, "What were you about, hiding among your family connections, and not once seeing the brethren around?"

In a newspaper clipping the following incident is recorded:

> He (Darby) shone not alone in matters scriptural and spiritual, but also in repartee, and, with St. Peter, hated any gaudy display in women's dress. On one occasion, seeing a lady of fine proportions sailing down the place of worship (where he presided as an honoured elder) wearing a bonnet with aggressive waving plumes, he remarked, in all solemnity, to the "brother" who was seated near him, "Poor woman! Moulting time will come."[32]

Darby was also well known for his consideration of the needs of others. Philpot said that he was "generous to the wasting of his substance."[33]

Darby once heard of a poor brother who thought of going to America because he was no longer able to support himself in England. He presented the astonished brother with a check to cover his travel expenses. But the man's circumstances took a turn for the better and he returned Darby's check to him. Darby replied, "So you are not going now; never mind, if you should want it, come to me again."

Darby was once missed at bedtime in the large house where he was staying as a guest during a conference. The others finally found him sleeping in a loft so that a poorer brother, whose loft-bed he now occupied, might have his more comfortable quarters in the house.[34]

Darby sought to be a help wherever he could, even helping out in a barbershop that belonged to a brother who had been taken ill. No one else thought of this brother's need, so Darby went and worked in his little shop as best as he could.

Darby and the Poor

Darby had a great affection for the poor and preferred to stay with them when traveling abroad rather than with well-to-do believers. This is all the more interesting when one considers the fact that he had been brought up in a rich family and had certainly never known any want as a child. Neatby recorded a memorable incident:

> He had arrived at the railway station of a Continental town where he was expected to make some little stay,

> and found himself, as he stepped from the train, face to face with a formidable contingent of the local brethren. Several ladies of good position were there, all jealous for the honor of becoming his host. Here was a delicate situation, but Solomon could not have been more equal to it. "Who [generally] puts up the [ministering] brothers?" said Darby. All eyes turned upon a very humble-looking brother, who had hitherto kept modestly in the background. Darby immediately went up to him, saying, "I will stay where the [ministering] brothers are in the habit of staying." And the entertainer of obscure itinerants became the host of the great man himself.[35]

Darby and Kelly were once invited to a sister's place for the study of the Word of God. When they arrived Darby was very disappointed to see that all the other guests were of the better class. This grieved him very much, and when he was asked to give thanks he begged Kelly to do so. He felt that the sister's act had been contrary to the mind of Christ since she had not given the more lowly saints an opportunity for hearing the Word.[36]

We find Darby's thoughts as to the poor in the following quotations:

> Christ preferred the poor; ever since I have been converted so have I. Let those who like society better have it. If I ever get into it, and it has crossed my path in London, I return sick at heart. I go to the poor; I find the same evil nature as in the rich, but I find this difference: the rich, and those who keep their comforts and their society, judge and measure how much of Christ they can take and keep without committing themselves; the poor, how much of Christ they can have to comfort them in their sorrows.[37]
>
> I love the poor, and have no distrust of them, living by far the most of my time amongst them, and gladly. When first I began such a life, I as to nature felt a certain satisfaction in the intercourse of educated persons: it was natural. If I find a person spiritually minded and full of Christ, from habit as well as principle I had

> rather have him than the most elevated or the most educated. The rest is all alike to me. The latter are apt to spare and screen themselves to get on in society: they want a fence round them. I would rather in general have a poor man's judgment of right and wrong than another's; only they are, from being thrown more together and the importance of character, apt to be a little hard on each other as to conduct, and jealous of favours conferred, but often very kind and considerate one toward another.[38]

Darby wrote in 1861, "I enjoyed hiding myself and presenting the Saviour to the poor."[39]

Once while Darby was traveling in Switzerland, he visited a brother who owned a factory. This brother was in the habit of offering strangers and poor people something to eat and a place to rest. Darby arrived and used the back entrance, the one used by the poor. He was not recognized by the servants and was treated as the rest. Darby apparently took this in his stride, without making use of his respected name. After refreshing himself he continued on his way.

Perhaps the thing to be feared most is the desire to be rich, as 1 Timothy 6:9 warns. If one is already rich then he might be able to use his wealth for the Lord and the Lord's own, but there is an admonition for him too in 1 Timothy 6:17-19.[40] Kelly wrote of Darby:

> He had a vigilant eye for the Lord, particularly with younger fellowlabourers; and I remember that when with me on first setting up house, he deliberately looked at a table-spoon or fork before him. Happily I passed muster; and nothing was said: they were only plated! So he lived himself. Even in such things he hated for Christians the pride of life, and justly felt that one little licence opens the way for many greater.[41]

Darby and Bellett

There were many who loved Darby, but he had few close friends; his closest ones were men like Wigram, Kelly, and especially Bellett. Darby was often a visitor in Bellett's house, sometimes for a number of weeks. Bellett always prided himself in saying, "If I deserve any credit it is that I early discerned what there was in John Darby!" Darby had great respect for Mrs. Bellett also, and once he said, "Mrs. Bellett has been my mentor for twenty years."[42]

Bellett passed into the Lord's presence during Darby's lifetime and their exchange of letters when he was dying is very touching. Here are two extracts. Bellett wrote to Darby:

> I came to know you, not slightly as before [he probably means as in their Dublin days] but in an apprehension that instinctively bound me to you, and this now for forty years [written in 1864] has never abated. What I do owe the God of my eternal life for feeding and strengthening that life, and enlarging its capacities through your ministry, in secret and in public! I have loved you as I suppose, in a certain sense, I have loved no other, and now, after so long a time, we are found together, still in the dear fellowship of the same confession.[43]

Darby replied:

> I have ever found in you, dear brother, everything that was kind; nor, be assured, was it lost upon me, though I am not demonstrative. Besides, the value I had for you, it was not a small thing to me that you, with dear Cronin and Hutchinson, were one of the first four, who with me, through God's grace the fourth, began to break bread in Dublin . . . It is to you, dear brother, my heart turns now, to say how much I own and value your love, and to return it; I rejoice that while I have been the object of many kindnesses on your part down here, it is one which will never cease, which has had Jesus our Master for its bond, though with many human kindnesses. But oh, what joy to know oneself united to Him! It adds a joy untold to every sweetness: it is the source of it too. Surely He is all.
>
> For me, I work on till He call me, and though it would be a strange Dublin without you, yet I go on my

John Gifford Bellett
(A very early edition of Chief Men Among the Brethren, *Pickering & Inglis)*

William Kelly
(The collection of Ulrich Bister)

> way, serve others, say little and pass on. Not that I do not deeply love others, but this will all come out in its truth in heaven, perhaps on one's death-bed; but I have committed my all to Him till that day. My hope is still to see you, my beloved brother; should I not, be assured there is none who has loved you more truly and thankfully than myself; it can hardly be unknown to you, though with me it is more within than without. Peace be with you. May you find the blessed One ever near you; that is everything. Faithful is He withal and true. In His eternal presence, how shall we feel that all our little sorrows and separations were but little drops by the way, to make us feel that we were not with Him, and when with Him, what it is to be there.[44]

The Lord did grant Darby a chance to see Bellett before he passed away. Bellett's daughter wrote that "the meeting of the two friends was very touching. Dear John held him in his arms, and expressed in ardent terms his great affection for him."[45]

After Bellett had passed away Darby wrote, "Dear Bellett is gone. I cannot quite account for the peaceful feeling I have as to it. But it is well, and he is well. There was truthfulness of heart, as well as joy in the blessed One, at the close."[46]

A Servant's Trials

We sometimes have a false impression of brothers who are very close to the Lord: we think that no one has it as good as they. But this is wrong in one sense. They are not spared the pains and burdens of the way any more than the simplest believer. On the contrary, their burden is often greater than that of others. The apostle Paul said, "Beside those things that are without, that which cometh upon me daily, the care of all the churches" (2 Corinthians 11:28, KJV). Their fellowship with Christ and their knowledge of Him perhaps makes them seem different.

Darby was not spared sickness. We have already noted his recurring problem with his eye, and his letters frequently mentioned this or that illness. However, it is beautiful to see that often a very serious sickness brought out a magnificent hymn from his pen. For example, when confined to a bed in a dark room because of difficulties with his eye, he wrote a hymn entitled "The Endless Song," which begins with the lines "Oh! the joy of the salvation / We possess around the throne!"[47]

Darby was once so ill that it was thought he was dying. During that illness he wrote "The Man of Sorrows." In two hundred lines this hymn portrays the life of our Lord from the manger to His coming again for His own. It begins, "O ever homeless Stranger! / Thus dearest friend to me."[48]

There was a period when Darby was sick at the same time every year. He attributed this to not being close enough to the Lord in service.[49]

Darby said, "God has made me a lonely person."[50] But in this loneliness the Lord was especially near and real to him. "I was always a solitary soul, thinking more for, than with people: but it is good to be more alone—most good, if it be more alone with Christ. What a place that is!"[51]

Darby also said, "I think I may say I never knew anything but sorrow as my portion."[52] But in his sorrow Christ was his joy, his all.

We usually forget that hardships are to be expected along the way. But God's Word tells us that "we must through much tribulation enter into the kingdom of God" (Acts 14:22, KJV) and "all that will live godly in Christ Jesus shall suffer persecution" (2 Timothy 3:12, KJV). Darby commented, "If any man serve Me, let him follow Me; that recalls a line I read many years ago, It is harder to live a Christian than to die a martyr."

Why is it that one believer appears to be more spiritual than another? Darby said, "The higher acknowledgement of Christ, the more spiritual energy in going through this world and overcoming it. If one believer is more spiritual than another, it is because he understands the person of Christ better."

True spirituality does not necessarily mean great intellectual understanding of all the doctrines of Scripture. In fact true spirituality is often found in the simplest brother whose all is Christ.

Darby said, "True spiritual superiority does not assert itself, but makes itself felt. It does not look for acknowledgement, but is acknowledged because real." Darby did not seek for himself a high place among believers, at least not in the way his opponents seemed to think. He wanted only to serve. Christ was everything to him and others recognized this. It was for this reason he held such an important place in the hearts of so many of the Lord's own. They saw something of Christ in him. "The only thing which can be truly blessing to our brethren, so precious because they belong to Him, is that which we reproduce of Him."[53]

Darby and Children

Darby was well known for his great love for and understanding of children. While laboring in eastern France and Switzerland Darby often stayed with poor mountaineers. When the mothers would be working out in the fields, he would be half-occupied with his studies and half-occupied with the children who sat about him, helping them with either their work or their play.

While visiting in the United States, Darby was invited to dinner by a poor man whose children kept pet rabbits. All were very happy and excited when the great man came—except for one little boy. His pet rabbit had been used for the main course. While dinner was being served Darby noticed how downcast the little boy was and asked him what was the matter. Despite previous instructions to the contrary, the boy blurted out the whole truth. Darby then declined to eat any of the rabbit dish, and as soon as the meal was over went outside with the boy. They both went to a large water tank and Darby took some mechanical toy ducks out of his pocket. He played with the little boy for about an hour in an attempt to console him in the loss of his pet.

Darby was known to have rolled up his overcoat to be used as a pillow for a sleeping child whose uncomfortable position had attracted his attention while he was addressing a meeting. On one of his many sea voyages Darby was seen at night walking up and down the deck with a restless child in his arms so that the worn-out mother might be able to sleep.

George Campbell Morgan, a well-known preacher and author of over sixty books, said that one of the cherished recollections of his boyhood was meeting Darby who had come to visit his father. Morgan recalled the almost reverential awe that came over him in the presence of such a great man; and then the awe disappeared, although the reverence remained, as the visitor spoke kindly to him about his studies.[54]

Regarding the conferences that took place in the 1870s in Vinton, Iowa, Anna Mabel Roberts wrote:

> At the conferences at the farm, dear Darby was present; also Christopher Wolston, Mons. Ponge, Captain Dunlop, and many whose names I cannot recall.
>
> As I am not able to speak worthily of dear J. N. D. as a teacher and servant of God, of his long years of devoted ministry, of his many and valuable writings and translations of Scripture, I must content myself with telling you a little of him as a man, and especially of those things which appeal to the young. Mr. Darby was a *grand* old man, in the vigour of manhood, although his hair was almost white. When, after one of the meetings, the barracks were being taken down, his hammer rang with the rest. When a young brother said to him: "This is too hard work for an old gentleman," Mr. Darby replied, with a twinkle in his eye, "Come out on the lawn and I'll show you which is the old man."[55] His features were rugged, but noble. He would have made a *kingly* king, so great was the dignity of his bearing; and yet, he was as simple as a child, and had a fine sense for humor.
>
> Your Aunt Anna (Mrs. Flemming) was not three years old. She was a little mischief, running all around and quite at home all over the house. Mr. Darby occupied the parlor bedroom. Going there after a meeting, he could not find his keys. At once he thought of Anna. Taking her by the hand, he began to hunt in the grass, where he had seen her playing. He soon found them—and then!—such a funny scolding he gave her, while she stood laughing all the time.
>
> I have heard that he was great at playing *bear* with little folks, running after them on all fours, and growling to their delight and terror.[56]

The following is a very touching and interesting letter Darby wrote to a young boy on the loss of some pet birds:

At last, dear______, I take up my pen to write a line to you in reply to your letter. As to your Brahmapootras, I feel it must have been a great chagrin to you, but as you had to reproach yourself—though this does not always soften our misfortunes—it has left you nothing to say. I feel with you in it. But even in these little things we have to see the Lord's hand, for nothing is little to Him which affects the souls of His children. How did you feel when you found it out in the morning—vexed, irritated, angry with those who did it or wishing vengeance against them? All this, you see, shows the state of your mind, and this is the real importance of the matter. I feared these Brahmapootras for you, not that there was anything wrong in keeping or taking care of them, but from the effect on your own spirit. The poor fowls were very innocent, and so is taking care of them. But I feared your heart had got engaged in them in a way that was doing you mischief, and now the Lord has taken them away. How good He is, to think even of the effect of fowl-keeping on your soul that lives for ever!

With regard to Lacrosse, healthy exercise for boys of your age is quite to be desired, but here too, I feared, and you have learned a lesson by this too. How many we have to learn in a way humbling to ourselves! And I am so thankful to see the Lord teaching you, and even in your letter I think I see the effect of it, and bless the Lord. I was very glad to get it. I could not have advised you to stay away, but I am not sorry you did; it is always well conscience should work, and the doubt you were brought into as to salvation will quicken your conscience and make you more watchful, and not only so, but make you feel your dependence on grace every moment, and help you to discern why such or such a thing is to be avoided; for you are now growing a great boy, and have to be exercised for yourself before God; and walking with a conscience exercised before Him, you will find yourself happy and strengthened too. I am glad you are in correspondence with______. At your age you need companions, and our hearts get knit with some, and it is a great point it should be with those who help and do not hinder us.[57]

Natural Gifts

Darby had an appreciation for music. According to William Kelly, Darby had a sweet voice and a good ear, but he feared music would become a distraction.[58] The following letter serves as an overview of Darby's thoughts on natural gifts.

> My Dear Brother, I am very thankful your conscience has been exercised about the music. I can sympathise with you, for as far as ear goes, music had the greatest power over me, though never taught to play. But the ground of those who wrote you to keep it up is all wrong and not true. It is not *for Christ* they wish you to keep the harmonium, and that decides the case. I am not a Jew, nor am I in the New Jerusalem where all will be to God's glory, though *not* in the highest way, for the Father does not come in there. I could suppose a person earning his bread by music, though I think it a very dangerous way, as Peter did by fishing, which is no excuse for a person spending his time fishing to amuse himself.
>
> All these pleas of "gifts of God" are bringing in nature—when it is fallen—into the worship or service of the new man and the Lord, and spoiling it.
>
> I have known hunting justified by the hounds having scent. No instrument can equal in effect (Haydn said so) the human voice. Besides, as I said, it is not true. It is merely helping the pleasure of fallen nature, not a thing evil in itself, but connecting sensual pleasure with spiritual life. It is not the thing to begin with a ruined soul, but we have to live by God's Word. Harps and organs down here began in Cain's city, when he had gone out from the presence of the Lord. In point of fact, artistic musicians as a general rule are not a moral class; the imagination is at work, not the conscience, nor the heart. Judaism did take up nature to see if they could have a religion of it, only to prove it could not be, but end in the rejection of Jehovah and His anointed. We are dead, and risen with Christ, and belong to another world. Hence I cannot seek my own enjoyment in what belongs to the old, though I may recognize

> God's work in it, but not seek it as a world I belong to now. It is not a legal prohibition, but the heart [is] elsewhere. If I could put a poor sick father to sleep with music, I would play the most beautiful I could find; but it only spoils any worship as bringing in the pleasure of sense into what ought to be the power of the Spirit of God. They cannot go really together, save as water may take away the taste of wine.
>
> It is a wholly false principle that natural gifts are a reason for using them. I may have amazing strength or speed in running; I knock a man down with one, and win a prize cup with another. Music may be a more refined thing, but the principle is the same. This point I believe to be now of all importance. Christians have lost their moral influence by bringing in nature and the world as harmless. All things are lawful to me. But as I said, you cannot mix flesh and Spirit. We need all our energies under grace to walk in the latter, always bearing about in the body the dying of the Lord Jesus, that the life of Jesus may be manifested in our bodies. Let Christ be all, and the eye is single and the whole body full of light. The converse is if our eye be evil, because it shuts out Christ; our affections are not set on things above where Christ sits at God's right hand. That is the point for us, happy affections *there*, and steadfastly, not being distracted.[59]

The reader may not agree with all the details of the above letter, but there are very important divine principles found in it that we should consider when we allow ourselves to do this or that. On what grounds do we justify our activities? What are our motives and goals?

The Hope of Day

written 1872

And is it so, I shall be like Thy Son,
Is this the grace which He for me has won?
Father of glory! Thought beyond all thought,
In glory to His own blest likeness brought!

O Jesus, Lord, who loved me like to Thee?
Fruit of Thy work! With Thee, too, there to see
Thy glory, Lord, while endless ages roll,
Myself the prize and travail of Thy soul.

Yet it must be! Thy love had not its rest
Were Thy redeemed not with Thee fully blest—
That love that gives not as the world, but shares
All it possesses with its loved co-heirs!

Nor I alone; Thy loved ones all, complete,
In glory around Thee with joy shall meet;
All like Thee, for Thy glory like Thee, Lord!
Object supreme of all, by all adored![60]

J. N. Darby

5

Ministry: Written and Oral

Always abounding in the work of the Lord.

1 Corinthians 15:58, KJV

William Kelly recorded the following in a letter dated February 22, 1901:

> The late Mr. Darby was a highly educated, as he was extremely able, man, of rare attainments in almost all branches of knowledge, of pre-eminent logical power, of moral and metaphysical analysis hard to match, to say nothing of his linguistic skill, ancient and modern.

As to the first few abilities mentioned, one has only to read the articles with which volume 32 of the *Collected Writings of J. N. Darby* begins—for example, "God in His Essence and Attributes," "The Absolute," "The Relative and the Absolute," or "Self-consciousness and the Infinite"—to see that what Kelly said is not exaggerated.

Darby knew ancient Latin, Hebrew, and Greek and modern French, German, and Italian. He could understand Dutch but had difficulties with it in conversation. While visiting New Zealand he learned the native language, Maori, and was able to preach in it.[1]

Many believers considered (many still do today) Darby a special servant of the Lord, fitted with great natural abilities and spiritual gifts for the accomplishment of an important task within the Christian church. Darby said, "I believe He [the Lord] has confided a testimony to me, however feeble I may be and unworthy. I do not say that to the exclusion of others of His servants, but as that for which I am responsible."[2]

William Kelly defined *calling* as follows: "Calling implies grace entering the world and separating unto God, bringing out of the condition in which people were." Darby remarked:

> God works in us to will and to do. It is not that we are mere pipes to carry something, but He acts in us and on us, and we have to take care that we give out purely what we have, taking care first, of course, what we take in.[3]
>
> The Lord chooses the vessel, and He chooses it in the wisdom which has prepared it for His use. And it is not the substitution of mere spiritual attainment for the creative wisdom which has prepared it, for the divine grace which has filled the vessel with His own gift, which will put God or man in his place.[4]

Many Christians who believe the Scriptural interpretation taught by Darby regarding the assembly and the Lord's coming for His own have never heard of Mr. Darby himself. Yet a large collection of his written ministry has been preserved, printed, and reprinted.

Published Works

The largest of Darby's published works is his *Collected Writings* in thirty-four volumes. William Kelly performed the difficult task of collecting and editing all the articles Darby had written and all the transcriptions of his lectures. It was a work of many years and involved translation from other languages. Darby wrote to Kelly:

> I had forgotten your enterprise, and am frightened when I see the extent of the publications. I should think some of the Notes would require some revising, but I have no objection to them if they are useful being printed as Notes. Even the sermons contain things I should not accept; they were first published with a notice that I had not revised them.[5] Some of the earlier publications would require a note or two, where clearer light was acquired, but had better not be altered.[6]

Volumes 4 and 5 of the miscellaneous section have been added to the original thirty-four. These two volumes were edited, compiled, and printed after Kelly's time.

The Collected Writings, containing works from the beginning to the end of Darby's ministry, reveals development of thought. This should be kept in mind. The content of earlier articles was not altered for the sake of consistency with later ones. The articles were reprinted the way they first appeared, and only seldom was a footnote added to mention later views. Thus one can trace the development of Darby's understanding of Scripture.

Darby also kept notebooks in which he recorded his thoughts. He mentioned these notebooks in his will and trusted his Brethren to make wise use of them after his decease. Parts of the notebooks began to appear toward the end of 1883. When publication was complete, there were seven volumes entitled *Notes and Comments.* These volumes are a valuable addition to Darby's other published works, but it should be kept in mind that the notes were actually for himself. They were clear to him, but the meaning of some statements may be difficult for others to ascertain.

Notes and Jottings first appeared in five thin volumes, but are now available in a one-volume edition. It contains notes from lectures and Bible readings that Darby held or attended.

Also available is a small volume containing the substance of lectures on the First Epistle of John. These lectures are not included in the other works named above.

Darby's synopsis of the Bible is perhaps his best-known work. Originally written in French, it was translated into English by Kelly.

There are three large volumes of Darby's letters, and other letters of his are in the French monthly *Le Messager*

Evangelique. A brother in the Lord's work in Canada once remarked to me that having a volume of Darby's letters with him on his travels was like always having an older brother with you; they are filled with encouragement, instruction, exhortation, and help.

Hymns

We have only one slim volume of Darby's hymns and poems. Neatby said:

> Of all the hymns of the Brethren—and no one can deny the exceptional beauty of very many of them—Darby's are unequalled (I had almost said unapproached) for depth, force and grandeur; though Darby put himself at a serious disadvantage . . . by his involved and uncouth style of composition.[7]

William Kelly remarked, "Mr. Darby wrote three or four [hymns] of unusual value, but rather marred by rugged phrase and lack of flow."[8] Turner explained the reason for what was lacking in these hymns:

> The hymns being the free utterance of what the heart learned with God, are without that careful finish that would have been given to mere composition. This however, increases their reality, and hence their attractiveness, for all who will appreciate their intrinsic excellence.[9]

Darby wrote of his own hymns, "They are real. They are not composed; perhaps one."[10] Turner described them as follows:

> A revelation of a devotion, deep, true and tender; the breaking of an alabaster box of choice spiritual perfumes; the outpouring of heartfelt piety in chaste and beautiful expression, which while it enchains the Christian heart constrains it to join its delightsome melody . . . there is no cloying sweetness, no mists of superstition, but a clear spiritual atmosphere where no breath of earthborn clouds intrudes.[11]

Of hymn-writing in general Darby said:

> We have the positive direction of Scripture to speak to one another in psalms, and hymns, and spiritual songs; but [these] mean compositions rhythmically and metrically arranged; so that I judge the use of such compositions is scripturally authorized. I would add that I think the spiritual mind will detect at once what is really given of the Spirit in such compositions and what is not even when merely added to make up the measure or rhyme. "Teaching and admonishing one another in psalms and hymns, and spiritual songs, singing with grace in your heart to the Lord." It enters into the affections, because that is the character of hymns and spiritual songs. It is not so much knowledge written down like a sermon, but it is where the heart answers in its affections to the revelation of Christ; perhaps something that I have heard in a meeting when Christ has been unfolded: it is the Holy Ghost raising up the affections in answer to the revelation of Christ. Then there is the expression of the heart that has received it in the affections of the new man, answering to this in the praise and adoration that it produces. It may not be the reproduction of the same ideas, but it is the adoration of the heart that is drawn out towards the Person that has been revealed.[12]

Darby believed, however, that *poetry* was "chiefly the effort of the human mind to create, by imagination, a sphere beyond materialism which faith gives in realities."[13]

Darby was given the task of revising the 1881 hymnal for the English Brethren. While doing so he wrote:

> There is a lack of worshipping the Father in them, but I know not how that suits hymns, or hymns it, and who is to give them.[14] Take hymns and see how many you have addressed to the Father, or continue to have Him and not ourselves for their subject after the first verse?[15]

After the above question had presented itself to him, Darby found much blessing in the study of the Christian's relationship with the Father.[16] Darby began the revision in 1875; three of his hymns addressed to the Father appear in the 1881 book, two written in 1879 and one in 1880 (a fourth, also written in 1879, is not included). From Darby's preface to the revised hymnal I quote:

> Three things are needed for a hymn book: a basis of truth and sound doctrine; something, at least, of the spirit of poetry, though not poetry itself, which is objectionable, as merely the spirit and imagination of man; and thirdly, the most difficult to find of all, that experimental acquaintance with truth in the affections which enables a person to make his hymn (if led of God to compose one) the vehicle, in sustained thought and language, of practical grace and truth which sets the soul's affections, rising in praise back again to its source. God alone can give this so as to meet the wants of an assembly. Like assembly prayer, it must not rise too completely beyond the state of the affections up to Him, so that what He is in grace developed in the affections of the soul be jointly proclaimed. It is not mere wants—that would be a hymn for the prayer meeting. A basis of truth has been spoken of, or, to speak more justly, the truth; this is evidently fundamentally necessary, but [there are] much feelings, experiences, and hopes, in which the soul moves, which ought to be Scriptural.
>
> Now in a vast number of hymns there is a real piety in the affections, but connected with statements which may not touch any great foundational truth, but are unscriptural, and thus the best affections are connected with unscriptural thoughts, and this is a very real injury to the soul. Thus, suppose uncertainty as to salvation, the absence of the spirit of adoption, a bright hope of being in glory when we die; these are merely taken as instances, for it applies to very many points, and souls are quite angry at losing a hymn which their piety has enjoyed, but which has connected their hopes and affections with what is not Scriptural . . . Hymns should be simple, full of Christ, and the Father's love, unaffected, and in some measure elevated, so as

> not to be mere prose. The singer must be there, but the singer associated in his thoughts with God filled from on high; yet not individualize himself and leave the assembly behind him. Many most sweet hymns are too individual, too experimental, for an assembly.

As to gospel hymns Darby wrote:

> There the difficulty is very great. Abstractedly you are making people sing as having certain feelings, and then preaching to them because they have not. But in actual Christendom things are not so sharply defined, and there are hidden souls and hidden wants which the hymn may give expression to, and set a soul free or make it apprehend God's love sometimes more effectually than the sermon; still there is very great danger of widespread delusion and loose apprehension of sin and grace, and the difficulty is real. You may often find the loudest singers where the conscience is the least reached.

Bible Translations

The last item on our list of Darby's written ministries is his Bible translation. Of the Bible itself he said:

> I have a profound (I believe divinely-given) faith in the Bible. I have, through grace, been by it converted, enlightened, quickened, saved. I have received the knowledge of *God* by it, to adore His perfections—of *Jesus,* the Saviour, joy, strength, comfort of my soul. Many have been indebted to others as the means of their being brought to God—to ministers of that gospel which the Bible contains, or to friends who delight in it. This was not my case. That work, which is ever God's, was wrought in me by means of the written Word. He who knows what the value of *Jesus* is, will know what the Bible will be to such a one.[17]

French, German, Dutch, English, Swedish, and Italian Bible translations are connected with Darby's name, though only the French, German, and English translations are really his work. Even one translation is work enough, and involves immense labor and energy.

Darby began work on the German translation with Carl Brockhaus. Julius A. von Poseck, who knew Greek (which Brockhaus did not), helped with the New Testament, which first appeared in 1854. Von Poseck wrote, "I helped him for a half year in my small way with the translation of the N. T. into German and had the opportunity to daily notice J. N. Darby's deep insight into the unfathomable depths of God's Word."[18] With the help of the Dutch brother Hermann Cornelius Voorhoeve, who was knowledgeable in Hebrew, Darby completed the translation of the Old Testament in 1871.

Darby's French Bible was translated for the French-speaking Swiss. The New Testament appeared in 1859 and the entire Bible in 1885. Mr. William Lowe, later a well-known Christian worker, was of great help to Darby. The proofs of the French New Testament had been casually passed to Lowe, and Darby was so impressed with the value of the improvements he suggested that he said, "You are just the man we want here, you must now stop and help us."[19] A friendship began which lasted until Darby died. Darby said that he knew of no one with the knowledge of the truth in its detail that Lowe had.

In 1868 Darby completed the English translation of the New Testament. He was not able to finish the Old Testament himself, but after his death it was completed with the help of his German and French translations and appeared in 1888.[20]

The following quote from one of Darby's letters refers to his work on the German Old Testament. The letter gives an idea of the amount of labor involved in completing such a project.

> I work by myself from soon after 7 a.m. to 9—breakfasting alone; then 9 to 12:30 p.m. at translation with them; from 3 to 7:30 again, and then I work through reserved hard passages alone, and then often until midnight alone—letters and what I have to do; so I am not idle. As to going out, I go to the Post at dinner time, or for ten minutes elsewhere.[21]

Though Darby made so many translations of the Bible

(which increased his familiarity with its contents) he never tried to publish a critical edition himself. He explained:

> ______wanted to publish an edition of what my translation has adapted as the reading to be accepted, but I declined. I feel no sufficient competency, though I have done the best I could, and am satisfied they have no adequate history of the text.[22]

Today, because of many new discoveries, the correct text is more or less certain.

To make an accurate translation, technical knowledge of Greek and Hebrew is not enough. Translation involves interpretation. An understanding of the thoughts and purposes of God is necessary. To make a good translation, one must be spiritual as well as learned in Greek and Hebrew. In his preface to the German translation Darby wrote, "In the issue of this translation, the purpose is not to offer to the man of letters a learned work, but rather to provide the simple and unlearned reader with as exact a translation as possible." In his preface to the 1871 edition of the Old Testament Darby wrote:

> We have been governed throughout by the thought, that the faithful rendering of the original text outweighs every other consideration; and the more so because we believe with the very fullest conviction the divine inspiration of the Holy Scriptures as the revelation of the infinite wisdom of God, and the expression of His gracious character in Jesus Christ. But since no one is able to grasp the whole expanse of this revelation, and often a meaning beyond the comprehension of the translator lies hidden in a sentence, which would be lost in a free translation but may be found in a more literal one, through deep teaching of the Holy Spirit—it is evidently necessary to reproduce the original text as in a mirror.[23]

Darby called his translation work "a service underground" and would rather have been serving the saints directly.

> I am very happy in the work, but a little anxious as to

> the time it will take . . . I accept my present work while it is so important in these last days that brethren should have the Word of God, and they should have it as pure as possible—and we must expect in these days to have the poor as always when the Church got into its own place in the world, at least for the great mass. And I feel I am serving the Lord in using the little knowledge I have of Greek and Hebrew, etc., in furnishing brethren who have them not, with the Word of God as nearly as possible as it is. Otherwise, the times call for building them up in the truth solidly as once given, so that I am jealous as to how much time I spend on what is means, however precious, for we cannot esteem the Word too precious. It is that which God has given us when the Church went wrong.[24]

Evaluations of Darby's Written Ministry

Darby's chief works, in his own opinion, were a pamphlet called "The Righteousness of God" and one on "1 Peter 2:24."[25] His best critique, according to William Kelly, was his examination of Newton's "Thoughts on the Apocalypse."[26]

The judgment of time is that Darby's greatest single work was his *Synopsis*. He wrote, "But as to my Synopsis, I go and learn from it myself sometimes. Nor am I aware of any changes. You may be quite at ease then."[27] But he also cautioned, "I fear souls may content themselves with it, instead of using it as a help to read the blessed Word with."[28] He wanted this *Synopsis* to be read constantly together with the Word itself. In the foreword Darby wrote:

> Though a commentary may doubtless aid the reader in many passages in which God has given to the commentator to understand in the main the intention of the Spirit of God, or to furnish philological principles and information, which facilitate to another the discovery of that intention; yet if it pretend to give the contents of Scripture, or if he who uses it seeks this in its remarks, such commentary can only mislead and impoverish the soul. A commentary, even if always right, can at

> most give what the commentator has himself learned from the passage. The fullest and wisest must be very far indeed from the living fulness of the divine Word. . . . My purpose is that the Word should be studied, and I even hope that it will be impossible to use these writings otherwise than in the study of the Word.[29]

Darby once compared human statements concerning the truth of God and the truth itself, the Word, with a living tree and sticks laid up in bundles.[30]

Von Poseck summed up Darby's ministry as follows:

> His writings show his deep insight and wide overview of the endless fields of divine truth, from the 1st to last chapter of God's Word, with which the Lord had fitted his excellent servant—be it in the explanation of the simple way of salvation in a full gospel, which even the Reformers only knew in part, or as regards the almost unknown nature, position, calling and hope of the Lord Jesus Christ to take up the Church, or, at last, the way in which the Spirit of God used him to scatter the old, confusing theological expressions and errors regarding the earthly calling, earthly blessings, earthly hopes and earthly worship and to present them in the light of the 2nd (Christian) part of God's Word.[31]

In spite of the fact that many see great spiritual value in Darby's writings, they are seldom read. And when they are read, it is with great difficulty. Darby delighted in concatenated sentences, sometimes with parentheses within parentheses, to express his views fully and guard against misconception. Kelly considered him to be occasionally "grand" here and there, but often obscure.[32] He greatly treasured Darby's writings though and was known for saying, "Read Darby!" Darby once playfully remarked to Kelly, "Kelly, you write to be read and understood. I only think on paper."

Darby found that writing on Scriptural subjects helped him learn. His writings reveal the development of his thoughts; he wrote them down as soon as they crossed his mind and made few changes. He said, "In writing I gain knowledge, and the subject becomes more familiar to me."[33]

Darby was aware of the difficulty his style of writing caused; comparing his style with someone else's he wrote, "His writings are most useful, and they attract the heart, and are much more easily understood than my own."[34] In his preface to "The Irrationalism of Infidelity"[35] Darby wrote:

> I would say, that as I am conscious I have no claim to literary honour, so I neither pretend to nor desire it. I hope I may have been, in general, sufficiently clear to be understood. I would only beg my reader kindly to remember, that sometimes the subjects are somewhat abstract; and while he who publishes anything must expect, of course, to be criticised (if what he writes is indeed worth it), I would so far claim indulgence as one may who has snatched from hours of rest almost the whole time occupied in composing what the reader has before him (service in ministering amongst souls from day to day, and other labours in the Lord's field, needless to mention, fully occupying all ordinary hours of toil). If I am useful to any, and the Lord accepts it as service done to Him, I am content.

G. K. Chesterton commented on the writings of George MacDonald: "He wrote nothing empty; but he wrote much that is rather too full, and of which the appreciation depends rather on a sympathy with the substance than on the first sight of the form."[36] This observation also sums up Darby's writings very well.

G. T. Stokes wrote about Darby:

> His style is execrable; his grammar bad; yet the criticism is just that "those obscure, uncouth, ungrammatical, torturous sentences, which excite our contempt, enter into the very bone of the victims, and paralyzes them in the inner man." So far as we may judge by his writings, he seems to be a man of iron will, without bowel or sympathies. . . . He certainly brings into theological literature and controversy a plainness of speech that has almost gone out of fashion in the churches.[37]

Neatby remarked about Darby's writing:

> He carried his neglect of appearances into his written and spoken composition; and that to such an extent that the style of his writing to the reader of today seems half ludicrous, half disgusting. . . . Darby's own account of the matter was that he could have equalled the rhetorical flights of the great masters, but he never thought it worthwhile. . . . it is hard to read Darby's better works without fancying that a noble eloquence was really at his command, if only he had chosen to cultivate it. Bad as his style is, it is the balance of an almost incredible carelessness, rather than a defective power.[38]

Yet Neatby also commented:

> In his expository writings he often drops a half hint that sets in strong light a passage that great commentators have left obscure. Sometimes he seems to explain with the ease and distinctness of one that had been in the secret of the author.[39]

Kelly said of Darby:

> What characterized our honoured brother as a saint and servant was a deeper insight into God's mind in Scripture than any other I ever knew, or heard of, approached in any age since the apostles; such was his spiritual power of bringing in Christ to decide questions great or small.[40]

The reader of Darby's works will probably notice that he was not a man of detail; this he fully admitted. He felt that others made beautiful things out of his gold.[41] "I am a miner, and bring the precious ore to the surface, which others coin."[42] "I always feel my work a very poor, imperfect one: I sow great principles, truths of God's blessed Word which I know to be truths and infinitely blessed; but I am no wise master builder."[43]

Turner's warning against a "passive acquiescence in all his (Darby's) teachings, as though it were impossible for such a man to err in any point of faith or practice" cannot be emphasized enough.[44] Darby's writings are often studied as carefully as the Scriptures themselves, and usually in the same way—that is, searching for hidden meanings and trying to divine what his "text" is really trying to say. One questions himself before he questions Darby if he does not understand a certain passage in his writings—as if they were infallible. This can become very dangerous. Stoney said it well: "It is to me an evidence of uncertainty when J. N. D.'s writings are quoted to establish a doctrine which, if known spiritually, would have been easily proved from Scripture."[45]

This is not to say that one cannot make use of Darby's writings, but that a right use of them should be made—namely, they should be used to gain a better understanding of the Scriptures themselves. His statements should be proved by Scripture, and the phrase *Darby says* should not be used as if it indicated a source of authority. The thought dare not be, How do the Scriptures fit into Darby's teachings? but rather, How does Darby's teaching correspond to Scripture truth?

The difficult style of Darby's writings makes them not very attractive to most believers. His collected writings should be more carefully and thoroughly edited and brought out in a shorter, more readable form. I know that many would not approve of this, and would see it as diluting wine with water, but Darby's writings are not Scripture. The intention is to make his writings accessible to a larger number of believers. It should not be that a teacher appears to be "as a specialist on a given subject, declaring his knowledge, to the interest of a few, the amazement of more, and the bewilderment of most."[46] Christopher Milne wrote, "Writing is a means of communication. It is not enough to speak; you must also be heard. The message must be received and understood."[47]

Darby was not at all in favor of what he called "brethren overwriting themselves." He said:

> I am not aware that I have written more than what God has given me for other's use when He has done so.[48] It is not the quantity but the quality of my labour which ever troubles me.[49] It is my habit scarcely to put one foot before the other in the study of the Word, and to give forth nothing until I am able, in measure, to say

> (while still liable to make mistakes, of course), "This is the mind of God." This makes me go on very slowly, but I seldom have to retrace my steps.[50]

Darby did not like calling himself the author of his tracts, for he felt that there was no good in anything of which God Himself was not the author.[51] Darby did not consider himself to be infallible, but this remark reveals that he was convinced that what he wrote was of God.

Interpretation of Scripture

As Darby grew older he felt that the truth became ever clearer for him, though he could say at the age of seventy-four, "For my own part, I teach, but I am always learning."[52]

Darby's mind, as Stoney wrote, was thoroughly dyed with Scripture. He advised others not only to go to Scripture for thoughts, but also to think in Scripture itself. He said he was always careful not to present a new interpretation of a passage until he had seen how it would be affected by all other portions of Scripture and how every other teaching of Scripture would be affected by it.[53] Darby's notes on John 14:12 say:

> I have spent or delayed several days waiting as to light on this verse, to know the Lord's mind on it . . . What I desire is to know His will, His mind in the matter; nothing else. Would to God I could do all miracles, were it His glory and will. Rather would I have Him glorified than all the miracles in the world.[54]

Elsewhere Darby wrote:

> I find two ways of reading Scripture: putting through grace my heart and conscience before it, so that it should act on me as subject to it; and studying it to seize it with its bearing, connection and depth. It should be a first thing to be filled; then draw from the stores of communion, and then when real the free action of the Holy Spirit. The Scripture speaks of order and method, as it does of free action of the Holy Spirit.[55]

Darby warned against studying the Word simply for the sake of knowledge and without communion with God:

> I think, indeed, dear brother, that, as you say, you have studied too much, and read the Bible too little. I always find that I have to be on my guard on this point. It is the teaching of God and not the labour of man that makes us enter into the thoughts and the purpose of God in the Bible. We search it without doubt, but the cream is not found through much labour of the mind of man: I do not think that any one will believe that I do not wish that it should be much read, but I do wish that it should be read with God. It seems to me that there is too much *labour* in your way of reading it; but in this, as in all else, man learns himself, and purifies himself. I doubt whether the literal application which you sometimes make is warrantable, and whether the ways and the scope and the purposes of God bend and limit themselves to *human* accuracy, to what man divines as to accuracy. I am perfectly sure that all is *divinely* accurate, but the subject being vast, and seen only in part, to reduce it to human accuracy is, at times, simply to falsify everything. I see two ends of an immense rainbow, I suppose that they never meet. Were I able to see the whole, I should only deem that my parallel line has only destroyed the bow; that not only are the beauty and the unity lost, but that which was in the nature even of the refraction which is necessary to the existence of the phenomenon. The Word of God is the communication of divine things to the understanding (rendered capable by the Spirit) of man; but we know in part, and the whole not being communicated as God knows it, as indeed it could not be, and ought not to be, we often lose it by attempting to put it into a frame.[56]
>
> It is not that there are not deep things in the Word of God, but if we search it with His grace and Spirit it is always plain for us on the top; then we have it from Him. The cream is on the surface, not that we do not search and study, but that when we get it from God it is plain and on the surface. Till then we must wait till He teaches us.[57]

Darby felt his understanding of Scripture growing from day to day:

> I almost fear sometimes that Scripture gets too clear for me sometimes, as a plan or system of God if the parts are not filled up with the fullness of Christ. But it is wonderfully clear, daily more so; yet so as that we know in part. In that we are little and narrow. However, all is true; and we shall find the fullness of it as a whole, and much more when with God.[58]

But Darby, as we all do, from time to time found difficulties in understanding a Scripture portion properly:

> This has not surprized me, ignorant as I am; but I have found these difficulties, one after another, to be but the means of entering more fully into the perfection, the wisdom, and the divine beauty of the revelation of my God. If I still find more of these difficulties, and I do so, I wait upon Him to solve them for me; I do not say, "The meaning is doubtful," but "The meaning is doubtful to me." I do not say, "There is inaccuracy, and I am accurate enough to judge it without divine light," but "I am ignorant, and God will enlighten me in due time."[59]

Darby readily acknowledged any help he received from others to better understand a particular portion of Scripture. He was thankful to Bellett, and to Kelly who wrote:

> It was very touching to observe that one, to whose richly suggestive help so many were indebted, was himself so frank to own any fresh thought of value in another, and to manifest his simple-hearted pleasure, not only in hailing the accession but in adding to the evidence of its truth, as he so well could and did, while pointing out its importance.[60]

Darby remarked, "I often find brethren who have received ideas from the Spirit of God, and I profit by these."[61] However, he could not always go along with the conclusions these brethren drew from the ideas.

> In general, I like better reading what is not according to my own thought, because one always gains (if there is piety, and the foundations are solid) something by reading it. Divine truth is of such vast extent, and is so many-sided, taking up the nature of God, His dispensations, His ways with men, their responsibility, the positive revelations of His counsels, the moral and eternal relations which flow from what He is, and from what other beings are; that on all points the truth may be looked at in many ways, and one fills up the gap left by others. I see this even in the apostles. John speaks of the nature of God; Paul of His counsels; Peter of His ways. All have the same truths; only as one goes on everything becomes increasingly absorbed in Christ; and if even there were mistakes in what the man writes, one eliminates them through grace, and one takes what is given of God, which is not according to one's own way of looking at things. So that it does not trouble me to find in your work ideas different from my own. Besides, if the foundations are well maintained, I like that there should be great breadth amongst brethren, and not a party formed upon certain views, provided also that devotedness and separation from the world, and the truths that lead us to this, be also maintained in all their energy, because the blessing of souls is in question in this.[62]

Of course Darby's attitude toward works containing flagrant error was completely different. He did have to read many works containing error in order to be able to deal with it and refute it. There is a story that a sister once asked Darby what books he read; he replied, "Only bad books, Madam." He wrote, "My books are quite alarming, as if I was regularly settled in the world; however, my life would hardly bear out the charge. But I use them diligently now."[63]

Darby followed a principle in reading books:

> It would require me to set about and grapple definitely with the books you mention, reading them for myself. I could not master the question otherwise. I always need to make a thing my own in my own mind to be able to

> deal with it. When I get hold of the bearing of the principle of the thing in connection with Scripture, I can deal more easily.[64] I do not like reading in fragments anything on which I have to form a judgment; I take the whole.[65]

Neatby said that if Darby was a scholar (and he was) then "he wore none of a scholar's trappings; he might be supreme in his own little world, but his habitual bearing showed no trace of self-consciousness."[66]

Despite his great learning Darby kept a humble mind. Once at a reading meeting a brother expressed a thought supposedly based on a statement from one of Darby's writings. Darby did not begin to defend himself, but said, "Then J. N. D.'s writings are entirely at fault, for it is obvious that this theory is unscriptural, and therefore unsound." As it was, the brother in question had actually misread, misquoted, and even read his own ideas into the book he was apparently quoting from.

Kelly told of a conference he attended in 1845 in London. Darby first rose to speak on the afternoon of the third day, and then only after a friend had referred to his silence. Darby's reason for not speaking was that so many brothers had so much to say. Many had spoken with considerable power and unction. So Darby gave a brief, well-organized summary of the main points of all the speakers and brought in a flood of fresh light from Scripture on the whole theme. Kelly called it a "most impressive discourse."[67]

Controversy

Some have desired to make use of Darby's writings for their own profit spiritually and have found difficulties with the style, but others have been actively and positively against that which came from his pen or mouth.

If Darby was aware of a calling and task he had been given to do, then he was also aware of what he felt to be a subtle evil constantly operating against him and seeking to destroy his work. This may explain the intensity of feeling and expression in his vehement attacks on all who sought to corrupt his view of the truth; for him error was something evil that directly affected the honor of the godhead. Even those who had been close friends for years were not spared if they fell into known and willful error.

Darby's enemies have attributed his reactions to love of controversy, ambition, and jealousy of position among the saints. But this judgment is not quite fair, since for him the important thing was the error, and not the person who had to be dealt with. "When you have to meet opponents, take care that it does not connect itself with anything of feeling as regards the individual" was his advice. Kelly wrote, "They are likely enough to cry out as once against J. N. D. because he did not mince his words when his soul fired up against outrage done to Christ or the truth. He was not at all animated by fleshly enmity or feeling."[68] He often used strong words, for which he was criticized, but remember what Jay E. Adams wrote:

> Don't be terribly impressed when you read a critic attacking someone for his language while avoiding much of what he has said. It is a cunning tactic that many persons employ when they do not know how to escape from a powerful exposé of their error. Rather than admit error, they attack the man who exposed it, often criticizing his language.[69]

After an exchange of letters of a controversial nature, one writer remarked that Darby wrote with a pen in one hand and a thunderbolt in the other.

It was only fundamental error that aroused Darby's deepest grief and indignation; his patience with honest mistakes became proverbial. "I think you will find, and it has been my comfort when I have returned to them, that in all my controversies, France and England, some great fundamental or practical truth has been in question. For disputation I have no taste."[70] Darby did not willingly enter controversy, but said:

> If I have to take my adversaries up, because they still carry on their warfare, and Satan is using them for mischief, I here declare I will not spare them, nor fail, with God's help, to make plain the tenets and doctrines which are at the bottom of all.[71]

Walter Scott wrote:

> Mr. Darby was a keen and able controversialist. His critical acumen in detecting principles where others, perhaps, would have dealt only with details, was truly marvellous. This character of mind led him on all controversial subjects treated of to lose sight of his opponent, and shun personalities, in order to present the subject on hand, in a broad, full, and comprehensive manner. The weakness of an opposed argument was soon apparent, and the truth got more firmly established. The strength of that mind consecrated to the defence and maintenance of Christianity is never more powerfully exhibited than in his "Examination of the Essays and Reviews"[72] and in other works of a similar character.[73]

Darby did not willingly enter controversies, and he had a natural dislike for conflict.[74] Yet in his life-time he had to meet many foes. In the early years of his public ministry he wrote, "I have been a man of contentions rather. God is my witness whether I loved it or not."[75] Toward the end of his public ministry Darby wrote, "I have only to add, dear brother, have patience and grace; a servant of the Lord must not strive. I know by my own experience how difficult it is. Without the most distant thought of an unkind feeling, we are not always gentle to all men."[76] Jay Adams said:

> In some circles, the fear of controversy is so great that preachers, and congregations following after them, will settle for peace at any cost—even at the cost of the truth, God's truth. The idea is that peace is all important. Peace is a biblical ideal (Rom. 12:18 makes that clear: "If possible, so far as it depends on you, be at peace with everybody"), but so is purity. The peace of the Church may never be bought at the cost of the purity of the Church. That price is too dear. But why do we think that we can get along in this world or for that matter, even in the Church, without conflict and controversy? Jesus didn't. Paul didn't. None of the preachers of the apostolic age who faithfully served their Lord

> were spared controversy. Who are we to escape controversy when they did not? The story of the advance of the Church across the Mediterranean world from Jerusalem to Rome is a story of controversy. When the gospel is preached boldly, there will be controversy. Most of the Epistles themselves were called forth to counter error of doctrines and sinfulness of life. In them there is controversy. The life of Paul is a life of controversy. Tradition tells us that every apostle, except John, who was exiled for his faith, died a violent death.[77]

One of the greatest Christian apologists of the twentieth century, C. S. Lewis, said, "A man can't be always defending the truth; there must be a time to feed on it."[78] Darby knew this sort of time well. Neatby said it was a natural thing, a delight for Darby to turn aside, either from the heat of controversy, or the involved study of unfulfilled prophecy, to the simple beauties of Philippians or the perennial calm of the writings of John.[79] The inner spiritual life in communion with God is far more important than all outward activity. "One great thing we have to seek is that communion with Christ be as strong as all the doctrines we hold or teach. Without that the doctrine itself will have no force: besides, we ourselves shall not be with God in it, and, after all, that is all."[80] "If I get knowledge merely to communicate it, I shall be as dry as a mill-stone. When we enjoy Him for His own sake it flows forth to others."[81]

Though Darby was very active (and activity has its time and place; it is not to be neglected) and often with other people, he would much rather have been alone with God. He found that incessant intercourse with men distracted him from communion with God.[82]

> In whatever weakness, I may almost say labouring night and day, with almost all round, either opposing, or expecting to be sustained and fed, and one's judgment exercised at every step. So that I assure you, with the danger of being dragged into the world one is working in (which is more than you suppose), or the loss of communion, which success with men is always apt to produce—while I have found my God gracious—the consciousness and enjoyment of communion with

those who are within the reclaimed country is not only pleasant, but profitable, as keeping before one's mind what one is labouring for.[83] If I serve the saints I am content.[84]

From 1858, Lonsdale Square was Darby's London home when he was not traveling. Cuendet visited it in 1888, six years after Darby's death, and wrote:

> I did not allow myself to be robbed letting myself be enchanted, in a serious and moving way, by the beauty of this honourable place, situated in a park, and to lift my eyes up to the high windows of the grey house where Darby spent the last 24 years of his life.[85]

Yet Darby wrote:

> I am, as few think, a pilgrim and a stranger upon earth. I see all kinds of evil in me, great laziness and sloth among the number. I have no home—though countless mercies; on earth my home, for the home belongs to the heart, is the place of His will; for the rest, it will really be in heaven; and Montpellier, Düsseldorf, or New Zealand—what is the difference?
>
> O Thou by long experience tried,
> Near Whom no grief can long abide;
> Where'er I roam my home I see,
> Secure of finding all in Thee.[86]

But Darby could also call his house in London his "den."[87] Writing from Germany in 1878 he said, "I shall feel happy when I turn my face towards London again. Not that I like the smoky city in itself, but it is my place of solitary labour, and, when my heart is able, of looking to the Lord.[88] Beautiful and peaceful Lonsdale Square was where he made the studious preparations for his three Bible translations, where he wrote his "Dialogues"[89] and most of his later works. He remarked, "I enjoy living thus among my books." Writing from his home in London in 1877 Darby said:

> I have not been sorry to be a little quiet here, working

> still as usual; but when I get there, it is more what is called for the priests a retreat. My own soul wants sometimes to be alone, and I always find myself more at the resources of grace when alone here: I may be very happy working elsewhere, and blessed, and very glad, as I am, to see the beloved brethren, but I find I am more in the sanctuary. I do not know that it ought to be so, but I am thankful that at least here it is so. We should find Him a sanctuary everywhere. But out, here and there, we are more in public (en scene), and I am glad to shrink back to be alone with Him, and more in His company; my work even is more directly with souls, does not distract, but the contrary. We may always be called out again to serve.[90]

At the age of eighty-one, several months before he passed away, Darby wrote:

> Do not reckon yourself lonely: it is a good thing to be alone with God. I have always been alone; but I bless God for it. Not that communion of saints is not happy and a blessing: Paul thanked God and took courage, but it is alone with Him that we get stuff, and there only; where else should we?[91]

Preaching

Darby's writings were, and are, difficult for many to understand. So was his handwriting, judging from his remark, "I have Revelation ready too, if the printer could print from my writing."[92] Yet his oral ministry was apparently quite the contrary.

A story is told about a brother who was invited to hear Darby preach. He had heard of this great man and was very interested in seeing him. The brother went to the address given him, but the place was not at all what he expected and he was perplexed. Darby was preaching in the poorer part of town in a simple and unpretentious building. The brother entered the building and had to descend several flights of stairs to reach the room where the meeting was being held.

John Nelson Darby, approximately 1878
(Neatby's A History of the Plymouth Brethren, *second edition, Hodder & Stoughton)*

Below: Lonsdale Square, London
(The author)
Right: Entrance to 3 Lonsdale Square
(Central Library, Islington)

"Down, down, down I went," he said, "but once I was there and heard the man speak I was lifted up to heaven."

H. C. Voorhoeve wrote:

> Not his own honour did he seek or aim for, but simply and alone the honour of Christ and the blessing of the Church of God. Combined with his great learning and deep knowledge of the Scriptures was his lowliness and simplicity, so that all came to him and could understand him, especially when he sought in an unequalled way to place the consciences [of others] in the presence of God, and to cause souls to enjoy the glory and work of Christ. I was often a witness of the deep impression his words made. At times it was as if a holy trembling shook the gathering, at times as if new life was communicated to the listeners hanging on his words. Constantly Christ—His glory, His love, His work—was in the forefront; and he never lost himself in making show for the sake of effect, or in nice and elegant speech. Simple and unaffected, earnest and heartfelt, interwoven with the true spirit of the Gospel, his addresses were the means of conversion and deliverance for thousands.[93]

Darby attended a conference in Vevey in 1871 and an outside observer gave his impression in the following words:

> He [Darby] proves, explains and answers questions the whole day and in the evening he can hold a 1½ hour (unprepared) lecture without showing signs of tiring. His manner reminds one of the speakers in the British Parliament, his style is more like a conversation. Although he speaks French with ease it is without any adornment; it is a naked, simple, confidential speech with great authority. He repeats himself often, as do the barristers in their counsel's speeches, but his repetitions, which generally deal with the important parts of Christianity, are like the blows of a hammer on the head of a nail. His expression is that of a man who is fully convinced, enthusiastic for the truth and in whose soul the heavenly glories are reflected. The unseen

> world is not *a* truth, but *the great* truth for him; he has seen them with his heart and spirit.[94]

Darby preached from the authorized version. He felt he never preached well on a subject until he had done it forty times.[95] He did not display his knowledge of Greek and Hebrew. This caused many people who had heard of his learning to wonder, but Darby had good reasons:

> I would suggest to distrust those who talk much about Greek *to those who do not understand it.* It is easy thus to impose on people. It is useful to know Greek, no doubt, in studying the New Testament, because it was written in Greek; and it is perfectly fair to refer to it with those who, knowing Greek, can judge of what is said; but it is very suspicious when much quoted to those who do not; for can they judge about it? Without pretending to be very learned, I know Greek, and I have studied the Greek Testament. The Spirit of God will guide more surely a plain man, if he be humble, in fundamental truths, than a little Greek will those who trust in it.[96]

When it came to public speaking Darby was anything but self-confident. Once when asked to preach in the open air, he declined and begged a younger brother to do so, saying, "I shrink from that line of work being afraid of sticking in the middle, from not knowing what to say."

Kelly once preached at a conference Darby was attending and for months afterwards Darby kept telling people, "Ah, I wish I could appeal to the people in the gospel as Kelly does!"[97]

It appears that Darby's shyness in public speaking in the open air developed later on in his ministry. Darby felt his lack of courage to be his thorn in the flesh to humble him and teach him that strength and ability to work come only from the Lord.

> No doubt we have to judge our want of courage. For my part, it is my greatest test, the want of aggressive courage, and the way in which I shrink back before the coarseness of the world. But there is the look towards God who has pity for us.[98]
>
> It was a dreadful cross to me to address myself to a

> stranger, and still more in public, so to speak. There was often legality; that is, conscience not grace drove me. But I found if I was near Christ in my soul, I found many opportunities and open doors, that I did not find when I was not. And this made my conscience work when I had difficulties. On the other hand, when conscious that I was with Christ and Christ with me, and at home in the service of His love, I felt more free to use opportunities (the true sense of redeeming the time in Eph. 5), freer and happier, at liberty so to use them, and not forced by conscience to do it when it was only bringing out evil—I do not quite say casting pearls before the swine, but at any rate, approaching it, which we are directed not to do. But I am too great a coward to be satisfied with myself in the matter, and have, alas, often had to act from conscience, yet felt happier afterwards; at least, confessing Christ, if not seeking souls in love.[99]

But Darby could also write to a brother:

> If you feel that the Lord has entrusted you with His Word, has put it into your heart, not only for yourself, but for others (Gal. 1:15-16), then fear nothing: faith tested is faith strengthened; it is to have learnt your weakness, but to have learnt the faithfulness of God, His tender care even in sending difficulties, that we may be there with Him.[100]

Darby was speaking from experience.

Conclusion

Darby summed up the sphere of his labors as follows: "I felt God, out of England, gave me the French speaking countries as a field of labour, perhaps America also, and in fact this did not fail. In His constant goodness He added part of Germany."[101]

During his travels Darby received public recognition, sometimes in unusual ways. Robert Louis Stevenson came up against Darby's influence while traveling in France and wrote about making the acquaintance of a helpful "Plymouth Brother" in his book *Travels with a Donkey in the Cevennes.* When taken ill in the United States in 1867, Darby even received flowers from the garden of Henry Wadsworth Longfellow.[102]

But fame, and a name in the world, meant nothing to Darby. As an old man of seventy-three he wrote:

> It is a joy to me now to see others raised up to continue the work, and I hope better than I, for that can well be, though I by no means doubt of a special work in these last days. But the workman is another thing. I have laboured, God knows; but I have been more of a hewer of wood and drawer of water for those who have more courage. But we are what God gives us and permits us to be.[103]

We close our look at Darby's ministry, written and oral, with quotes that serve as a sort of summary.

In 1860 he wrote, "If I were able to serve Him—as I am sure He is precious in service—it would be famous. Outwardly in quantity I could hardly do more; what I want is a deeper well of Christ in my own soul to draw from for the blessing of others."[104]

In 1869 Darby wrote in a letter:

> I have been profoundly moved in seeing, on reading over old tracts, all the principles on which the fate of the world and the Church now turns, brought out from 30 to 39 years ago! God was in it in a way I did not know, though I felt it personally to be God's truth. But what a solemn thing! It has made me feel the responsibility of bringing it all out systematically, before the professing Church.[105]

In 1879 he wrote, "What set me free in 1827 is still the theme on which my soul dwells, with, I trust, much deeper sense of its importance—something much nearer to me, but the same truths. And blessed truths they are; and the hope, what a hope!"[106]

In 1881 Darby wrote:

> All I have taught has come back to me as divine truth from God, and that is a great comfort. I have nothing to regret but my own poor walk, though I had no *object* but Christ. But of *Jacob and Israel* it shall be said, according to this time—the end of the wilderness—"What hath *God* wrought."[107] It was a comfort to me that all I had taught and laboured in was of God and from God. It was not on this a question of the workman at all, but of the truth: I had long known, and gladly, that I was nothing.[108]

The Scriptures tell us that "we are his workmanship, created in Christ Jesus unto good works, which God hath before ordained that we should walk in them" (Ephesians 2:10, KJV). And the Lord Himself said, "I have chosen you, and ordained you, that ye should go and bring forth fruit, and that your fruit should remain" (John 15:16, KJV).

The Road

It is not with uncertain step
That we tread our homeless way;
A well-known Voice has called us up
To everlasting day.

The voice of Him who, whilom, trod
Alone the trackless way,
(And marked the road that leads to God),
Where we once, as lost, did stray;

Nor leaves us now alone to trace
Our path across the waste,
But leads us still with living grace
To the home to which we haste.

May abide His will, for the longer road
Where patience and faith are tried,
And count on a love which bears each load,
And our hearts from trial may hide.

He will still be there, be it long or brief,
Our strength in every need;
Himself our joy, our sure relief,
Till from care in His presence we're freed.[109]

J. N. Darby

6
A Word in Closing

Use a sharp knife with yourself, say little,
serve all, pass on.
This is true greatness, to serve unnoticed
and work unseen.
J. N. Darby

Let us look at a letter written by Darby to a brother who had translated and published one of his works. In the preface the brother had remarked that Darby was one of the most advanced in the Christian career, and an eminent servant of Christ. Darby's reaction to the remark is in the letter:

> My dear friend and brother in Jesus Christ: It gives me much pleasure to see your translation of ______. I reserve the pleasure of reading it, or rather of having it read to me, for moments in which the Lord says to us, as He did to the Apostles, "Come ye yourselves apart and rest a while." But I cannot refrain from telling you, my dear friend, that the pleasure that the appearance of your work gave me has been somewhat abated by the too favourable opinion which you have expressed in your preface respecting me. Before I had read a word in your translation, I made a present of a copy to a very

dear and sincere friend of mine, who brought me word that you had spoken in praise of my piety in your preface. The passage produced the same effect on my friend that it did on me, when I afterwards saw it. I hope, therefore, that you will not take in ill-part what I am about to say to you on the subject, and which is the fruit of a tolerably long experience.

Pride is the greatest of all evils that beset us, and of all our enemies it is that which dies the slowest and hardest: even the children of the world are able to discern this. Madame De Stael said, on her death-bed, "Do you know what is the last to die in man? It is self-love." God hates pride above all things, because it gives to man the place that belongs to Him who is above, exalted over all. Pride intercepts communion with God, and draws down His chastisement, for "God resists the proud." He will destroy the name of the proud, and we are told that there is a day appointed when "the loftiness of man shall be bowed down, and the haughtiness of men shall be made low." I am sure, then, my dear friend, that one cannot do another greater injury than by praising him and feeding his pride. "He that flattereth his neighbour spreadeth a snare for his feet," and "A flattering mouth worketh ruin." Be assured, moreover, that we are too short-sighted to be able to judge of the degree of our brother's piety; we are not able to judge it aright without the balance of the sanctuary, and that is in the hand of Him who searches the heart. Judge nothing, therefore before the time, until the Lord come, and make manifest the counsels of the heart, and render to every man his praise. Till then let us not judge of our brethren, whether for good or evil, but with becoming moderation, and remember that the surest and best judgment is what we form of ourselves when we esteem others better than ourselves.

If I were to ask you how you know that I am one of the most advanced in the Christian career, and an eminent servant of God, you would no doubt be at a loss to reply. You would perhaps cite my published works; but do you know, my dear friend and brother—you who can preach an edifying sermon as well as I can—

that the eyes see further than the feet go? and that unhappily, we are not always, nor in all things, what our sermons are; that "we have this treasure in earthen vessels, that the excellency of the power may be of God, and not of us"? I will not tell you the opinion I have of myself, for in doing so, I shall probably all the while be seeking my own glory; and while seeking my own glory, appear humble, which I am not. I had rather tell you what our Master thinks of me—He that searcheth the heart—and speaks the truth, who is "the Amen, the Faithful Witness" and has often spoken in my inmost soul, and I thank Him for it; but, believe me, He has never told me I am an "eminent Christian and advanced in the ways of godliness." On the contrary, He tells me very plainly that if I knew my own place, I should find it that of the chief of sinners, and least of all saints. His judgment, surely my dear friend, I should take rather than yours.

The most eminent Christian is one of those of whom no one has ever heard speak, some poor labourer, or servant, whose all is Christ, and who does all for *His* eye, and His alone. The first shall be last. Let us be persuaded, my dear friend, to praise the Lord alone. He only is worthy of being praised, revered, and adored. His goodness is never sufficiently celebrated. The song of the blessed—Rev. 5—praises none but Him who redeemed them with His blood. It contains not one word of praise for any of their own number—not a word that classes them into eminent, or not eminent—all distinctions are lost in the common title, the *redeemed,* which is the happiness and glory of the whole body. Let us strive to bring our hearts into unison with that song in which we all hope that our feeble voices will one day mingle. This will be our happiness, even here below, and contribute to God's glory, which is wronged by the praise that Christians too often bestow on each other. We cannot have two mouths—one for God's praise, and one for man's. May we, then, do now what the seraphim do above, who with two wings cover their faces, as a token of their confusion before the holy presence of the Lord; with two cover their feet, as if to

> hide their steps from themselves; and with the remaining two fly to execute their Lord's will, while they cry, "Holy, holy, holy is the Lord of Hosts; the whole earth is full of His glory."
>
> Excuse these few lines of Christian exhortation, which I am sure will, sooner or later, become useful to you, by becoming part of your own experience. Remember me in your prayers, as I pray that the blessing of the Lord may rest upon you and your labors. If ever you print another edition—as I hope you will—strike out, if you please, the two passages to which I have drawn your attention; and call me simply "a brother, and minister in the Lord." This is honour enough, and needs no addition.

Our story comes to a close with one more quotation. Looking back on Darby's life, William Kelly said:

> This then is my conclusion, that a saint more true to Christ's Name and Word I never knew or heard of. He used to say that three classes, from their antecedents, are apt to make bad brothers; clergymen, lawyers, and officers. He himself was a brilliant exception, though a lawyer first and a clergyman afterward. A great man naturally, and a diligent student as if he were not highly original, he was a really good man, which is much better. So, for good reason, I believed before I saw him; so taken all in all I found him, in peace and in war; and so, in the face of passing circumstances, I am assured he was to the end. Do I go too far if I add, may we be his imitators, even as he also was of Christ?

Expectation

Lord Jesus, source of every grace,
Glorious in light divine,
Soon shall we see Thee face to face,
And in that glory shine;

Be ever with Thee, hear Thy voice,
Unhindered then shall taste
The love which doth our hearts rejoice,
Though absent in this waste.

In peaceful wonder we adore
The thoughts of Love divine,
Which in that world for evermore
Our lot with Thine entwine![1]

J. N. Darby

Appendix A

Darby Family Tree

Descent from Edmund Darby of Gaddesby, near Melton Mowbray, Leicestershire. Descent traced from Edmund's son to brother of John Nelson through the heir.

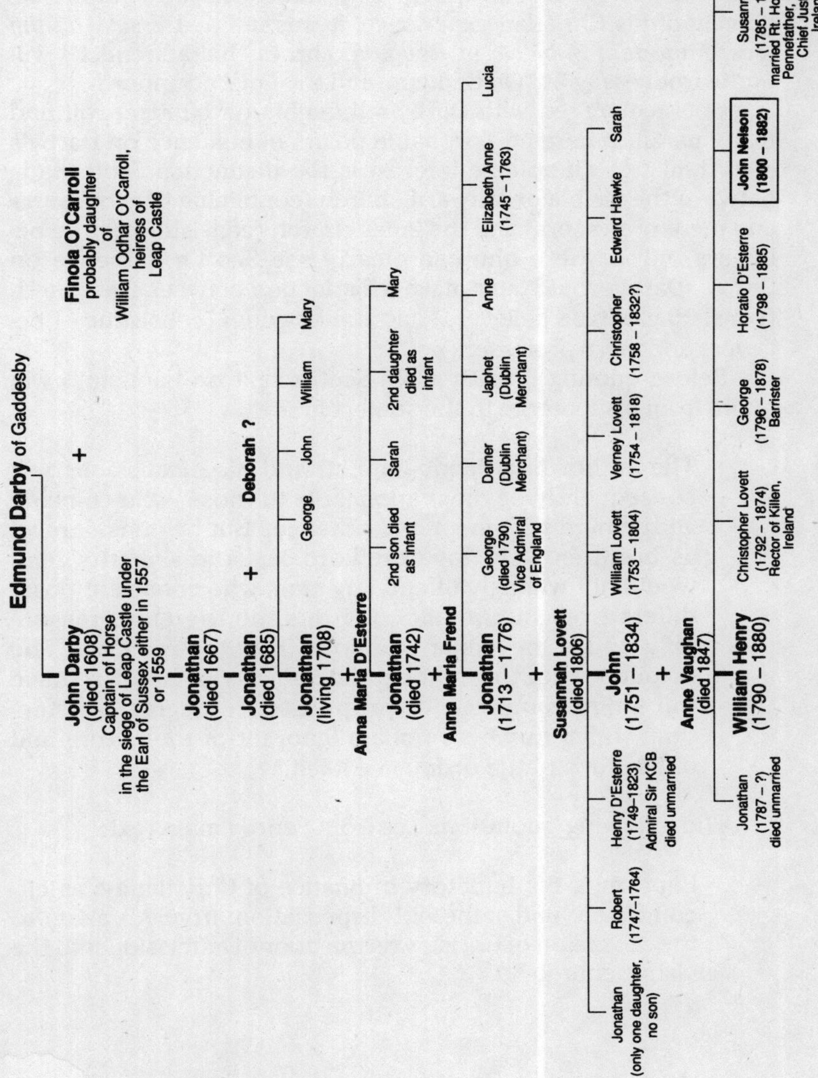

Appendix B

Baptism

In the course of this biography I quoted several times from a work by Thomas Scott that greatly influenced Darby in the beginning of his Christian experience. It was entitled *Essays on the Most Important Subjects in Religion*, and in this appendix I will quote from essay 24 "On Baptism, and the Lord's Supper."

One acquainted with Darby's thoughts on baptism will find many parallels here and probable points of influence on Darby's own thinking. Of notable interest is the distinction Scott made between the visible or outward church (containing true believers and mere professors) and the inner church (consisting of true believers only). Here one can clearly see Scott's influence on Darby. Darby would later make a distinction between the church (consisting of true believers) and the kingdom (consisting of believers and mere professors).

Before quoting directly from Scott's text on baptism, I will quote from his footnote to the subject first:

> The author is a Paedo-baptist; and his discussions will consequently be most applicable to those, who coincide with him in sentiment and practice. But he considers all as brethren who "love the Lord Jesus in sincerity" and would not willingly offend any man, who conscientiously differs from him in such matters; he therefore reasonably hopes for similar candour from his readers. The disputes about the *mode* and *subjects* of Baptism have too long occupied a disproportionate degree of attention; whilst numbers remain ignorant of the nature and obligations of the ordinance itself.[1]

The following quotations are from Scott's main text:

> Baptism is the initiatory ordinance of Christianity; as circumcision, under the old dispensation, from Abraham to the ascension of Christ, was the door of admission into the visible church.[2]

The appointment of this emblem, in the initiatory ordinance of Christianity, emphatically testifies the doctrine of original sin and the necessity of regeneration: for it declares every man, as "born of the flesh," to be so polluted, that unless he be washed with purifying water, he cannot be received even into the outward church of God; and unless he be inwardly cleansed by the Holy Spirit, he cannot be a member of the true church.[3]

When the apostles went forth "to teach," or disciple "all nations," to baptize them in this name, and afterwards to teach them more fully all things which Christ had commanded, that they might observe them; the converts, whether made from among the Jews or gentiles, were baptized on an intelligent profession of repentance and faith. When the Jews made proselytes to their religion, they circumcised the adult males on such a profession, according to the nature of their dispensation; and Paedo-baptists, in similar circumstances, would baptise adults both male and female on a profession of faith in Christ. But we maintain (for reasons which have been repeatedly assigned) that as the Jews also circumcised all the males in the families of the proselytes, who were incapable of personally rejecting the Jewish religion; so the apostles baptised the households of their converts, including the females, and only excluding such, as, being able to answer for themselves, gave evidence, by word or deed, that they did not obey the truth. Nay, we are of opinion that those children, who had one believing parent, though the other continued an unbeliever, were thus admitted, as relatively holy, into the visible church of Christ (Matt. 28:19-20; Acts 16:15,33; Rom. 11:16-25; 1 Cor. 1:16; 7:14).[4]

The adult convert, by receiving baptism, virtually acknowledged, according to the obvious meaning of the ordinance, that he was a sinner by nature and practice, that he repented of his sins, and believed in Christ for the forgiveness of them; that he renounced idolatry, and all other objects or forms of worship, "to serve the one living and true God," in whose name he was baptised; that he cordially believed the truths of the gospel, and relied on the mercy of the Father, on the mediation of the incarnate Son, and on the grace of the Holy Spirit, for complete salvation; and that he sincerely purposed to forsake all his sins, and every confidence, pursuit, interest, or indulgence which interfered with these engagements.[5]

The baptism of the infant offspring, of such converts, was likewise a solemn declaration, that they desired the same blessings for their children, as they had chosen for their own portion: and they thus pledged themselves to the church, "to bring them up in the nurture and admonition of the Lord"; giving them every instruction, and using all means of rendering them wise unto salvation. When they brought the children, which were afterwards born to them, to be baptised; they virtually renewed their former profession and engagements, and declared their persevering purpose of instructing and commanding their households in the fear of God: and as the children grew up, such of them, as profited by these means, would personally accept of the privileges, and enter into the engagements peculiar to Christianity, in the manner which will be shortly considered.[6]

But when a Christian parent is persuaded, notwithstanding all these crimes and abuses, that the baptism of the infant offspring of believers accords with the word of God, and, in compliance with what he judges his duty, presents his children to be baptised; he solemnly ratifies and renews the profession and engagements of his own baptism; he avows his earnest desire, that the covenant made with him may be for the good of his seed also (Jer. 32:38-40; Acts 2:33,39); and he engages to bring them up in the faith and obedience of the gospel, as far as his instructions, discourse, example, and prayers can have influence. As they grow up, he, or other pious relations, may profitably explain to them the nature, meaning, and engagements of baptism; the blessings it signifies; the advantages of being thus early admitted into the visible church, and trained up as her children; and the aggravated guilt of deliberately rejecting the salvation and service of God, from pride and carnal affections; or even of neglecting the means of appropriating these advantages, and complying with those engagements, which their parents, or senior friends, had entered

> into, in their name, and for their benefit. Thus an additional avenue is opened to the consciences of young persons, and an additional restraint imposed on their passions.[7]
>
> The outward sign certainly will not profit those who live and die without "the inward and spiritual grace," even "a death unto sin, and a new birth unto righteousness": and the conduct of multitudes, who act in direct opposition to the most solemn engagements entered into for themselves or others, will render their doom more dreadful at the last day, than that of Jews, Mohammedans, pagans, or avowed infidels [see Luke 12:47].[8]

Darby was very firm as to what he considered to be the teaching of Scripture on baptism. In 1844 he wrote, "I am deeply convinced that a Christian handles evilly if he does not baptize his children."[9] Yet, not all Brethren associated with him shared his views. For example, William Kelly could not agree and favored so-called "believer's baptism." These two different views existed side by side within the Brethren group and this difference was the cause of some difficulties, particularly toward the end of Darby's life.

Though Darby held strong views on baptism he favored the stance taken by the apostle Paul: "Christ sent me not to baptize, but to preach the gospel" (1 Corinthians 1:17, KJV). In a letter to a brother in 1852 he wrote:

> I will write to you more at length, beloved brother, what I think on the baptism of infants, but I care much more for the peace of the church than for any opinion about that. I have never tried to persuade anybody. I believe that everyone must act according to his own conscience.[10]

Appendix C

Darby's Marginal Notes

Next to 2 Timothy 3
in His Greek New Testament

I will here mention one thing about myself as an object of grace. I had once had my soul brought I knew not where—so deep as no . . . tongue, I suppose, could tell; others may have felt it, I know it not—hardly before I began to preach repentance. (I had, previously, a good while given myself to God, having myself been brought to deep repentance and self-sacrifice.) After that I went on, learning the way of salvation, or my mind opening upon its reality, with occasional trials of unbelief, some of them painful, but none such as the one I mentioned.

I think Scott's essays gave a strong determination to my thought at one time, while my mind was working upon it. I had always recognized the truths, but I am speaking of their power, for my mind had passed, after its own repentance, under the dark cloud of the popish system (i.e., to look for the powers of Christ's agency in the visible authority of the Church), though God was with me through it all. And I used to hold up Christ to my brother as availing against the claim of men on their points, yet it prevailed so far as to prevent my mind from finding comfort in the truths I honestly urged on him, which I had found in what poor reading of Scripture I had.

And yet God was with me all the while, and I was in my . . . affections framed on the doctrines of grace, and abhorred the world, and sought non-conformity to it. But I had not, though [I] loved Christ, I have no doubt sincerely and growingly since June or July 1820, or 21, I forget which. I had not certain peace, though I trusted in Him for salvation, and, since the deep trial I mentioned, had (first indeed, in preaching, I began with holiness, but soon felt it was not the way) avowed salvation only by Christ, and stated the truth of Scripture as I have no doubt was in it, and, I believe, not without profit to souls.

It was only latterly at Calary I began generally to proclaim love. Then I was totally stopped in the work, and suffered long confinement. After I had been confined something more than three months, I was tried, with indeed very different support from what I had before through the grace I had received, and which will explain how I was led into this long statement. It issued in assurance, in love, as I trust to be perfected ere long, so as either by my life or death to glorify God.

It took occasion from a great trial of judgment on a matter in which, while my weakness was very apparent, God's hand secured very remarkably. So it brought my soul by much and various exercise, by night and day, to this point: Would I rest the faith of my soul as a living man on the Word of God? Grace determined me to do so. The trial passed away in various exercises of conscience, searching whether there was anything of offense in it towards God or towards man, with some intervals of thankfulness for evidences of love in circumstances brought before me, till it all began to give way before the apprehension of His love in Christ, in a way I could not describe, settling into steadier and calmer assurance of love by a progress which I cannot state, but of which I felt the work from day to day.

But the Scriptures have coincidently approved themselves to be the perfect manifestation of God in Christ, and though I used them in everything before, it is only since then that they supplied themselves to me on every side as altogether Divine and all-sufficient. I would remark that humiliation was the method in which God wrought with my soul from the beginning to reveal His love, and I could not doubt, by the issue of peace, Whose hand had been there; and in very minute circumstances—as man would judge—Providence shewed itself indeed.

The whole trial arose from a paper of directions being left out of a parcel by mistake, while the paper it referred to was sent to the printer, and laid there, he not knowing what to do with it or whose it was, till I found it out afterwards by the carelessness of a messenger to the post, and, a third time, by his delay two letters were arrested in the [?] and each of them had their part in the passages of the trial.

I have been led to mention these things merely as shewing God's hand. Another passage of the trial, as I recollect [it], was: Would I endure all things for the elect's sake? In this, grace also determined me. I had a further trial in which some persons related to me—who I believe were under grace, but a cloud was over the exercises of it in them, doubtless under God's gracious wisdom—were proposed to me: Suppose them mere reprobates, would you give them up? And they were presented to my mind as such. In this I submitted to God—since this, I preached the gospel I believe in its simple power for a short time at Calary, but that was not, as I believe, the work the Lord had appointed me; I wait now only for His permission, trusting He is preparing me for it—that is, I preached not merely that there was no other salvation than Christ, but also that Christ was the power of Divine love unto salvation, and the difference was felt.

Indeed, this made all instruction different. Before, it dealt more exclusively with principles, now more fully with souls, and though it had not been without, to me, most blessed testimony before, yet, together with a great deal of practical, weekly dealing with their souls, I thought the Word was ploughing much deeper than heretofore. The day will declare it indeed, though the result of weakness in me. I am not sure that in Divine wisdom it was not suitable. I am quite sure that, in all, I am debtor to Divine grace, and have perfect need of the Divine mercy.

The previous account, though strictly accurate, is very imperfect. I did not feel led to speak of more; it is possible I may elsewhere. [I] may rather speak nothing but of the Lord, as I trust in measure I have for some time, for He is the rock; His work is perfect.

Appendix D

Calary

Calary is described in *A Topographical Dictionary of Ireland* (1837, vol. 1, 242) as "containing 2533 inhabitants . . . situated in the rugged table lands which extend southward from the great Sugar Loaf mountain to the vicinity of Roundwood; and lies embosomed between the lower range hills among which the Downs hill claims pre-eminence, and the more elevated chain of heights above which the lofty Djouce rises in towering grandeur. It comprehends a dreary tract of poor elevated land, bog, and barren mountain, extending on the east to the glen of the Downs, and on the west to Luggelaw, comprising more than 9720 statute acres of productive land, with a large tract of unprofitable waste. The Sugar Loaf mountain rises to the height of 2000 feet above the level of the sea."

Appendix E

Lost Sheep

It is difficult to place the following account by Darby. The title in one edition is "An Incident in the Early Life of J. N. Darby." As it deals with Kerry and not Calary, it probably took place *after* Darby's time there. Yet he seemed to be introducing himself to the boy as a priest. The general "spiritual" impression of the story suggests the time after Darby attained inner peace and full assurance of salvation.

At the close of a cold February day Darby was disturbed at his work by a knock on the door. A poor man had come to see him, one whom he did not know and had not seen before. The man asked pardon for coming at such a late hour, but explained he had a son who was ill. The father feared his son was dying and requested that Darby come and see the boy. Darby rose and followed the man in willing response to his request. Darby wrote:

> After upwards of an hour's toilsome walking (for the roads which in some places led over steep hills were in others scarcely passable on account of the heavy marshes), on entering the little cottage I looked round me and at first found no sign of any inhabitant, except an old woman who sat crouching over the embers of a peat fire. She rose as I entered, and with the natural courtesy of the Irish poor offered me the low chair or rather stool on which she had been seated.
>
> I thanked her, and passing on to the object of my visit discovered in one corner of the hut a heap of straw on which lay the poor sufferer. Some scanty covering, probably his own wearing apparel, had been thrown over him, but as to bed or bed clothes there was none discernible in this humble dwelling.
>
> I approached, and saw a young lad about seventeen or eighteen years of age evidently in a state of extreme suffering and exhaustion, and it was to be feared in the last stage of consumption. His eyes were closed, but he opened them on my approach and stared at me with a kind of wild wonder, like a frightened animal.

I told him as quietly as possible who I was, and for what purpose I had come, and put a few of the simplest questions to him respecting his hope of salvation. He answered nothing, he appeared totally unconscious of my meaning. On pressing him further, and speaking to him kindly and affectionately, he looked up, and I ascertained from the few words he uttered that he had heard something of a God and future judgment, but he had never been taught to read. The Holy Scriptures were a sealed book to him, and he was consequently altogether ignorant of the way of salvation as revealed to us in the gospel. His mind on this subject was truly an utter blank.

I was struck with dismay and almost with despair. Here was a fellow creature whose immortal soul, apparently on the verge of eternity, must be saved or lost for ever; and he lay before me now, the hand of death close upon him; not a moment was to be lost and what was I to do? What way was I to take to begin to teach him, as it were at the eleventh hour, the first rudiments of Christianity?

I had scarcely ever before felt such a sinking within me. I could do nothing, that I knew full well, but on the other hand God could do all; I therefore raised up my heart and besought my heavenly Father for Christ's sake to direct me in this most difficult and trying position, and to open to me by His Spirit of wisdom a way to set forth the glad tidings of salvation so as to be understood by this poor benighted wanderer. I was silent for a few moments whilst engaged in inward prayer and gazing with deep anxiety on the melancholy object before me. It struck me that I ought to try to discover how far his intelligence in other things extended, and whether there might not be reasonable hope of his understanding me when I should commence to open to him (as I was bound to do) the gospel message of salvation. I looked down upon him with an eye of pity, which I most sincerely felt, and I thought he observed that compassionate look, for he softened towards me as I said: "My poor boy, you are very ill, I fear you suffer a great deal!"

"Yes, I have a bad cold; the cough takes away my breath and hurts me greatly."

"Have you had this cough long?" I asked.

"Oh, yes, a long time; near a year now."

"And how did you catch it? A Kerry boy, I should have

thought, would have been reared hardily and accustomed to this sharp air!"

"Ah," he answered, "and so I was until that terrible night—it was about this time last year when one of the sheep went astray. My father keeps a few sheep upon the mountains and this is the way we live. When he reckoned them that night there was one wanting, and he sent me to look for it."

"No doubt," I replied, "you felt the change from the warmth of the peat fire in this close little hut, to the cold mountain blast."

"Oh! that I did; there was snow upon the ground, and the wind pierced me through; but I did not mind it much, as I was so anxious to find father's sheep."

"And did you find it?" I asked, with increased interest.

"Oh, yes, I had a long, weary way to go, but I never stopped until I found it."

"And how did you get it home? You had trouble enough with that too, I daresay. Was it willing to follow back?"

"Well, I did not like to trust it, and besides, it was dead beat and tired, so I laid it on my shoulders and carried it home that way."

"And were they not all at home rejoiced to see you when you returned with the sheep?"

"Sure enough, and that they were," he replied. "Father and mother, and the people round that heard of our loss, all came in the next morning to ask about the sheep, for the neighbours in these matters are mighty kind to each other. Sorry they were, too, to hear that I was kept out the whole dark night; it was morning before I got home, and the end of it was I caught this cold. Mother says I will never be better now, God knows best; anyways, I did my best to save the sheep."

Wonderful! I thought, here is the whole gospel history. The sheep is lost, the father sends his son to seek for and recover it. The son goes willingly, suffers all without complaining, and in the end sacrifices his life to find the sheep, and when recovered he carries it home on his shoulders to the flock, and rejoices with his friends and neighbours, over the sheep which was lost, but is found again. My prayer was answered, my way was made plain, and by the grace of God I availed myself of this happy opening.

I explained to this poor dying boy the plan of salvation, making use of his own simple and affecting story. I read to him the few verses in Luke 15, where the care of the shepherd for the strayed sheep is so beautifully expressed, and he at once perceived the likeness, and followed me with deep interest while I explained to him the full meaning of the parable.

The Lord mercifully opened not only his understanding, but his heart also, to receive the things spoken. He himself was the lost sheep, Jesus Christ the good Shepherd, who was sent by the Father to seek for him, and who left all the joys of that Father's heavenly glory to come down to earth and search for him and other lost ones like himself; and as the poor boy had borne without murmuring the freezing snowstorm and the piercing wind, so has the blessed Saviour endured the fierce contradictions of sinners against Himself, and the bitter scorn and insults heaped upon Him, without opening His mouth to utter one word of complaint, and at last laid down His precious life, that we might be rescued from destruction and brought safe to our everlasting home. Neither will He trust His beloved ones, when rescued, to tread the perilous path alone, but bears them on His shoulders rejoicing to the heavenly fold.

My poor sick lad seemed to drink it all in. He received it all; he understood it all. I never saw a clearer proof of the power of the divine Spirit to apply the word of God.

He survived our first meeting but a few days. I had no time to read or expound to him any other portion of the Scripture. At times we could hear nothing but stifling, rending cough; at times he slumbered heavily for a little, but whenever he was able to think and listen, these verses in Luke 15 satisfied and cheered him. He accepted Christ as his Saviour, he earnestly prayed to be carried home like the lost sheep in the heavenly Shepherd's arms. He died humbly, peacefully, almost exulting, with the name of Jesus, my Saviour and my Shepherd, the last upon his lips.

"The Son of man is come to seek and to save that which was lost" (Luke 19:10).

Appendix F

Petition

Addressed to the House of Commons

To the Commons of the United Kingdom of Great Britain and Ireland, in Parliament assembled; the Petition of the Archbishop of Dublin and Bishop of Glandelagh, and of the said Clergy of the said dioceses,

Humbly Sheweth,

That your Petitioners, influenced by a love of peace, and by a desire of avoiding even the appearance of political discussion, have been hitherto withheld from approaching your Honorable House, and appealing to it for protection against the hostility and calumny with which they and their religion have been, for a length of time, systematically assailed, under the pretence of seeking civil and religious liberty, but with the real design of obtaining powers subversive of both, and with the hope of overturning the Established Religion, by the defamation of its Clergy, and the misrepresentation of their faith.

Whilst any doubt could remain, that such designs and such hopes existed, your Petitioners were desirous, though exposed to daily vexations, and insults, and injuries, to submit in silence, and to endeavour by the quiet discharge of their proper duties, to soften the violence of their enemies, although they had but too great reason to be convinced that these their enemies were such, from being enemies to their Church.

But now, that all disguise as to the true design entertained to their prejudice, has been entirely thrown aside; now that direct hostility against the Protestant faith of the Reformed Church, established in England and Ireland, has been openly and vauntingly avowed; now that the Reformation has been publicly pronounced a curse, and the Establishment an usurpation;—when the hatred which Popery has always evinced against Protestantism has displayed itself with increased and acrimonious activity, and even the spirit of persecution has anticipated the power of enforcing its dictates; when the whole body of those in this part of the United Kingdom who profess themselves the spiritual subjects of the See of Rome, have, the better to effect the objects of that See, and to establish its despotism over conscience, enlisted themselves unqualifiedly in the service of a Priesthood, all whose principles are at direct variance with those of the Protestant faith, and who are triumphantly announced, as eager to confederate themselves with a foreign enemy, against the institutions and the very existence of the Realm, both in Church and State.

Your Petitioners think, that they would be unworthy of the station to which they have been appointed as guardians of the Protestant religion, did they not earnestly implore your Honorable House to protect that religion, against the machinations of its inveterate adversaries, and to continue to its professors all those privileges and securities, which under Divine Providence, have hitherto proved its safeguard against the schemes and operations of enemies, who boast themselves unchanged and unchangeable, and who, at least, in their desire for its extinction, but too manifestly prove that they are so.[1]

Appendix G

Edward Pennefather

The following remarks on Edward Pennefather are taken from *The Irish Nation: Its History and Its Biography.*[1]

> In Court, his language and appearance bespeak the scholar and the gentleman. His forehead is smooth and open, yet somewhat over anxious; his expressive and intelligent countenance indicates deep meditation, but seems to say that all is peace within; his manner is artless and candid, his deportment erect and independent. When he commences his address, your attention is at once arrested; you perceive at a glance that he is master of his subject, and feels himself to be so; with perfect self-possession, he details the numerous and complicated facts of a chancery case—unfolds with ease and applies with judgment arguments the most intricate, and principles the most abstruse, and deduces his inferences, with unrivalled clearness. . . .
>
> During the sitting of the Courts when at the bar, a little after four o'clock in the morning, winter and summer, found him in his study; this enabled him to pass a great portion of the evening with his family, when he heartily joined in whatever engaged their interest. He was blessed with a wife of great talent and cultivation, and no doubt this in no small degree added to the enjoyment of his hours of recreation. His spirits were cheerful and even, and his temper singularly calm. With great dispatch of business, he never appeared hurried; and without being rigid in requiring punctuality from others, he was invariably punctual himself. He was a very good artist, and greatly enjoyed drawing in pencil and water colours. He always travelled with a sketch book, and being fond of reading, especially history and biography, he was never unoccupied. He was, in body as well as in mind, till towards the close of life, very active when free from gout; he was a good rider and a good shot; and in

> the vacations used to appear on horseback in leather breeches and top boots long after they had disappeared except in the hunting field.
>
> He had a family of ten children, to each of whom he was as if he had but one. He ruled by example much more than precept, and the result was the devotion of one and all to him. With his two elder sons (the two others being several years younger) he was on the terms more of a brother than a father; their intercourse was ever of the most unreserved kind. . . .
>
> His charity was very liberal, and equally unostentatious. With all the work he had to do, though often the demands on his time were most urgent, yet he never did any sort of business on Sunday. That day was entirely devoted to the purposes for which it was set apart.

In a letter dated October 8, 1827, Francis Newman wrote his impressions of the Pennefathers to his brother John:[2]

> Mr. P. is astonishingly simple-minded, and circumspect not to have more to do with worldly concerns than absolute duty requires: and he is in everything so indifferent to the world, that I am sure Tacitus would have branded him for *culpable sloth.* But he is very active where he thinks it his duty to act, or where he thinks it is the cause of Christ. . . .
>
> If you knew Mrs. P. it would nearly follow as a sort of corollary that her children all knew and loved divine truth. She is so anxious for that one thing; and has such caution not to press it indiscreetly at the same time. I was rather interested to find that she considers Sunday to be no *direct* obligation.[3] She says that she thinks she sees reason for thinking it conformable to Christ's will to keep it, though it is not commanded; at any rate this is one of the principal means we have of *professing* religion without ostentation; just as the Jews professed by it their belief in the Creator. But she lets her little girls read their books on Natural History etc. on Sunday: and says we are under no bondage. I have been much struck at the clearness with which she discusses questions of conscience, and the direct way in which she brings the first principles of the Christian temper to bear on the

minute actions of daily life. So too the gentle way in which she insinuates her advice to her sons, every word of which *implies* the principle that this world's judgment is nothing. . . .

She strikes me as the most *perfect* character I have ever seen. But perhaps I have seen few *so experienced* Christians for many days together. I never gained before so clear an idea of what was meant by a Christian's being opposed to the spirit of the world. It is not *merely* to avoid the pomps and vanities, or *merely* to judge of actions by opposite rule; but it is to feel that *the time is short,* and to be *looking for* the Lord Jesus from heaven.

Appendix H

Letter to Darby

from His Parishioners[1]

Calary School House
March 28th 1829

Dr. & Rev'd. Mr. Darby,

We the Inhabitants of Calary as a testimony of our love and grateful thanks feel it our duty to pay our tribute of filial affections and heartfelt thanks to your Reverence for your manifest love towards us in the bowels of our Lord and *Saviour* in commending us to *his Grace* and the patient waiting for *him*. Indeed we have I trust with unutterable pleasure heard your most tender affections for us, and we whom it pleased *Providence* to order you once to be the shepherd of us and amongst whom you have first sown the *seed of life* to the comfort of many, do most humbly implore at the throne of *mercy* that where you began to labour in the *vineyard* willing to spend and be spent in the *glorious* cause of establishing *his* Kingdom amongst us, that *he* may in mercy bless us and grant we may behold your face again. It is unnecessary to multiply words as we only intend simply to declare our feelings which we most earnestly request our acceptance, at the same time hoping your Reverence will present our sincere regard may be communicated to that most valuable ornament of *Grace* who made known to us in so plain and distinguished a manner your zeal for our *eternal* happiness and the consolatory admonition delivered to us from the 12 of Romans. We candidly declare that some of us could plainly read the second or great Commandment of the *law* in his countenance and shall now close by praying that our Lord and *Saviour* may bless you, and mark your zeal for *his* cause in Calary in the Book of remembrance above, Malachi 3.

We are . . .

Ellen Fox
Jane Fox
Margaret Fox
Martha Leeson
John Hatton
John Delamare
Samuel Fox

Sutton Delamare
Anthony Sutton
Janet Sutton
John Sutton
D. O'Brien
S. Master

Appendix I

Other Groups

If Darby did not know of Cronin's group, he did know of others, as this invitation found among Darby's papers in the Darby Collection shows.

> 1827
> For as much as there exists a desire in the hearts of many believing people, I give public expression to a deep sense of existing evils in all professing churches, to "sanctify a fast," to "call a solemn assembly," and to "cry unto the Lord." It is proposed to take a room in 49, Upper Sackville St. four mornings in the year with a view to supply this necessity. For which purpose that room will be opened Wednesday Jan. 21 from 8 till 3 o'clock, that all denominations thus feeling and acknowledging their sins as the sins of one man, may meet in fasting, humiliation, and confession, to supplicate Him "to Whom belongeth mercies and forgivenesses," to bring speedy deliverance in His own way, to "hear, forgive, hearken, do, and not defer for His own sake." "Alas for the day! for the day of the Lord is at hand and as a destruction from the *Almighty* shall it come. Is not the meat cut off before our eyes, joy and gladness from the house of our God." "*O Lord, to Thee will I cry.*" "We have no might neither know we what to do, *but our eyes are unto Thee.*"
>
> There will be (the Lord permitting) lectures on the evening of the 3rd Tuesday in every month at No. 49, Upper Sackville St. commencing at 7 o'clock, on subjects chiefly connected with the day of the Lord.

Appendix J

Darby's Concluding Remarks

in an Article Entitled "The Assembly of God, its Present State, and the Duties that Result"[1]

Summary

I conclude by a few propositions:

(1) The object to be desired is the gathering of all God's children.

(2) The power of the Holy Spirit alone can effect this.

(3) Any number of believers need not wait till that power produces the union of all, because they have the promise that, where two or three are gathered together to the name of the Lord, He will be in their midst; and two or three may act in reliance on this promise.

(4) The necessity of ordination in order to administer the Lord's Supper nowhere appears in the New Testament; and it is clear that it was to break bread Christians came together on the Lord's day (Acts 20:7; 1 Cor. 11:20-23).

(5) A commission from man to preach the gospel is unknown to the New Testament.

(6) The choosing of presidents and pastors by the assembly is altogether unwarranted by the New Testament. The election of a president is merely human and quite unauthorised. It is a mere intervention of our wilfulness in the concerns of God's assembly, an action pregnant with evil consequences. The choice of pastors is a daring encroachment on the Holy Spirit's rights who distributes according to His own will. Alas! for him who does not profit by the gift which God grants to another. When elders were appointed, it was either by the apostles, or by those whom they directed for the purpose to the assemblies. If the assembly is in ruin, even for such a state God is sufficient; who will lead on and guide His children if they walk in humility and obedience, without setting about a work to which God has not called them.

(7) It is clearly the duty of a believer to separate from every act that he sees to be not according to the word, though bearing with him who unintelligently does so. And his duty requires this of him, even though his faithfulness should cause him to stand alone, and though, like Abram, he should be obliged to go out, not knowing whither he goes.

Conclusion

My design in these few pages has not been to shew, either the ruined condition of the assembly, or yet that the present dispensation cannot be again set up, but rather to propose a question which usually is altogether misapprehended by those who undertake to organise churches. The ruin of the assembly has been briefly considered in another tract. But as a brother, to whom these pages were read, felt that this question of present ruin was awakened in his mind, and desired to have some proof to satisfy such as were in like manner exercised, I add a few sentences.

(a) The parable of the wheat-and-tare field gives us the Lord's judgment on this point—that the evil wrought in the field where the good seed had been sown was not to be remedied but to continue until the harvest. Let it be borne in mind that the parable has nothing to do with discipline among God's children, but relates to the question of a remedy for evil brought in by Satan whilst men slept, and to the restoring the economy to its primitive footing. The question is decided with summary authority by the Lord *in the negative*; for He tells us that throughout its course no remedy shall be applied to the evil,—that the time of the harvest, or the judgment at the end of the age, will extirpate it, and that till then the evil is to go on. Let us here call to mind that our separation from evil, and the enjoyment of Christ's presence with the "two or three," are altogether distinct from the pretension to set up again this economy now that the evil is come in. The former is both a duty and a privilege; the latter is fruit of pride and neglect of the word.

(b) Rom. 11, already quoted, expressly tells us that the present dispensation shall be dealt with like that which went before it, and that, if it continued not in God's goodness, it would be cut off, not restored.

(c) 2 Thess. 2 teaches us that "the mystery of iniquity" was already working, and that, when an obstacle which then existed was to be taken out of the way, the "wicked one" would be revealed, whom the Lord is to consume with the breath of His mouth and to destroy with the manifestation of His coming. Thus the evil that began in apostolic days was to continue, ripen and manifest itself, when it would be consumed by the Lord's appearing.

(d) 2 Tim. 3 shews the same thing, that is, the ruin (not the restoration) of the dispensation; for in the last days perilous times are to come and men be lovers of their own selves (from whom the Spirit calls us to "turn away"), evil men and seducers waxing worse and worse, deceiving and being deceived.

(e) Jude also shews that the evil which had already crept into the assembly would be the object of judgment when the Lord came (compare verses 4 and 14); and this awful truth is confirmed by the analogy of all the ways of God with man. For man has perverted and corrupted what God had given him for his blessing; and God has never repaired the evil, but brought forth something better after judging the iniquity. And this better thing has been in its turn corrupted, until at length everlasting blessing is brought in. When the economy was a revelation to sinners, God gathered a feeble remnant of believers from among the unbelieving, and transferred them into that new blessing which He established instead of what had been corrupted; as for example the residue of Jews into the assembly at Pentecost, and so on. So in Rom. 11 we are taught that the Lord will similarly deal with the present dispensation.

(f) The same thing is seen in the Revelation. As soon as "the things that are," or the seven churches, are brought to a close, the prophet is taken to heaven: and all that follows has to do, not with anything acknowledged as an assembly, but with divine providence in the world.

I have done no more than refer to a few express passages; but the more God's word is studied, the more do we find this solemn truth confirmed. I say then, Do all that you can, but pretend not to do what exceeds that which the Lord has given you, which would but betray the pretensions and the weaknesses of the flesh. Humility of heart and spirit is the sure way not to be found fighting against the truth; for God giveth grace to the humble. May His name of grace and mercy be for ever blessed!

Appendix K

Darby and Newton

Darby held the view that when dealing with teachings designated as evil, one should occupy himself with combating the teaching itself and not become tangled up in making personal attacks on the teacher. The following two extracts are of great interest in this respect.

The first is from *B. W. Newton and Dr. S. P. Tregelles: Teachers of the Faith and the Future* edited by G. H. Fromow. Ardent Darby followers tend to question the reliability of the account, but there is really no justifiable ground in doing so as it in no way contradicts Darby's general attitude and behavior as observed elsewhere. The hostility is probably so strong because the "evil teacher" Newton appears to receive something like indirect praise from Darby.

> The Editor of *Watchword and Truth* and author of *Scriptural Truth About Our Lord's Return*, Dr. R. Cameron of Seattle, said:
>
> > Over forty years ago, at my own table in New York City, Mr. Darby called Mr. Newton "dear brother Newton." I expressed my deep surprise at the use of such an endearing term concerning the one whom he had freely called "that dangerous man," and other equally harsh terms. At once Mr. Darby replied: "Mr. Newton is the most godly man I ever knew." I said: "Well, then, what was all this trouble and condemnation about, if Mr. Newton is such a godly man?" He answered promptly: "Oh, but Mr. Newton had taught blasphemous doctrines about the person of our blessed Lord, and these had to be dealt with." "But," I said, "Mr. Newton withdrew the tract on which this charge was made, and afterwards published another tract that is the clearest, most scriptural and most reverential treatment of that delicate question that has ever been published."[1] "Yes," said Mr. Darby, "but there never was any adequate

> repentance for the sin!" Here the conversation ended, because Mr. Darby (for I loved him) was too old and too venerable a man to admit of my giving "adequate expression" to my indignant feelings.

The second extract is a letter taken from the Fry collection, written by Darby to Mrs. Newton on the occasion of his hearing that her husband was ill. This letter was written after the separation of Darby and Newton and the "Bethesda" troubles:

> Dear Mrs. Newton,
>
> My name I am sure cannot but be now painful to you though I am not unmindful of many kindnesses received—but I write having heard that Newton is very ill to assure you that however I may have felt it my duty, after long delay, in public matters to cut with uncompromising opposition to his path—I have only unfeigned sympathy with you in his illness and have not one other desire but blessing for him. The position in which I stood afforded no occasion for the expression of any sentiment—it would have been misplaced—but his illness does and I gladly embrace it and I should be quite glad, if the opportunity offered, without doing him any harm that you should communicate it to him. Unchanged as these may be in my judgment as to duty, I have never ceased to mourn over him individually.
>
> I trust the Lord's mercy may be extended to him and to you in his illness—it is my earnest desire—I have often prayed for him since I have acted so decidedly in what, I do not conceal from myself, must have been personally painful to you all.
>
> I assure you I have no feeling but an earnest desire for his blessing in every way—I do not venture to say any more to you now lest I should trespass on feelings instead of soothing them but beg you to believe me unfeignedly and in the remembrance [of him] and with my prayer for his blessing and the Lord's mercy to be fully towards him.
>
> Yours in the Lord,
>
> J. N. D.

Appendix L

What Do I Learn from Scripture?

(from *Collected Writings of J. N. Darby*, 23:127-133)

The following paper was drawn up, on the request being made to the writer to give a statement of his faith.

It was replied that the writer would not sign a confession of faith which he had drawn up himself; that all human statement of truth was so inferior to scripture, even when drawn from it [the written word], that he could not do it; and the drawing up of this has only the more convinced him of it.

In the first place, there might be important points left out, or that put in which had better not be there. And supposing everything right that was there, it was like a made tree instead of a growing tree. The word gives truth in its living operations. It is giving in connection with God, in connection with man, with conscience, with divine life, and is thus a totally different thing. To use another image, it is not the growing tree, but supposing all there, sticks laid up in bundles. The writer had, however, no objection personally to say what he believed, to give an answer when asked the question. What follows is given with a deeper conviction than ever of the imperfection of a human assemblage of truth; the writer adding that there are many things more which he should teach. But he could say: "I believe this"; I have learnt this from scripture.

I learn from the scriptures that there is one living God (1 Tim. 2:5; 4:10 and others), fully revealed to us in Christ (John 1:18), and known through Him as Father, Son, and Holy Ghost (Matt. 3:16-17; 28:19; Eph. 2:18), in the unity of the Godhead (John 5:19; 1 Cor. 12:6), but revealed as distinctively willing (John 6:38-40; John 5:21; 1 Cor. 12:11), acting (John 5:17; 1 Cor. 12:11), sending, sent (John 14:26; 15:26; 5:24,37; 1 Cor. 12:11; 1 Pet. 1:12; 1 John 4:14), coming (John 15:26; 16:7-8,13), distributing (1 Cor. 12:11), and other actings; or, as habitually expressed amongst Christians, three persons in one God, or Trinity in Unity. God is the Creator of all things; but the act of creating is personally attributed to the Word and the Son, and the operation of the Spirit of God (Gen. 1:1-2; Job 26:13; John 1:1-3; Col. 1:16; Heb. 1:2).

I learn that the Word, who was with God and was God, was made flesh, and dwelt among us (John 1:1-2,14), the Father sending the Son to be the Saviour of the world (1 John 4:14). That He, as the Christ, was born of a woman (Gal. 4:4), by the power of the Holy Spirit coming on the Virgin Mary (Luke 1:35), true man (Phil. 2:7; Heb. 2:14,17; 1 John 4:2; 2 John 7), without sin (Luke 1:35; 1 John 3:5), in whom dwelleth all the fulness of the Godhead bodily (Col. 2:9), the promised seed of David according to the flesh (Rom. 1:3; Acts 2:30; 13:23; 2 Tim. 2:8), the Son of man (Matt. 16:13 and others), and Son of God (John 1:18,34 and others), determined to be the Son of God with power according to the Spirit of holiness by resurrection from the dead (Rom. 1:4), one blessed Person, God and man (Phil. 2:6-10; 2 Cor. 5:19-21; Heb 1–2; 1 John 2:23; 3:3; 5:20; Rev. 22:12-13; John 1:1,14; 8:58 and many others), the man Christ Jesus (1 Tim. 2:5), the anointed man (Acts 10:38), Jehovah the Saviour (Matt. 1:21; the word Christ or Messiah means anointed, and Jesus or Joshua, Jehovah or Jah the Saviour).

I learn that He died for our sins according to the scriptures (1 Cor. 15:3), having appeared once in the consummation of ages to put away sin by the sacrifice of Himself (Heb. 9:26); that He has borne our sins in His own body on the tree, suffering for sins the just for the unjust, that He might bring us to God (1 Pet. 2:24; 3:18); and that He is our righteousness before God (1 Cor. 1:30; Heb. 9:24).

I learn that He is risen from the dead (1 Cor. 15:20; Matt. 28:6 and many others), raised by God, by Himself, by the glory of the Father (Acts 3:15; John 2:19; Rom. 6:4; Eph. 1:20), and ascended up on high (Mark 16:19; Luke 24:51; Eph. 4:8-10 and others), having by Himself purged our sins, and sits at the right hand of God (Heb. 1:3; 10:12; Eph. 1:20-21 and others).

I learn that after Christ's ascension the Holy Ghost has been sent down to dwell in His people individually and collectively, so that in both ways they are the temple of God (John 16:7; 7:39; Rom. 8:9; the Father sends, John 14:26; Christ sends from the Father, 14:16-17, 26; Rom. 8:11; 1 Cor. 6:19; 3:16; Eph. 2:22; 1 Cor. 12:13; Eph 5:30; 1:23, &c). We are sealed (Eph. 1:13; 2 Cor. 1:22) and anointed with this Spirit (2 Cor. 1:21; 1 John 2:20,27), the love of God being shed abroad in our hearts (Rom. 5:5); we are led by Him (Rom. 8:14), and He is the earnest of our inheritance (Eph. 1:14; 2 Cor. 1:22; 5:5); we cry, Abba, Father, knowing we are sons (Rom. 8:15; Gal. 4:6).

I learn that Christ will come again to receive us to Himself (John 14:3), raising those that are His, or changing them if living, fashioning their bodies like His glorious body, according to the power by which He is able to subdue all things to Himself (1 Thess. 4:16-17; 1 Cor. 15:23,51-52; Phil. 3:20-21), and that those of them who die meanwhile will depart and be with Him (2 Cor. 5:8; Luke 23:43; Acts 7:59).

I learn that God has appointed a day in which He will judge this habitable world in righteousness by that man whom He has ordained, whereof He has given assurance unto all men, in that He has raised Him from the dead (Acts 17:31), and that at the end He will sit on the great white throne, and judge the dead, small and great (Rev. 20:11-12).

I learn that every one of us shall give an account of himself to God (Rom. 14:12), and receive the things done in the body, whether they be good or evil (2 Cor. 5:10); and as the righteous inherit eternal life (Rom. 6:22-23; Matt. 25:46), so the wicked shall be punished with everlasting destruction from the presence of the Lord, will go into everlasting punishment, be cast into the lake of fire prepared for the devil and his angels; and that whosoever is not found in the book of life will be cast into the lake of fire (2 Thess. 1:7-9; Matt. 25:46; Rev. 20:15).

I learn that this blessed one, the Lord Jesus Christ, died for all, has given Himself a ransom for all, testified in due time (2 Cor. 5:14; 1 Tim. 2:6; 1 John 2:2), that He has made propitiation for our sins, and not for ours only, but for the whole world.

I learn that He has thereby obtained an eternal redemption (Heb. 9:12), and that by one offering of Himself once for all the sins of all that believe on Him are purged (Heb. 1:3; 9:22; 10:2), and that by faith in Him their consciences are also purged (Heb. 9:14; 10:2), and God remembers their sins and iniquities no more (Heb. 10:17), that called of God, they receive the promise of an eternal inheritance (Heb. 9:15), being perfected for ever, so that we have boldness to enter into the holiest by His blood, by the new and living way He has consecrated for us (Heb. 10:14,19-20).

I learn that to enter into the kingdom of God we must be born of water and the Spirit, born again (John 3:3,5), being naturally dead in sins, and by nature children of wrath (Eph. 2:1-3; 2 Cor.

5:14). That which God employs in order to our being born again is His word (James 1:18; 1 Peter 1:23). Hence it is by faith that we become His children (Gal. 3:26).

I learn that God so loved the world that He gave His only-begotten Son, that whosoever believeth in Him shall have everlasting life (John 3:16), but that to this end, God being a righteous and holy God, the Son of man had to be lifted up upon the cross (John 3:14-15), that there He bore our sins in His own body on the tree (1 Pet. 1:24), and was made sin for us, that we might be made the righteousness of God in Him (2 Cor. 5:21).

I learn that He loved the church, and gave Himself for it, that He might sanctify and cleanse it by the washing of water by the word, that He might present it to Himself a glorious church, without spot or wrinkle, or any such thing (Eph. 5:25-27).

I learn that the God and Father of our Lord Jesus Christ has chosen us in Him before the foundation of the world, that we might be holy and without blame before Him in love (Eph. 1:4).

I learn that those that believe are sealed with the Holy Spirit, who is the earnest of our inheritance till the redemption of the purchased possession (Eph. 1:13-14; 2 Cor. 1:22); that by Him the love of God is shed abroad in our hearts (Rom. 5:5), that we have not received the spirit of bondage again to fear, but the Spirit of adoption, whereby we cry, Abba, Father (Rom. 8:15; Gal. 4:6; John 14:20); that they who have received this Spirit not only cry, Abba, Father, but know that they are in Christ, and Christ in them; that thus not only He appears in the presence of God for them, but they are in Him who is sitting at the right hand of God, expecting till His enemies be made His footstool (Eph 2:6; Heb. 9:24; 10:12-13); that they are dead to sin in God's sight, and to reckon themselves so; having put off the old man, and put on the new; alive to God through Jesus Christ (Christ is their new life); crucified to the world, and dead to the law (Col. 3:3-4,9-10; Rom. 6:6,11; Gal. 2:20; 6:14).

I learn thus that if they are in Christ, Christ is in them and they are called upon to manifest the life of Jesus in their mortal flesh (John 14:20; Rom 8:10; 2 Cor. 4:10), and to walk as He walked (1 John 2:6), God having set them in the world as the epistles of Christ (2 Cor. 3:3), whose grace is sufficient for them, and whose strength is made perfect in their weakness (2 Cor. 12:9).

I learn that they are converted to wait for God's Son from heaven (1 Thess. 1:10; Titus 2:12-13; Luke 12:35-37), and taught to do so; and that they have the promise that they shall never perish, nor shall any man pluck them out of Christ's hand (John 10:29), but that God will confirm them to the end, that they may be blameless in the day of our Lord Jesus Christ (1 Cor. 1:7-9).

I learn that they have part in these privileges through faith in Christ Jesus, in virtue of which righteousness is imputed to them (Rom. 5:1-2; Gal. 3:11,14,24-26; Rom. 4:16,24-25; Eph. 2:8; 2 Cor. 5:7; Gal. 2:20; Heb. 11:4; Acts 13:39; Gal. 3:6,9 and many others); that Christ, who has obeyed even unto death, and wrought a perfect work upon the cross for them (Phil. 2:8; John 17:4; Heb 7:27; 9:25-28; 10:12,18), is now their righteousness, made such of God to them (1 Cor. 1:30), and that we are made the righteousness of God in Him (2 Cor. 5:21); that as His precious blood cleanses us from all sin, so we are personally accepted in the beloved (Eph. 1:6); that as by one man's disobedience many were constituted sinners, so by the obedience of One many shall be constituted righteous (Rom. 5:19).

I learn that we are sanctified, or set apart to God, by God the Father, through the offering of Jesus Christ once for all, and by the operation and power of the Holy Ghost through the truth, so that all Christians are saints (Jude 1; Heb. 10:10; 2 Thess. 2:13; 1 Cor. 6:11; John 17:17,19; 1 Pet. 1:22; Rom. 1:7; 1 Cor. 1:2; Eph. 1:1 and others), and that in our practical state we have to follow after holiness (Heb. 12:14; 2 Pet. 3:14), and grow up to the measure of the stature of the fulness of Christ, being changed into His image, to whom we are to be perfectly conformed in glory (Eph. 4:13,15; 2 Cor. 3:18; 1 John 3:2-3; Eph. 4:1; Col. 1:10; 1 Thess. 2:12; 5:23).

I learn that the Lord has left two rites, or ordinances, both significative of His death; one initiatory, the other of continual observance in the church of God—baptism and the Lord's supper (Matt. 28:19; Mark 16:16; Acts 2:38; 8:12,16,36; 9:18; Eph. 4:5; 1 Cor. 1:17; 1 Pet. 3:21; Rom. 6:3; Col. 2:12; Matt. 26:26-28; Mark 14:22-23; Luke 22:19-20; 1 Cor. 11:23-26; 10:3-4).

I learn that, when Christ ascended up on high, He received gifts for men, for the perfecting of the saints, for the work of the ministry, for the edifying of the body of Christ; and that from Christ the whole body, fitly joined together and compacted by that which every joint supplieth, maketh increase of the body, to the edifying of itself in love (Eph. 4:6-13; Acts 2:33; 1 Cor. 12:28; Rom. 12:6; 1 Pet. 4:10-11; Matt. 25:14; Luke 19:13).

I learn that, as the grace and sovereign love of God is the

source and origin of all the blessing (John 3:16,27; 1 Cor. 2:12; 4:7; Eph. 2:7-10; Titus 2:11), so continual and diligent dependence on that grace is that by which we can walk after Him and to His glory, who has left us an example that we should follow His steps (John 15:5; Phil. 2:12-13; 1 Thess. 5:17; Rom. 12:12; Luke 18:1; 2 Pet. 1:5-10 and many others; John 8:12; 10:4; 12:26; 17:10; 2 Cor. 5:15; 1 Cor. 6:19-20; Rom. 14:7-8; 1 Cor. 10:31; Col. 3:17; 1 John 2:6; 1 Pet. 2:21).

I learn from the example and authority of the Lord and His apostles that the scriptures of the Old and New Testament are inspired of God, and are to be received as the word of God, having His authority attached to it, and which works effectually in those that believe (Matt. 4:4,7,10; Luke 24:25-27,44-46; John 5:39; 10:35; Matt. 5:17-18; John 20:9; Matt. 1:23, and a multitude of passages; Matt. 26:54; 2 Pet. 1:20-21; Gal. 3:8; 2 Tim. 3:14-17; 1 Thess. 2:13; 1 Cor. 2:13; 14:36-37; 15:2-3; Rom. 16:26, where it is not "the scriptures of the prophets," that is, at any rate scriptures, but New Testament, not Old; 2 Pet. 3:16); and that the testimony of the Lord is sure, making wise the simple, discerning the thoughts and intents of the heart, being understood, not by the wisdom of man, but by the teaching of God, being spiritually discerned, they are revealed, communicated, and discerned by the Spirit (Ps. 19:7; Heb. 4:12-13; Luke 24:45; 1 Cor. 2:10; 1 John 2:20,27; John 6:45; 1 Cor. 2:12-14).

I learn that, while God alone is immortal in and by Himself (1 Tim. 6:16), the angels are not subject to death (Luke 20:36), and that the death of a man does not affect the life of his soul, be he wicked or renewed, but that all live still as to God, though dead (Luke 12:4-5; Matt. 10:28; Luke 16:23; 20:38), and that the wicked will be raised again as well as the just (John 5:28-29; Acts 24:15).

I learn that every assembly of God is bound by the exercise of discipline, according to the word, to keep itself pure in doctrine and godly walk (Heb. 12:15-17; 1 Tim. 3:15; Titus 3:10-11; 1 Cor. 5:7,13).

Notes

Foreword to the German Edition

1. David Bebbington, *Patterns in History* (Leicester: InterVarsity Press, 1979), 5,16.

Chapter One - Beginnings

1. Leap Castle's exact origin is not known, nor the exact meaning of its name, Leím Uí Bhanáin, or Leap of O'Bannon. In all probability it had been built in the fourteenth or fifteenth century on the site of an earlier fortification as a tower house, with additions and alterations later. It came to be considered as the most haunted castle in Ireland until its destruction in the 1922 revolution when it was bombed. Today it is only a ruin, but an impressive one, and apparently plans are being made for its restoration.
2. Sources of information on Leap Castle and Darby family: *The Clans of Ireland. Their Battles, Chiefs, and Princes* (Dublin: Sullivan); *Burke's Irish Family Records; The Landed Gentry–Ireland*; G. Cunningham, *Illustrated Guide Roscrea and District* (Roscrea: Parkmore, 1976); Cooke, *History of Birr* (1875); A. C. Fox Daries, *Armorial Families* (1929); James Fleming, *Historic Irish Mansions No. 51: Leap Castle, Co. Offaly, Seat of the Darby Family;* D. F. Gleeson, *Roscrea, Sign of the Three Candles* (Dublin: Fleet Street); Irish Tourist Board, Dublin; The Landscape of Slieve Bloon; Leicestershire Library Division for Melton Mowbray; Edward Maclysaght, *More Irish Families* (Irish Academic Press, 1982).
3. Newton said that John Darby, through his brother Henry D'Esterre, was aided by Lord Nelson in getting orders for supplying the navy with foodstuffs.—B. W. Newton, *Letters and Account of Early Years of the Brethren in the so-called Fry Manuscripts,* 61.
4. Between 1818 and 1825 the street was apparently renumbered; number 9 was changed to number 10.
5. J. N. Darby, *Letters of J. N. D.* (Lancing, Sussex: Kingston Bible Trust), 2:292.
6. Newton, *Fry Manuscripts,* 250-251.
7. J. B. Stoney, *Letters from J. B. Stoney* (Lancing, Sussex: Kingston Bible Trust), 2:267-268.
8. J. N. Darby, *Collected Writings of J. N. Darby* (Lancing, Sussex: Kingston Bible Trust), 6:37.
9. *Letters of J. N. D.*, 2:15-16.
10. Ibid., 3:89.
11. Since this biography was published in German, several persons

have voiced their doubts as to whether this Anne Darby really was J. N. Darby's mother and have suggested that she was John Darby's second wife whom he married after the first Anne died. J. N. Darby's own words are also turned around in the attempt to explain away his not seeing her after his early childhood. Yet the fact remains that this Anne Darby really is the Anne Vaughan that John Darby married and not another. The fact also remains that they separated and the only point that is still left unclear is why they did. It is understandable that for many this throws a shadow on J. N. Darby's early home life, but trying to explain something away because it seems damaging to the reputation of a person one honors is not justifiable. This is not the way to deal with the problem. In any case, the only person who could be cast in a bad light is John Darby and not his son John Nelson. For J. N. Darby one can only feel sorry that his mother was so soon taken from him, causing a deep and lasting pain his own words only all too clearly testify to.

12. W. Kelly, *Kelly Letters,* February 22, 1901.
13. *Letters of J. N. D.,* 1:205.
14. *Collected Writings of J. N. Darby,* 14:330.
15. Sources of information on London, Warbleton, and Westminster: Boase, *Modern English Biography* vol. 1 (1982); Elizabeth Doff, *The Darby Influence in Warbleton, 1819-1939* and personal letters to the author; East Sussex County Council, John Darby letter and Anne Darby death register; Canon C. A. Empey, *The Priory, Kells,* information supplied on Christopher Darby; T. W. Horsfield, *History and Antiquities of the County of Sussex* (1834); Record of Old Westminster vol. 1; Public Record Office for John Darby will (prob 11/1841) CP 3968 and Sir Henry D'Esterre Darby will (prob 11/1691) CP 3839; Muniment room and library, Westminster Abbey, London, J. N. Darby baptism record; City of Westminster Archives Department, London, with special thanks to Miss M. J. Swarbrick, chief archivist; Guildhall Library, London; Holborn Library, Borough of Camden, London; Hackney Archives Department, London; headmaster, Westminster school.
16. *Letters of J. N. D.,* 2:45.
17. "I remember a teacher of mathematics sought to show by a tangent, an indivisible angle, but he had only to make a circle with a longer radius and division was made"—J. N. Darby, *Notes and Comments* (Lancing, Sussex: Kingston Bible Trust), 4:270.
18. R. B. McDowell and D. A. Webb, *Trinity College, Dublin, 1592-1952: an Academic History* (Cambridge University Press, 1982), 121.
19. Inns: so-called because they were originally places of residence and study for the students and apprentices of law.
20. Sources of information on Trinity/law: *Irish Genealogy—A Record Finder,* 181; Trinity College, Dublin, for manuscripts, early printed books, and various records relating to J. N. Darby and G. and J. G. Bellett; The Honorable Society of Lincoln's Inn, London, for William Henry and George Darby information; King's Inn's library, Dublin, for J. N. Darby's law papers.
21. *Collected Writings of J. N. Darby,* 27:368.

22. *Letters of J. N. D.*, 1:20; *Collected Writings of J. N. Darby*, 6:27-28.
23. Rev. T. Scott, *Essays on the Most Important Subjects in Religion*, 9th ed. (London: L. B. Seeley, 1822), 17.
24. *Letters of J. N. D.*, 2:466.
25. W. G. Turner, *John Nelson Darby, A Biography* (C. A. Hammond, 1901, 1926, 1944) 1926.
26. *Letters of J. N. D.*, 1:285.
27. *Kelly Letters*, June 22, 1899.
28. *Letters of J. N. D.*, 2:310.
29. *Collected Writings of J. N. Darby*, 27:92.
30. T. Scott, *Essays*, 276-277.
31. Newton, *Fry Manuscripts*, 242. The brother he mentioned here was probably William Henry, who was once a Catholic, later joined the Brethren, and later still left them. William Henry wrote at least three short tracts—"Faith and Works," "The Canon of Truth," and "Baptism and Conflict with Indwelling Sin," published by George Morrish, London. My copies of these tracts were stamped February 11, 1859, and they were written while he was still among the Brethren (Morrish was a publisher of Brethren literature).
32. *Collected Writings of J. N. Darby*, 18:156.
33. *Letters of J. N. D.*, 2:254.
34. Ibid., 3:247.
35. G. Bellett, *Memoir of the Rev. George Bellett, M. A.* (London: J. Masters, 1889), 28.
36. J. N. Darby, Darby Collection, Foundation of Archives of Church History, DeBilt, Netherlands.
37. Ibid.
38. "Ecclesiastical Intelligence," *Christian Examiner and Church of Ireland Magazine* (October 1825), 339.
39. Rev. A. C. Downer, *Thomas Scott the Commentator* (London: Chas. J. Thynne, 1909), 8.
40. A curate was a clergyman in charge of a parish.
41. J. C. Philpot, *The Seceders* (London: Banner of Truth Trust), 44.
42. "The consistent believer, however, will be influenced by his principles to retrench a variety of superfluous expenses, and exceedingly to moderate his desires of providing for his family, that he may raise a fund for charitable and pious uses; and while he shews a readiness for every good work, by which the wants and miseries of men may be relieved; he will especially endeavour to render all his liberality subservient to the more important interests of religion" (T. Scott, *Essays*, 256).
43. "Active kindness, however, does not consist merely in giving; but a man may express much love by denying his own inclination or foregoing his ease, that he may serve others. That charity, of which the apostle speaks so highly, (1 Cor. 13), is especially distinguished by its unfeigned desire and aim to promote both the temporal and eternal good of men; and may be shewn in a vast variety of inexpensive services, and in minute instances of self-denial, accompanied with alacrity and kindness. The consistent Christian, in the lowest condition, will never want an occasion of convincing his little circle,

that he wishes to do them good, and is habitually ready to put himself to trouble and inconvenience for that purpose; while he will always be able to pray for numbers, to whom he can render no other service. . . . Surely then, they who have received such a ministry, should renounce the 'works of darkness' and 'the hidden things of dishonesty'; they 'should take heed to themselves and to their doctrine'; and they should 'labour and not faint,' but 'endure hardship' and face danger 'as good *soldiers* of Jesus Christ.' They should be 'instant in season, out of season'; and, laying aside all worldly pleasures, diversions, and pursuits; all avarice, ambition, and mere secular studies, which subserve not the end of their holy calling, they should devote their time, health, abilities, and influence to the service of the sanctuary, 'giving themselves wholly thereunto.' Nothing, however lucrative, creditable, or congenial to their taste, should engross those powers and that time, which they have most solemnly engaged to employ in seeking the salvation of souls: for, the desire of spending their lives in this good work, in preference to more lucrative and easy employments, seems to be that very 'call of the Holy Ghost,' by which men are indeed 'moved to take this sacred office upon them' " (T. Scott, *Essays,* 220,255).

44. *Letters of J. N. D.,* 3:453-454.
45. Ibid., 2:376.
46. Pennefather also had a house in Dublin, as noted before. There is some difficulty as to where this country house was. Pennefather had two country seats, one called Templecarrig in Delgany (Francis Newman, who succeeded Philpot, has letters bearing the address Templecarrig for the time he was in Pennefather's service) and one called Rathsallagh in upper Talbotstown. Philpot was apparently at Rathsallagh. Samuel Lewis's work, *A Topographical Dictionary of Ireland* (London: S. Lewis & Co., 1837), describes it as comprising 1753 statute acres (Templecarrig had 30 acres), containing 271 inhabitants and belonging entirely to E. Pennefather (vol. 2, 508). There was also a school in the area maintained entirely by the Pennefather family. This is of interest for Philpot wrote in *The Seceders:* "I have taught in the Sunday-school a class of barefooted, ragged little fellows, whose habiliments smelling of turf, the least unpleasant of their odours, were sufficiently repulsive to the young collegian fresh from the elegancies of Oxford; and remember, almost with a smile, to this day the careful way in which I had to put my foot down, lest it should inadvertently tread on some of the many naked surrounding toes" (44). The school he mentioned is probably the one connected with Pennefather, and not the one in which Darby preached, though a Sunday school was held there. If it *was* the one in which Darby was active, their contact with one another was very close.
47. *Letters of J. N. D.,* 3:167.
48. "An address delivered by a bishop, archdeacon, or other ecclesiastical person at a visitation of the clergy under his jurisdiction"—*The Concise Oxford Dictionary of the Christian Church,* ed. E. A. Livingstone (Oxford University Press, 1986), 101-102.

49. "Ecclesiastical Intelligence" (March 1827), 242. See Appendix F.
50. *Interesting Reminiscences of the Early History of Brethren,* 2-3.
51. Darby, *Notes and Comments,* 7:261-262.
52. J. N. Darby, *Notes and Jottings* (Lancing, Sussex: Kingston Bible Trust), 99-100. I will cover Darby's distinction between "appearing" and "coming" in chapter 3.
53. "Humility may be considered as most essential to the Christian temper, and as radical to every part of it" (T. Scott, *Essays,* 202).
54. *Collected Writings of J. N. Darby,* 1:36.
55. Ibid., 1:38.
56. *Letters of J. N. D.,* 3:299.
57. Ibid.
58. Ibid., 2:165.
59. J. N. Darby, *Pilgrim Portions for the Day of Rest* (London: G. Morrish), 167.
60. L. M. Bellett, *Recollections of the Late J. G. Bellett* (London: James Carter, 1895).
61. *Letters of J. N. D.,* 2:7.
62. *Kelly Letters,* June 22, 1899.
63. *Letters of J. N. D.,* 1:34.
64. W. Kelly, Marginal Notes in W. B. Neatby's *A History of the Plymouth Brethren* (London: Hodder & Stoughton, 1902), 46.
65. W. Robbins, *The Newman Brothers* (London: Heinemann Educational Books, 1966), 12.
66. T. Scott, *Essays,* 19-21.
67. *Letters of J. N. D.,* 1851, 1:189.
68. J. N. Darby, *Spiritual Songs* (Dublin, 1883).

Chapter Two - A Great Recovery

1. *Letters of J. N. D.,* 1:344.
2. Ibid., 1:515.
3. Ibid., 3:301.
4. Ibid., 3:246.
5. Ibid., 2:379.
6. Ibid., 2:244.
7. Ibid., 2:386.
8. Ibid., 3:301.
9. Ibid., 2:368.
10. The exact date or circumstances of Darby's meeting with Hutchinson I have not, sad to say, been able to determine. It could have come about through Rev. Robert Daly, as he was well acquainted with the family of Powerscourt and Howard. The Howards were related to the Powerscourts through marriage. There is more on the connection of Theodosia Howard with Richard Wingfield V (Viscount Powerscourt) in our next chapter. In the diary of Lady Anne Jocelyn (cousin to Theodosia Howard and sister of Lady Powerscourt—i.e., Richard Wingfield's first wife) a Mr. and Mrs. Synge are mentioned several times as family acquaintances (MS 18,430 in *Manuscript Sources for the History of Irish Civilization* in the

National Library of Ireland, Dublin). This Mr. Synge was John Synge, Francis Hutchinson's cousin. He too would play a role in the early history of the Brethren movement. (See "John Synge and the Early Brethren" by T. C. F. Stunt in *Christian Brethren Research Fellowship Journal* 28; "A Comprehensive History" by the same author in *The Harvester* of May 1968; and page 36 of *A History of the Brethren Movement* by F. R. Coad, Paternoster Press, Exeter, 1976.)

11. *Reminiscences,* 3-4.
12. This year 1829 has caused great confusion and misled many. The real date was 1827, as the testimony of other writers shows (Darby, Kelly, Miller) and other conclusive evidence proves. Bellett is not to be depended upon when it comes to naming dates that seen from the time of his writing were for him long past. In other places he made some obvious mistakes. Neatby wrote of Bellett's account: "The accuracy may be gauged by the fearlessness of the detail." William Kelly wrote in the margin beside that statement: "By no means." And so it is. (In a letter dated January 7, 1907, Kelly called Neatby's book "faithless" and in "no way reliable.") The account is not accurate in its dates. Bellett said of his own account, "I may fail in accuracy of recollection, and, of course, I may mistake when I was not personally engaged, but I will follow just as my memory suggests to me, bethinking myself, of course, as I proceed, and praying the Lord to guide in all simplicity and truth" *(Reminiscences,* 2). If we take the year 1827 as correct, all other parts fall into their proper places; otherwise one has a lot of contradicting material to reconcile.
13. In all the directories checked, Francis Hutchinson's address is given as number 8 and not number 9—viz., Wilson's Dublin directory for the years 1829 to 1832 and the post office annual directory for 1832 and 1833. Either Andrew Miller was wrong in giving number 9 as the right house in his Brethren history, or the mix-up has something to do with the fluctuation of house numbers at that time because of building going on in the district and new houses being erected.
14. *Reminiscences,* 5-6.
15. The only support for an 1829 date is the fact that Francis Hutchinson appears in no Dublin directory that I was able to refer to until 1829, but this might be due to other circumstances.
16. W. Kelly, ed., *Bible Treasury* (Winschoten, Netherlands: H. L. Heijkoop Verlag), 14:269.
17. *Kelly Letters,* January 7, 1902. In an article in the *Bible Treasury* (16:368) dealing with a letter written to Darby by Groves we find: "It may be added that Mr. G. was known to hold principles 'entirely at variance' with Brethren's. What could one expect from a person who failed to see the difference between 'the kingdom of heaven' and 'the church'? He consequently misused the parable of the wheat-and-tare field to oppose the godly separateness of the saints. Like Papists, &c., he applied to *the church* what our Lord said of *the world.* For the field is the world, not the church; and in the world there can be no righteous separation till judgment. Was it intentionally to be so in the church of God?"

18. H. Craik, *Passages from the Diary and Letters of Henry Craik* (London: J. F. Shaw), 79.
19. *Reminiscences,* 4.
20. Craik, *Passages,* 81.
21. Mrs. A. N. Groves, *Memoir of the Late Anthony Norris Groves by His Widow* (Bristol: James Nisbet, 1856), 30.
22. Ibid., 29.
23. Ibid., 31.
24. Ibid., 35-36.
25. J. G. Bellett had been influenced by others in the past in a direction his brother George did not approve of. George wrote: "In the beginning of this summer [1821], I believe it was, I paid a visit to North Lodge, and to my dear mother's great delight preached in dear Kilgobbin Church for Mr. Kearney, who had been my master and teacher for so many years. My preaching satisfied all, I believe, but one—my dear John; but he and I had begun before this to diverge a good deal from one another on doctrinal points; for his views had become more decidedly Calvinistic, and the friends with whom he associated in Dublin were all, I believe, without exception, of this school, and my own feelings against the system had not lessened" (George Bellett, *Memoir,* 41-42). Darby was certainly one of the Dublin friends mentioned above.
26. Craik, *Passages,* 89.
27. *Reminiscences,* 4.
28. H. H. Rowdon, *The Origins of the Brethren* (London: Pickering & Inglis, 1967), 39.
29. *Reminiscences,* 4.
30. Lower Pembroke Street was where Edward Cronin lived and had for some time been practicing what Groves was talking about.
31. *Reminiscences,* 4-5.
32. Mrs. A. N. Groves, *Memoir,* 34.
33. Ibid., 39.
34. Once again there is confusion as to the right house numbers. L. M. Bellett's *Recollections* (page 36) gives the number 2 for this period, whereas all the directories have number 5 for the years 1826, 1828, and 1829. Number 2 appears in 1834.
35. *Reminiscences,* 5.
36. Ibid., 16-17.
37. Ibid., 14.
38. *Letters of J. N. D.,* 3:301.
39. Ibid., 2:208.
40. Ibid., 1:515.
41. Ibid., 2:438.
42. Ibid., 1:515.
43. Rowdon, "Secession from the Established Church in the Early Nineteenth Century," *Vox Evangelica* (1964), 3:76-88. Rowdon wrote: "In private, Walker and his followers practised the Breaking of Bread (as they called the Lord's Supper) on the first day of the week, engaged in teaching and admonishing one another, apparently without any distinction between clergy and laity, exercised discipline

and introduced the use of the holy kiss. Walker urged the view that, as in Apostolic days, there should be one church in each place, but denied that he believed that his church in Dublin, and those associated with it, comprehended all the true disciples of Christ in the country. He insisted, however, that 'they do comprehend all, whom I know or can acknowledge as such.' A true church, in Walker's estimation, was a 'collection of disciples; who are gathered together into one body by their agreement in that Truth, who unitedly confess it, walk under its influence, and are regulated by its influence.' Since it must be an 'insulated body,' its members must withdraw from unbelievers (2 Cor. 6:14-15), heretics (Tit. 3:10-11) and disciples who walk disorderly (2 Thess. 3:14-15). Though he distinguished between those who realized the error of maintaining their existing church connections and those who did not, Walker looked for the drawing together of all true disciples in separation from both the world and the false church. In this, there were eschatological undertones: Walker denied that the Christian gospel was intended to improve the condition of the world and directed hope to the second advent of Christ to the earth" (77-78). Walker left for London in 1819, returning in 1833. It would be of great interest to know when and how much Darby knew of this group. But anything really concrete must yet be found.

44. *Reminiscences,* 15-16.
45. *Letters of J. N. D.,* 1:515.
46. G. W. Ware, *A Review of Certain Contentions for the Faith,* 73.
47. Mrs. A. N. Groves, *Memoir,* 532.
48. *Letters of J. N. D.,* 1:185.
49. Ibid., 1:182.
50. Ibid., 1875, 2:340-341.
51. Darby, *Notes and Jottings,* 38.
52. *Letters of J. N. D.,* 2:386.
53. Ibid., 1:73.
54. Ibid., 3:479.
55. Newton, *Fry Manuscripts,* 243.
56. *Collected Writings of J. N. Darby,* 2:310-311,319.
57. *Letters of J. N. D.,* 1:42.
58. J. N. Darby, *Miscellaneous Writings* (Bible Truth Publishers), 4:164.
59. Ibid., 5:143-147.
60. *Letters of J. N. D.,* 2:388.
61. Kelly, *Bible Treasury,* 16:303.
62. See *Letters of J. N. D.,* 2:437.
63. *Collected Writings of J. N. Darby,* 20:456.
64. The following are extracts from Darby's letters quoted in Neatby's *History,* 225-226.

"I am requested to say, that inasmuch as you have now placed yourselves in the same position as Mr. G.—viz., outside the communion of the saints gathered together in the name of Christ in London—the gathering in Rotherham being in fellowship with those in London, cannot possibly receive any statement of the particulars of the matter, either written or by word of mouth. To do so they feel would be to ignore the discipline of the assembly in London, and practically to set aside discipline everywhere; as it virtually denies the unity of the body, and reduces every assembly to an independent congregation.

"I understood the breach arose between you and Rotherham [i.e., between the exclusive meetings at Sheffield and Rotherham] by reason of your reception of Goodall. With the main facts of his case I am acquainted, for I took part in what passed, and now allow me to put the case as it stands as to him. I put it merely as a principle. He (or anyone else) is rejected in London. The assembly in London have weighed, and I with them, the case, and counted him as either excommunicated or in schism. I put the two cases, for I only speak of the principle. I take part in this act, and hold him to be outside the Church of God on earth, being outside (in either case) what represents it in London; I am bound by Scripture to count him [*sic*] so. I come to Sheffield; there he breaks bread and is—in what? Not in the Church of God on earth, for he is out of it in London, and there are not two churches on earth, cannot be, so as to be in one and out of another. How can I refuse to eat with him in London and [yet] break bread with him in Sheffield? have one conscience for London, and another conscience for Sheffield? It is confusion and disorder. I do not apprehend I am mistaken in saying you received Goodall without having the reasons or motives of the Priory or other brethren in London. If you have had their reasons, the case is only the stronger, because you have deliberately condemned the gathering in London and rejected its communion; for he who is outside in London is inside with you."

65. *Letters of J. N. D.*, 2:422.
66. Ibid., 1:374.
67. Ibid., 2:393.
68. Ibid., 1:205.
69. Kelly, *Bible Treasury*, 5:50.
70. *Letters of J. N. D.*, 2:422.
71. Ibid., 3:49.
72. Contrast Groves' view: "I would *infinitely* bear with all their evils, than separate from their good"—G. H. Lang, *Anthony Norris Groves* (London:Thynne, 1939), 221.
73. *Letters of J. N. D.*, 2:385.
74. Ibid., 1:94.
75. Darby Collection.
76. *Letters of J. N. D.*, 2:362.
77. *Reminiscences*, 8.
78. Rev. R. Braithwaite, *The Life and Letters of Rev. William Pennefather, B.A.*, 4th ed. (London: John F. Shaw), 23-24.
79. Newton, *Fry Manuscripts*, 250.
80. Kelly, *Bible Treasury*, 6:255.
81. *Collected Writings of J. N. Darby*, 1:36.
82. See volume 1 of *Collected Writings of J. N. Darby* for this and two other papers written later, "Separation from Evil, God's Principle of Unity" and "Grace, the Power of Unity and of Gathering."

83. *Letters of J. N. D.,* 2:316-317.
84. Ibid., 2:132-133.
85. Ibid., 3:300.
86. Ibid., 2:469-470.
87. Ibid., 2:9.
88. Ibid., 2:306.
89. Ibid., 1:304.
90. *Collected Writings of J. N. Darby,* 26:324.
91. *Letters of J. N. D.,* 1:301-302.
92. Kelly, *Bible Treasury,* 10:302-303.
93. *Letters of J. N. D.*, 3:434.
94. Ibid., 1:31.
95. Adolf Brennecke, *Alt England* (Essen:Magnus-Verlag), 63.
96. *Letters of J. N. D.,* 2:111.
97. Ibid., 2:35.
98. Darby, *Pilgrim Portions,* 110-111.
99. Braithwaite, *Pennefather,* 25.
100. John Parnell was related to William Parnell, who in 1811 had married Frances Howard, the sister of the later Lady Powerscourt (Theodosia). John Parnell, according to William Collingwood in *The Brethren: A Historical Sketch* (Glasgow: Pickering & Inglis), had begun to meet for the breaking of bread together with William Stokes and others about the year 1825. Henry Groves' *Memoir of Lord Congleton* (London: Walter G. Wheeler) does not go into this, and begins with Parnell's connections with Bellett and Hutchinson.
101. *Reminiscences,* 6.
102. Ibid., 7-8.
103. George Bellett, *Memoir,* 73-74.
104. *Letters of J. N. D.,* 1:2.
105. *Collected Writings of J. N. Darby,* 1:187.
106. Wigram married Catherine Parnell, the daughter of William and Frances (Howard) Parnell, in 1835. According to Newton (*Fry Manuscripts,* 263) Wigram came into contact with the Brethren first in Dublin, later in Plymouth.
107. *Letters of J. N. D.,* 3:53.
108. Ibid., 3:245.
109. W. H. Cole quoted in David J. Beattie's *Brethren. The Story of a Great Recovery* (Kilmarnock, Scotland: John Ritchie, 1944), 20-21.
110. *Letters of J. N. D.,* 3:230.
111. Ibid., 1:9.
112. Ibid., 3:237.
113. Ibid., 3:26.
114. Ibid., 2:129.
115. Newton, *Fry Manuscripts,* letter.
116. John G. Bellett's brother George married Sir Edward Denny's sister in 1831.
117. Turner, *Darby,* 1944:70-71.
118. Müller married Groves' sister Mary in 1830.
119. *Letters of J. N. D.*, 1:8.

120. *Reminiscences,* 19-20.
121. Darby, *Spiritual Songs* (1883).

Chapter Three - Prophecy and a Lady

1. Viscountess Theodosia A. Powerscourt, *Letters and Papers by the Late Theodosia A. Viscountess Powerscourt,* ed. R. Daly (London, 1838), 108.
2. Mrs. H. Madden, *Memoir of the Late Right Rev. Robert Daly, D.D.* (London: James Nisbet, 1875), 53.
3. Powerscourt, *Letters and Papers,* vii.
4. Craik, *Passages,* 168.
5. Mrs. A. N. Groves, *Memoir,* 355.
6. Braithwaite, *Pennefather,* 47.
7. Newton, *Fry Manuscripts,* 237.
8. Ibid., 283.
9. Ibid., 284.
10. Desmond Bowen wrote: "Although Lord Powerscourt was not religious, his wife was exceedingly so, as was her brother, Lord Jocelyn, who later became the Earl of Roden. It was Lady Powerscourt who greatly helped Daly to advance in Evangelical circles"—*The Protestant Crusade in Ireland, 1800-1870* (Gill & MacMillan, 1978), 74.
11. Powerscourt, *Letters and Papers,* 109.
12. From *A Selection of Poems by Christian Authors,* comp. G. H. S. Price (London: Copper & Budd), 19.
13. Powerscourt, *Letters and Papers,* vi.
14. Braithwaite, *Pennefather,* 115.
15. *Reminiscences,* 3.
16. Kelly, *Bible Treasury,* 12:352.
17. Ibid.
18. *Letters of J. N. D.,* 3:298-299.
19. Ibid., 1:516.
20. *Collected Writings of J. N. Darby,* 2:108.
21. Ibid., 11:185.
22. Darby, *Notes and Jottings,* 197.
23. Ibid., 195.
24. *Letters of J. N. D.,* 1:329-330.
25. Darby, *Notes and Jottings,* 99.
26. Ibid., 194.
27. *Collected Writings of J. N. Darby,* 11:156.
28. Ibid., 11:119,153.
29. Darby, *Notes and Jottings,* 86.
30. Ibid.
31. Ibid.
32. Ibid., 84.
33. Ibid.
34. Ibid., 196.
35. Ibid., 184.
36. *Collected Writings of J. N. Darby,* 4:10.

37. Darby, *Notes and Jottings,* 184.
38. Darby's view, and that of the Brethren, was that the Lord's coming for His own (the rapture *before* the millennium) and the destruction by fire in 2 Peter (at the *end* of the millennium, and ushering in the eternal state) are two different events.
39. F. W. Newman, *Phases of Faith: or Passages from the History of My Creed* (London, 1850).
40. *Collected Writings of J. N. Darby,* 11:67.
41. Kelly, *Bible Treasury,* 4.
42. Mr. Stunt mentioned Tweedy in his article "Leonard Strong: the Motives and Experiences of Early Missionary Work in British Guiana": "The last of the early Brethren to come to Demerara was Thomas Tweedy who had seceded from the Church of Ireland in the early 1830's soon after his graduation from Trinity College, Dublin, in 1833. As a roving evangelist in Ireland he had decided that missionary work was his vocation, but partly on account of ill health and perhaps also because of discouragement from his family he remained in Ireland for some years. It was only in 1842 that he set out for Demerara where he arrived after a 'fine passage' of only 33 days. How effective was Tweedy's work as a missionary is hard to say, as his health was, at the best of times, fragile and the only account we have of his life is written by one who was not particularly interested in the spiritual side of his work. He married a local coloured lady, Elizabeth Thomas, by whom he had 2 children"—Coad, *Prophetic Developments, with Particular Reference to the Early Brethren Movement,* Christian Brethren Research Fellowship (Exeter: Paternoster Press, 1966), 103. (The year 1833 seems to support the statement that Darby's letter to Newton was in 1833, unless Tweedy had contact with Darby before leaving the church.)
43. Much has been made of Darby's visit to Scotland, mentioned in chapter 2, as the source of his rapture views. Darby has been accused of borrowing or stealing "his" ideas as to the rapture from a Miss Margaret MacDonald who prophesied while he was there. Dave MacPherson professed to have "uncovered" this purposely covered-up fact. Having read MacPherson's book *The Incredible Cover-up,* I find it impossible to make a just comparison between what Miss MacDonald "prophesied" and what Darby taught. It appears that the wish was the father of the idea. Roy A. Huebner in his book *The Truth of the Pre-Tribulation Rapture Recovered* has very ably smashed the MacPherson theory with the hammer of reality. I refer all who are interested to his book, though I do not agree with him in all points. The fact that Darby's stay must have influenced him in some way cannot be ignored, but *how* must still be looked into in greater depth. The *contents* of Miss MacDonald's prophecy do not correspond with Darby's rapture view, yet an indirect influence through other experiences or events during his stay in Scotland are certainly a possibility.
44. *Letters of J. N. D.,* 1:371.
45. Darby, *Spiritual Songs* (1883).

Chapter Four - Character and Personal Traits

1. According to Dr. David Martyn Lloyd-Jones, "The fundamental elements in our personality and temperament are not changed by conversion and by re-birth. The 'new man' means the new disposition, the new understanding, the new orientation, but the man himself, psychologically, is essentially what he was before"—Iain H. Murray, *The First 40 Years* (Edinburgh: Banner of Truth Trust, 1982).
2. Darby, *Notes and Jottings,* 420-421.
3. *Kelly Letters,* January 23, 1901.
4. J. A. von Poseck, *Christus oder Parkstreet? Gottes wort oder Menschenwort* (1882), 48-49.
5. Walter Scott, *J. N. Darby, A Memorial,* 2nd ed. (London), 7.
6. Coad, *History,* 107.
7. Turner, *Darby,* 1944:61-62.
8. F. Cuendet, *Souvenez-vous de vos conducteurs* (Vevey, 1935), 41,59.
9. Kelly wrote in November 1881 of "the general awe and idolatry paid him."
10. Von Poseck, 49.
11. *Kelly Letters,* October 19, 1881.
12. Ibid., November 22, 1882.
13. Newton, *Fry Manuscripts,* 244-245.
14. Ibid., 216.
15. Turner, *Darby,* 1944:21-23.
16. Ibid., 70.
17. *Letters of J. N. D.,* 2:421.
18. Ibid., 3:285.
19. Ibid., 2:20.
20. Ibid., 2:59.
21. Darby, *Pilgrim Portions,* 118.
22. Neatby wrote that Darby was jealous of Kelly in later years (Neatby's *History,* 289, preface dated September 1901). Kelly wrote in the margin, "I am slow to allow [jealousy] save at passing moments of irritation [in] a [man] quite above such a temptation." And in a letter dated January 23, 1901, and thus written before Neatby's book, Kelly wrote of the same circumstances that prompted Neatby to mention jealousy: "The letter writer imputes jealousy to Mr. Darby about me. When I heard this . . . I indignantly refuted it." Kelly then wrote of others who were trying to run him down, were jealous because of lectures he gave in London, and sought to turn Darby against him: they "at last succeeded in arousing some feeling in our honored brother's mind. Even then I laughed at it as only a little weakness; till I grieve to say facts before my own eyes and many more compelled me to fear the enemy had insinuated a feeling so beneath him, especially toward one who venerated him as I did and do [note the present tense]. In the same letter Kelly wrote that he was "slow to believe that he had any jealousy of B. W. Newton." Darby was being influenced by others; his problem was not a state or condition of heart. If jealousy did surface, then it was in a passing moment as Kelly said. In August 1903 Kelly wrote with reference

to Darby that he had "an unbroken deep regard to a great and good man, an uncompromising champion for Christ's glory and God's truth" (*Bible Treasury,* 4:316-317).

23. Turner, *Darby,* 1901:18.
24. *Letters of J. N. D.,* 1:71.
25. Darby, *Miscellaneous Writings,* 4:236.
26. Ibid., 4:236,242.
27. Unpublished memoir. Anna Mabel Roberts was married to Timothy O. Loizeaux, one of the two brothers who founded Loizeaux Brothers, a publishing house that was known for its Brethren literature and today still publishes well-known works of C. H. Mackintosh and F. W. Grant.
28. Neatby, *History,* 196.
29. *Kelly Letters,* January 23, 1901.
30. *Letters of J. N. D.,* 1:408.
31. Kelly, Marginal Notes, 198.
32. Darby Collection.
33. Turner, *Darby,* 1901:18.
34. N. Noel, *The History of the Brethren* (Denver, 1936), 52.
35. Neatby, *History,* 196-197.
36. Turner, *Darby,* 1944:74.
37. *Letters of J. N. D.,* 1:205.
38. *Collected Writings of J. N. Darby,* 10:277-278.
39. Cuendet, 31.
40. Howard A. Snyder in his excellent book *The Problem of Wine Skins. Church Structure in a Technological Age* wrote in his chapter "The Gospel to the Poor": "Renewal in the Church has usually meant the Church's rebirth among the poor, the masses, the alienated. And with such resurgence has usually come the recovery of such essential N.T. emphases as community, purity, discipleship, the priesthood of believers and the gifts of the Spirit." He warned: "It is not surprising that Christians do, with time, tend to prosper materially. Increased faithfulness at work, more careful stewardship of money, a new concern for education, and similar factors, do bring economic and social advancement. Christian faithfulness generally brings material blessings. The problem is not that Christians prosper; it is that in prospering they tend to turn their backs on the poor and adopt the social attitudes of their newly acquired status. Consciousness of the gospel's special call to the poor is either forgotten or spiritualized" (InterVarsity Press, Downers Grove, IL, 1975, pages 47-48,51).
41. Turner, *Darby,* 1901:38.
42. L. M. Bellett, *Recollections,* 28,53.
43. *Reminiscences,* 21-22.
44. *Letters of J. N. D.,* 1:383-384.
45. L. M. Bellett, *Recollections,* 119.
46. *Letters of J. N. D.,* 1:393.
47. Darby, *Spiritual Songs* (1883), 87.
48. Ibid., 90.
49. *Collected Writings of J. N. Darby,* 26:264.
50. *Letters of J. N. D.,* 2:263.
51. Darby, *Pilgrim Portions,* 174.

52. *Letters of J. N. D.*, 2:383.
53. Darby, *Pilgrim Portions*, 190.
54. John Harris, *G. Campbell Morgan, The Man and His Ministry* (Fleming H. Revell, 1930), 27.
55. Neatby's *History* speaks of Darby having extraordinary bodily strength and being able to do with three or four hours of sleep in twenty-four even in the midst of immense exertions (198).
56. Anna M. Loizeaux, "Sketches for My Grandchildren."
57. *Letters of J. N. D.*, 2:14-15.
58. Turner, *Darby*, 1944:74.
59. *Letters of J. N. D.*, 3:475-476.
60. Darby, *Spiritual Songs* (1883).

Chapter Five - Ministry: Written and Oral

1. Peter J. Lineham, *There We Found Brethren* (New Zealand: G. P. H. Society, 1977), 54.
2. *Letters of J. N. D.*, 1:187.
3. *Collected Writings of J. N. Darby*, 26:318.
4. Ibid., 3:330.
5. Ibid., see footnote to table of contents in vol. 12.
6. *Letters of J. N. D.*, 1:397.
7. Neatby, *History*, 195.
8. *Kelly Letters*, May 12, 1897.
9. Turner, *Darby*, 1944:56.
10. J. N. Darby, *Spiritual Songs* (Nachdruck, Sussex: Kingston Bible Trust, 1974), VII.
11. Turner, *Darby*, 1944:55-56.
12. Darby, *Spiritual Songs* (1974), VII-VIII.
13. Heyman Wreford, *Memories of the Life and Last Days of William Kelly* (London: F. E. Race), 81.
14. *Letters of J. N. D.*, 2:346.
15. Ibid., 3:173-174.
16. Ibid., 3:93.
17. Kelly, *Bible Treasury* (new series), 8:1.
18. Von Poseck, 47-48.
19. *A Brief Account of the Life and Labours of the Late William Lowe* (London: C. A. Hammond), 3.
20. Information on translation work was taken from various sources including Arnold D. Ehlert, ed., *The Bible Collector*, vols. 9-10 (CA, 1967) and Gerhard Jordy, *Die Brüder Bewegung in Deutschland, Teil 1* (Wuppertal: R. Brockhaus Verlag, 1979).
21. *Letters of J. N. D.*, 2:63.
22. Ibid., 2:131.
23. *Collected Writings of J. N. Darby*, 13:168.
24. *Letters of J. N. D.*, 2:65-66.
25. *Collected Writings of J. N. Darby*, 7.
26. Ibid., 8.
27. *Letters of J. N. D.*, 3:130.
28. Ibid., 1:118.

29. J. N. Darby, *Synopsis of the Books of the Bible, J. N. D.* (Lancing, Sussex: Kingston Bible Trust, 1965), vol. 1, pp. v,ix.
30. *Collected Writings of J. N. Darby,* 23:27. See appendix L.
31. Von Poseck, 47.
32. *Kelly Letters,* February 22, 1901.
33. *Letters of J. N. D.,* 2:363.
34. Ibid., 2:73.
35. This work fills 358 pages of volume 6 of *Collected Writings of J. N. Darby.*
36. From the foreword to *George MacDonald and His Wife* by Greville MacDonald.
37. G. T. Stokes, "John Nelson Darby," *Contemporary Review* (1885), 48:12.
38. Neatby, *History,* 49-50.
39. Ibid., 332.
40. *Kelly Letters,* February 22, 1901.
41. *Letters from J. B. Stoney,* 3:242.
42. *Kelly Letters,* February 22, 1901.
43. *Letters of J. N. D.,* 2:60.
44. Osborne and Woodward asked: "There is a strong movement today toward rigid doctrinal statements which take dogmatic stands on controversial issues. These stands are often based not on the Bible's teaching but on the denomination's position. Is it possible that the church is regressing to a medieval situation where the individual can no longer challenge his church's interpretation of scripture and still remain within? Christians must never allow tradition to take precedence over scripture in the church." They stressed a return to Scripture: "People will know what they believe rather than merely knowing what they have been told. It will also prevent church splits. . . . The church must get back to the Bible in a new way, and this means getting INTO the Bible"—*Handbook for Bible Study* (Grand Rapids, MI: Baker Book House, 1979), 17-18.
45. *Letters from J. B. Stoney,* 1:121.
46. G. Campbell Morgan, *Discipleship* (Grand Rapids, MI: Baker Book House, 1973).
47. *The Enchanted Places* (London: Methuen, 1983).
48. *Letters of J. N. D.,* 1:468.
49. Darby, *Pilgrim Portions,* 158.
50. *Letters of J. N. D.,* 3:259.
51. Ibid., 3:390.
52. Ibid., 2:330.
53. *Letters from J. B. Stoney,* 1:242.
54. Darby, *Notes and Comments,* 7:243-244.
55. *Letters of J. N. D.,* 1:302.
56. Ibid., 3:256-257.
57. Ibid., 3:134.
58. Ibid., 2:62.
59. "Darby wrote thus to his brother: 'I hope that as to these things I may not be given over to hopeless Pyrrhonism'—a thing that his proud mind and intellect couldn't bear to feel. (Pyrrho lived about 300 B.C., he taught that nothing can be certainly known, for to everything a

teacher may state a plausible contradiction may be advanced. A truly wise man therefore will suspend judgment about everything and be sure of nothing.)"—Newton, *Fry Manuscripts*, 277-278.

60. Kelly, *Bible Treasury* (new series), 4:315-316.
61. *Letters of J. N. D.*, 3:259.
62. Ibid., 3:255-256.
63. Ibid., 1:189.
64. Ibid., 1:188.
65. Ibid., 3:259.
66. Neatby, *History*, 195.
67. Turner, *Darby*, 1944:21.
68. Kelly, *Bible Treasury* (new series), 4:25.
69. Jay E. Adams, *Grist from Adam's Mill* (Phillipsburg, NJ: Presbyterian and Reformed, 1983), 48.
70. *Letters of J. N. D.*, 1:348.
71. *Collected Writings of J. N. Darby*, 7:140.
72. Ibid., 9.
73. W. Scott, *Memorial*, 8.
74. *Letters of J. N. D.*, 1:185.
75. Ibid., 1:1.
76. Ibid., 2:301.
77. Adams, *Preaching to the Heart* (Phillipsburg, NJ: Presbyterian and Reformed, 1983), 17.
78. C. S. Lewis, *Reflections on the Psalms* (London: Collins Fount Paperbacks, 1977), 14.
79. Neatby, *History*, 194.
80. Darby, *Miscellaneous Writings*, 4:60.
81. *Collected Writings of J. N. Darby*, 16:347.
82. *Letters of J. N. D.*, 1:9.
83. Ibid., 1:12.
84. Ibid., 2:87.
85. Cuendet, 28.
86. *Letters of J. N. D.*, 1:229-230.
87. Ibid., 1:129.
88. Ibid., 2:448.
89. "Familiar Conversations on Romanism," which continued through several volumes of *Collected Writings of J. N. Darby.*
90. *Letters of J. N. D.*, 2:413.
91. Ibid., 3:208.
92. Ibid., 1:30.
93. H. C. Voorhoeve, *Mededeelingen omtrent het werk Gods in onze dagen*, vol. I, Nr. 41, 198.
94. *Chretien Evangelique* (October 20, 1871).
95. *Letters from J. B. Stoney*, 1:33.
96. *Collected Writings of J. N. Darby*, 7:1.
97. Turner, *William Kelly As I Knew Him* (C. A. Hammond), 6.
98. *Letters of J. N. D.*, 2:243.
99. Ibid., 2:27-28.
100. Ibid., 2:243.
101. Ibid., 3:164.

102. Ibid., 3:382.
103. Ibid., 2:244.
104. Ibid., 3:326.
105. Darby, *Notes and Comments,* 1:1.
106. *Letters of J. N. D.,* 2:499.
107. Ibid., 3:162.
108. Ibid., 3:166.
109. Darby, *Spiritual Songs* (1883).

Chapter Six - A Word in Closing

1. Ibid.

Appendix B

1. T. Scott, *Essays,* 269.
2. Ibid.
3. Ibid., 270.
4. Ibid., 270-271.
5. Ibid.
6. Ibid., 271-272.
7. Ibid., 272-273.
8. Ibid., 273.
9. Cuendet, 59.
10. *Letters of J. N. D.,* 3:278.

Appendix F

1. *Commons Journal,* vol. 82 (1826-1828) and *Christian Examiner* (March 1827).

Appendix G

1. J. Wills and F. Wills, *The Irish Nation: Its History and Its Biography,* vol. 3 (Edinburgh: A. Fullarton, 1873), 699,703,705.
2. From the collection at the Birmingham Oratory.
3. See *Letters of J. N. D.,* 3:225-228.

Appendix H

1. Darby Collection.

Appendix J

1. Kelly, *Bible Treasury,* 15:55-56.

Appendix K

1. "Ancient Truths Concerning the Deity and True Humanity of Christ" (1858).

No specific reference to Translation in any of these titles.

Bibliography

"Archbishop Magee." *Dublin University Magazine* 26 (October 1845), 28 (December 1846).

Balderston, T. "On Re-Reading Some Early Tracts by J. N. Darby." *Scripture Truth*, May, July, 1982.

Bass, C. B. *Backgrounds to Dispensationalism.* Grand Rapids, MI: Baker Book House, 1977.

Beattie, David J. *Brethren. The Story of a Great Recovery.* Kilmarnock, Scotland: John Ritchie, 1944.

Beckett, J. C. *The Making of Modern Ireland.* London: Faber & Faber, 1981.

Begley, D. F. *Irish Genealogy—A Record Finder.* Dublin: Heraldic Artists, 1981.

Bellett, G. *Memoir of the Rev. George Bellett, M.A.* London: J. Masters, 1889.

Bellett, L. M. *Recollections of the Late J. G. Bellett,* London: James Carter, 1895.

Bowen, D. *The Protestant Crusade in Ireland, 1800-1870.* Gill & MacMillan, 1978.

Braithwaite, Rev. R. *The Life and Letters of Rev. William Pennefather, B.A.* 4th ed. London: John F. Shaw.

"A Brief Account of the Life and Labours of the Late W. J. Lowe." *Letters of Interest,* 1927.

Burke's Irish Family Records.

Carpenter, A., ed. *My Uncle John: Edward Stephen's Life of J. M. Synge.* London, 1974.

Carron, T. W. *The Christian Testimony Through the Ages.* 1956.

Chretien Evangelique, October 20, 1871.

Christian Examiner and Church of Ireland Magazine, September 1825-December 1828.

The Clans of Ireland. Their Battles, Chiefs, and Princes. Dublin: Sullivan.

Coad, F. R. *A History of the Brethren Movement.* Exeter: Paternoster Press, 1976.

______. *Prophetic Developments, with Particular Reference to the Early Brethren Movement.* Christian Brethren Research Fellowship. Exeter: Paternoster Press, 1966.

Collingwood, William. *The Brethren: a Historical Sketch.* Glasgow: Pickering & Inglis.

Craik, H. *Passages From the Diary and Letters of Henry Craik.* London: J. F. Shaw.

Cuendet, F. *Souvenez-vous de vos conducteurs*. Vevey, 1935.
Darby, J. N. *Catalogue of the Library of the Late J. N. Darby, Esq.* London: Sotheby, Wilkinson & Hodge, 1889.
______. *Collected Writings of J. N. Darby*. 34 vols. Lancing, Sussex: Kingston Bible Trust.
______. Darby Collection in the Foundation of Archives of Church History, c/o Dr. W. J. Ouweneel, DeBilt, Netherlands (letters, papers, etc., formerly known as Sibthorpe Collection).
______. *How the Lost Sheep Was Found*. Lancing, Sussex: Kingston Bible Trust.
______. *Letters of J. N. D.* 3 vols. Lancing, Sussex: Kingston Bible Trust.
______. *Miscellaneous Writings*. vols. 4-5. Bible Truth Publishers.
______. *Notes and Comments*. 7 vols. Lancing, Sussex: Kingston Bible Trust.
______. *Notes and Jottings*. Lancing, Sussex: Kingston Bible Trust.
______. *Pilgrim Portions for the Day of Rest*. London: G. Morrish.
______. *Spiritual Songs*. Dublin, 1883.
______. *Synopsis of the Books of the Bible*. 5 vols. Lancing, Sussex: Kingston Bible Trust, 1965.
Daries, A. C. Fox. *Armorial Families*. 1929.
Dictionary of National Biography.
Downer, Rev. A. C. *Thomas Scott the Commentator*. London: Chas. J. Thynne, 1909.
"Edward Pennefather." *Dublin University Magazine*, November 1859.
Ehlert, Arnold D., ed. *The Bible Collector*. vols. 9-10. California, 1967.
Fleming, James. *Historic Irish Mansions, No. 51: Leap Castle, Co. Offaly, Seat of the Darby Family*.
Foster, R. F. *Charles Stewart Parnell: the Man and His Family*. Hassocks, 1976.
Fry. See B. W. Newton.
Fuller, J. F., F.S.A., M.R.I.A. Bellett article in *Journal of the Cork Historical Archaeological Society*. 2nd series, vol. 28. 1922.
Geldbach, E. *Christliche Versammlung und Heilsgeschichte bei J. N. Darby*. Wuppertal: R. Brockhaus Verlag, 1975.
Gleeson, D. F., M.A., D.Litt., M.R.I.A. *Roscrea, Sign of the Three Candles*. Dublin: Fleet Street.
Groves, Mrs. A. N. *Memoir of the Late Anthony Norris Groves by His Widow*. Bristol: James Nisbet, 1856.
Groves, Henry. *Memoir of Lord Congleton*. London: Walter G. Wheeler.
Guinness, D. and Ryan W. *Irish Houses and Castles*. London: Thames and Hudson, 1971.

Huebner, R. A. *The Truth of the Pretribulation Rapture Recovered.* New Jersey: Present Truth Publications, 1982.

Interesting Reminiscences of the Early History of Brethren with letter from J. G. Bellett.

Ironside, H. A. *A Historical Sketch of the Brethren Movement.* Neptune, NJ: Loizeaux, 1985.

Ischebeck, G. *John Nelson Darby.* Witten: Bundes Verlag, 1929.

Jordy, Gerhard. *Die Brüder Bewegung in Deutschland, Teil 1.* Wuppertal: R. Brockhaus Verlag, 1979.

Kelly, W., ed. *Bible Treasury,* a monthly magazine of papers on Scriptural subjects. Reprint. Winschoten, Netherlands: H. L. Heijkoop Verlag.

______. *Kelly Letters.*

______. Marginal Notes in Neatby's *History.*

Kritik, bzw. Stellungnahme, zu Geldbach "Christliche Versammlung und Heilsgeschichte bei J. N. Darby," MS.

The Landed Gentry—Ireland.

Lang, G. H. *Anthony Norris Groves.* London: Thynne, 1939.

Last Days of J. N. Darby. 2nd ed. Christchurch, 1925.

Leslie, Rev. Canon J. B. Biographical Succession List of the Clergy of Glendalough Diocese with additional remarks by Rev. Canon N. D. Emerson, Ph.D.

Lewis, Samuel. *A Topographical Dictionary of Ireland.* London: S. Lewis & Co., 1837.

Lineham, Peter J. *There We Found Brethren.* New Zealand: G.P.H. Society, 1977.

Livingstone, E. A., ed. *The Concise Oxford Dictionary of the Christian Church.* Reprint. Oxford University Press, 1986.

Maclysaght, Edward. *More Irish Families.* Irish Academic Press, 1982.

MacPherson, D. *The Incredible Cover-up,* New Jersey: Logos International, 1975.

Madden, Mrs. H. *Memoir of the Late Right Rev. Robert Daly, D.D.* London: James Nisbet, 1875.

Marshall, S. *Royal Naval Biography.* 1823.

Maxwell, Constantia. *A History of Trinity College, Dublin, 1591-1892.* Dublin, 1946.

McDowell, R. B. and Webb, D. A. *Trinity College, Dublin, 1592-1952: an Academic History.* Cambridge University Press, 1982.

Miller, A. *The Brethren ("Commonly so-called"), A Brief Sketch of their Origin, Progress and Testimony.* London.

______. *Miller's Church History.*

Moede, G. F. "Assemblies of Brethren." *Ecumenical Review* 24, no. 2 (April 1972).

Neatby, W. B. *A History of the Plymouth Brethren.* London: Hodder & Stoughton, 1902.

Newman, F. W. *Phases of Faith: or Passages from the History of My Creed.* London, 1850.

Newton, B. W. *Letters and Account of Early Years of the Brethren in the so-called Fry Manuscripts.*

Noel, N. *The History of the Brethren.* 2 vols. Denver, 1936.

O'Brien, R. B. *The Life of Charles Stewart Parnell, 1846-1891.* vol. 1. Reprint. New York, 1969.

Oulton, J. E. L. "The Study of Divinity in Trinity College Dublin, Since the Foundation." *Hermathena* 58 (1941).

Ouweneel, Dr. W. J. *Het verhaal van de "Broeders."* vol. 1. Winschoten, Netherlands: Uit het Woord der Waarheid, 1977.

Pennefather, Susanna. Notebook Engagements: MS3503 in National Library of Ireland.

Philpot, J. C. *Letters and Memoir of Joseph Charles Philpot.* Grand Rapids, MI: Baker Book House, 1981.

______. *The Seceders.* London: Banner of Truth Trust.

Pickering, Hy. *Chief Men Among the Brethren.* Neptune, NJ: Loizeaux, 1986.

Poseck, J. A. von. *Christus oder Parkstreet? Gottes wort oder Menschenwort.* 1882.

Powerscourt, Theodosia A. *Letters and Papers by the Late Theodosia A. Viscountess Powerscourt.* Edited by R. Daly. London, 1838.

Price, G. H. S., comp. *A Selection of Poems by Christian Authors.* London: Copper & Budd.

Pyle, F. *Trinity College Dublin.* The Irish Heritage Series, no. 24. Dublin: Eason, 1979.

Robbins, W. *The Newman Brothers.* London: Heinemann Educational Books, 1966.

Rowdon, H. H. "The Early Brethren and the Ministry of the Word." *Christian Brethren Research Fellowship Journal,* January 1967.

______. *The Origins of the Brethren.* London: Pickering & Inglis, 1967.

______. "Secession from the Established Church in the Early Nineteenth Century." *Vox Evangelica* 3 (1964).

Sandeen, E. R. *The Roots of Fundamentalism.* Grand Rapids, MI: Baker Book House, 1978.

Scott, Rev. T. *Essays on the Most Important Subjects in Religion.* 9th ed. London: L. B. Seeley, 1822.

Scott, Walter. *J. N. Darby, A Memorial.* 2nd ed. London.

Stevenson, R. L. *Travels with a Donkey in the Cevennes.*

Stokes, G. T. "J. N. Darby." *Contemporary Review* 48 (1885).

Stoney, J. B. *Letters from J. B. Stoney.* 2nd series. Lancing, Sussex: Kingston Bible Trust.

Stunt, T. C. F. "A Comprehensive History." *The Harvester.* May 1968. (A review of Coad's *History.*)

______. "Early Brethren and the Society of Friends." *Christian Brethren Research Fellowship Occasional Paper* 3 (1970).

______. "John Synge and the Early Brethren." *Christian Brethren Research Fellowship Journal* 28.

______. "Leonard Strong: The Motives and Experiences of Early Missionary Work in British Guiana." *Christian Brethren Research Fellowship Journal* 34.

______. *Some Contemporaries of Early Brethren.*

The Symbols of Heraldry Explained. Dublin: Heraldic Artists, 1980.

Taylor, W. B. S. *History of the University of Dublin.* 1845.

Trotter, Mrs. E. *Undertones of the 19th Century.* London: J. Clarke, 1905.

Turner, W. G. *John Nelson Darby, A Biography.* C. A. Hammond, 1901, 1926, 1944.

______. *William Kelly As I Knew Him.* C. A. Hammond.

Veitch, T. S. *The Story of the Brethren Movement.* London: Pickering & Inglis.

Voorhoeve, J. N. *Innerlich Bewegt.* Schwelm: Heikoop Verlag.

Walford's Country Families. 1893.

Ware, G. W. *A Review of Certain Contentions for the Faith.*

Wills, J. and Wills, F. *The Irish Nation: Its History and Its Biography.* Edinburgh: A. Fullarton, 1873.

Wilson, Bryan R., ed. *Patterns of Sectarianism.* London, 1967.

Wreford, Heyman. *Memories of the Life and Last Days of William Kelly.* London: F. E. Race.

Unpublished Doctoral Theses

Bass, C. B. "The Doctrine of the Church in the Theology of J. N. Darby, with special reference to its contribution to the Plymouth Brethren Movement." University of Edinburgh, July 1952.

Goddard, J. H. "A Synthesis of the Bibliology, Theology Proper, Angelology, and Anthropology of J. N. Darby." Dallas Theological Seminary, May 1947.

Hagan, M. R. "The Concept of Christian Ministry Revealed in the Writings of J. N. Darby." 1967.

Sturgeon, H. E. "The Life of J. N. Darby." Southern Baptist Theological Seminary, August 1957.

Acknowledgments

The author gratefully acknowledges unpublished material provided by the following individuals:

F. J. Egan, proprietor of Dooly's Hotel, Birr, Ireland—information on Leap Castle.

Canon C. A. Empey, The Priory Kells, Kilkenny—information on Christopher Darby.

F. B. Gill—"Matthew 18:20," manuscript dealing with the early years of the Brethren movement.

Rev. T. R. Jennings, Newcastle, Co. Wicklow—information on Darby as priest.

Marie D. Loizeaux—information from Anna M. Loizeaux's "Sketches for My Grandchildren."

The author gratefully acknowledges help provided by the following libraries and their staffs:

British Library, London.

Central Library, Borough of Islington, London, E. A. Willats, principal reference librarian.

Dorset County Council, Mrs. R. M. Popham, A.L.A., assistant reference librarian.

East Sussex County Council, County Record Office, C. R. Davey, B.A.

Evangelical Library, London.

Guildhall Library, London.

Holborn Library, Borough of Camden, London, Lesley Marshall.

House of Commons, Public Information, Sue Robbins.

Irish Tourist Board, Dublin, Imelda Guerrini.

King's Inns Library, Dublin, Jonathan Armstrong, assistant librarian.

Lincoln's Inn, London, Miss B. Bates, Student's Administration.

Rose Lipman Library, Borough of Hackney, London, David Mander, archivist for head of library services.

Melton Mowbray Library, Leicestershire, G. W. Belton, divisional librarian.

National Library of Ireland, Manuscript Sources.

National Maritime Museum, London, P. Pelowski.

Offaly County Library.

Oratory, Birmingham.

Ordinance Survey, Dublin, maps.

Public Record Office of Ireland, Dublin, David V. Craig, senior archivist; M. Hewson, director.
Public Record Office, London.
Representative Church Body Library, Dublin, Raymond Refaussé, librarian and archivist.
Roscrea Heritage Society, George Cunningham.
John Rylands Library, University of Manchester, David Brady.
Trinity College Library and Department of Early Printed Books, Dublin, M. Pollard; Charles Benson, S.O., senior assistant librarian; Bernard Meehan, manuscripts assistant; Dr. A. K. Swift, keeper of early printed books.
Warbleton and District History Group, Heathfield, East Sussex, Mrs. Elizabeth Doff.
Westminster Abbey, Muniment Room and Library, London, Howard M. Nixon.
City of Westminster, Archives Department, London, Miss M. J. Swarbrick, chief archivist.
Westminster School, London, headmaster; J. C. P. Field, librarian and archivist.
Dr. Williams' Library, London, John Creasey, M.A., A.L.A.
Worcester College, Oxford, L. Montgomery.